30130 088639702

SABOTAGE & SUBVERSION

Stories from the Files of the SOE and OSS

SABOTAGE & SUBVERSION

Stories from the Files of the SOE and OSS

IAN DEAR

ARMS AND
ARMOUR

Arms and Armour Press
An Imprint of the Cassell Group
Wellington House, 125 Strand, London WC2R 0BB

Distributed in the USA by Sterling Publishing Co. Inc.,
387 Park Avenue South, New York, NY 10016-8810.

Distributed in Australia by Capricorn Link (Australia) Pty.
Ltd, 2/13 Carrington Road, Castle Hill, NSW 2154.

British Library Cataloguing-in-Publication Data:
a catalogue record for this book is available from the
British Library

ISBN 1-85409-260-X

Designed and edited by DAG Publications Ltd.
Designed by David Gibbons; edited by Michael Boxall;
printed and bound in Great Britain.

Contents

Acknowledgements

I should like to thank Peter Masters for his help in researching documents for this book and obtaining some of the photographs from OSS archives. I should also like to thank the following who took the time and trouble to read parts of the manuscript: Dr John Brunner, Professor M.R.D. Foot, Themis Marinos, Terence O'Brien and R.A. Rubinstein. Dr Brunner, Themis Marinos, Charles Messenger, Mike Langley, Mrs Shirley Cannicott and the Special Forces Club, London, were kind enough to lend me photographs, and Mrs Sue Rodgers of the Special Forces Club answered my barrage of requests with great efficency and cheerfulness. Pictures indicated as Crown Copyright are reproduced with the permission of the Controller of HMSO.

Introduction

Sabotage and subversion have always been part of warfare. But the global nature of the 1939–45 conflict, combined with the increasing sophistication of the means to implement sabotage and subversion during those years, make the manner and extent in which they were carried out during the Second World War of especial interest.

In the context of warfare, sabotage – defined by David Stafford in his book *Britain and European Resistance*, 1940–45 as the physical dislocation of supplies useful to the enemy – needs no further definition here, except to say that Hugh Dalton, SOE's first political head, believed that armed support for guerrilla forces behind the enemy lines was a natural part of a sabotage organisation, and it is therefore included in this book. 'We must organise movements in every occupied territory,' he wrote in July 1940, 'comparable to the Sinn Fein movement in Ireland, to the Chinese guerrillas now operating in Japan, to the Spanish irregulars who played a notable part in Wellington's campaign.'

Incidentally, the word sabotage comes from the French word *sabot*, the wooden clogs worn by French industrial workers. Disgruntled workers disabled machines by throwing their clogs into the working parts.

Subversion can be said to be the undermining of the enemy's government, armed forces, collaborating authorities, and allies by methods other than military ones. These methods included 'black' radio broadcasts and 'black' propaganda – 'black' meaning that the government disseminating it did not acknowledge its existence as opposed to 'white' propaganda which it did – were both used for subversive purposes by OSS and SOE, the two organisations that implemented sabotage and subversion for the American and British governments. Chapters on these esoteric arts are therefore included here as are examples of black market currency manipulation, forgery, blackmail, smuggling, pornography, and kidnapping, when used for subversive purposes; and, to set the scene, there are chapters on the training and equipping of saboteurs, the latter describing weapons and special devices which both organisations co-operated to improve.

But this book is not a history of SOE and OSS. What it attempts to do, with the help of new documentation that has become available in recent years, is to highlight a few of their more outstanding sabotage and subversive operations, sometimes for comparison, sometimes to show what their individual strengths and weaknesses were, sometimes to highlight the character and bravery of those involved in their operations; but, especially, to illustrate to what lengths the two Allied governments would go to achieve their ends.

Although the text has been confined to the activities of SOE and OSS, the reader must not infer from this that the Axis did not have similar organisations. The Germans, for example, had the Abwehr's *Abteilung* (Department) II which formed the Brandenburger Regiment for sabotage and was very active in the field of subversion. For example, it helped organise the pro-German uprisings in the Sudetenland in 1938 which in turn led to the eventual annexation of all of Czechoslovakia by the Nazis; and actively encouraged local *Volksdeutsche* (German-speaking nationals living outside the Reich) to subvert the government of the country in which they were living and to help the Wehrmacht when it invaded. In this respect it was particularly successful in Poland in September 1939 and in Yugoslavia in April 1941.

The Japanese, too, were active in using local populations to subvert the governments and local troops of the European colonies before invading them. They had Special Service Organisations, or *Kikan*, which operated in such countries as Malaya, Burma and the Netherlands East Indies for this purpose. Perhaps the best-known examples are the Minami *Kikan* which secretly organised the anti-British Burma Independence Army and Major Fujiwara Iwaichi's F *Kikan* which fostered the anti-British Indian Independence League and recruited the Indian National Army that fought against the British in the Burma campaign.

However, because the Axis occupied much of Europe and south-east Asia for most of the Second World War (in some cases for all of it), it was necessarily the Allies who developed sabotage and subversion to a greater degree. It therefore seems logical to base this book on the activities of the two largest Allied organisations to carry out these forms of warfare in occupied territory.

1
OSS and SOE – What Were They?

The Special Operations Executive was formed on Churchill's orders in July 1940 from three smaller organisations: Section D, part of the Secret Intelligence Service which dealt in sabotage; EH, a semi-secret Foreign Office department which handled propaganda; and an obscure branch of the War Office known as MI(R). Its objective was, in Churchill's well-known phrase, to 'set Europe ablaze' – the prime minister's order to Dalton, the Minister of Economic Warfare, who was SOE's first political head. Its inspiration were the Fifth columnists who were supposed to have been so active throughout Europe, including Britain, and were much feared at the time (although except for the examples of *Volksdeutsche* activity mentioned in the introduction, they proved to be largely a myth). It was, of necessity, a secret organisation. By that is meant that it was not one that the government would officially acknowledge as existing.

Being new, SOE had its difficulties with the other two long-established British secret services. These were the Security Service, which was primarily responsible for the security of the United Kingdom (counter-intelligence), and the Special Intelligence Service, whose business was the gathering of information in enemy-occupied territory by spying (intelligence). Both were numbered as being part of the Military Intelligence Directorate – MI5 and MI6 respectively – though, in fact, the former reported to the Home Office and the latter to the Foreign Office. SOE, on the other hand, was responsible to the Ministry of Economic Warfare, or the Ministry of Ungentlemanly Warfare as its first political minister, Hugh Dalton, called it.

SOE's differences with MI5 were minor, but with MI6 it had a fundamental problem in that spies need anonymity and a tranquil, unsuspecting enemy; the whole object of sabotage and subversion is to create mayhem and confusion. This fundamental difference in approach was one of the reasons that made co-operation between the two organisations difficult. Having different political heads was another. Nor was their early relationship made easier by the fact that until April 1942 SOE had to rely on MI6's radio network. Initially, it also had to rely on MI6 to supply it with the necessary forged documents for agents entering the field. As MI6 calculated, not unreasonably, that the risk of a forged document being discovered was in direct proportion to the number in circulation, SOE found it difficult to obtain any.

One senior SOE staff officer, Bickham Sweet-Escott, even hinted that inaccurate documents were deliberately foisted on to SOE. 'There were one or two ugly cases', he wrote after the war, 'where our people were arrested because they said the papers they had been given were not in order. In the end we were forced to break 'Z's' [MI6] monopoly and do our own forging, but our right to do so was not won without a tremendous campaign of mutual vilification.'

During the course of the war SOE survived several crises of confidence in it, and numerous clashes with rival organisations and with the armed forces. Initially it was organised into three parts: SO1 (propaganda), SO2 (operations), and SO3 (planning). SO3 was soon absorbed into SO1, and in August 1941 SO1 became the Political Warfare Executive (PWE), controlled by the Foreign Office.

This new arrangement did not prevent SOE from continuing to take an active part in 'black' subversion. This often provoked angry confrontations with the PWE – a secret department of which took over the dissemination of 'black' propaganda and 'black' broadcasts from SO1 – and the Ministry of Information (MOI) which disseminated 'white' propaganda. A good example of these clashes is illustrated in a letter sent to a member of SOE in India in July 1944 by a London staff officer when the former proposed creating a 'black' propaganda station to broadcast to the Japanese.

'You were, I think, in London when some at least of the great Middle East radio SOE versus PWE uproar was going on,' the staff officer wrote, and went on to explain that that débâcle was similar to the position in India in that there had been a definite need for propaganda broadcasts in the Middle East and SOE had been the only organisation on the spot with the technical and political knowledge, and the skilled personnel, to do it. So while accepting that it was for the PWE to initiate policy – described by the writer as 'wishy-washy directives' – SOE went ahead with its propaganda broadcasts. When the PWE sent their own representatives out to Cairo and demanded that SOE relinquish control of the stations, however, 'a tremendous battle of words and paper followed'. Telegrams flew between Cairo and London in abundance and the Foreign Office even joined in on the PWE's side with the ambassador to Greece wiring the Foreign Office from Cairo. The upshot was that the PWE took the credit for everything that went well, and SOE took the blame for anything that did not. SOE was also accused of interfering in policy which was none of its business, of promoting an attitude in various Balkan peoples which flew in the face of Foreign Office policy, and of misinterpreting directives. All this reached ministerial level, and even Churchill, which did SOE no good at all. Such conflicts, the writer concluded firmly, 'must not occur again'.

It is not surprising that with infighting on such a scale SOE's first executive head, Sir Frank Nelson, became a victim of overwork and was replaced in April 1942 by his deputy, Sir Charles Hambro. After a disagreement with his political boss, Lord Selborne (who replaced Dalton in February 1942), Hambro was himself replaced in September 1943 by his deputy, Major-General Colin Gubbins who remained SOE's executive head until the organisation was disbanded in January 1946. The executive head was always known by the initials CD.

Initially, SOE came directly under the supervision of the heads of the three armed services which formed the Chiefs of Staff, a committee which advised Churchill on military strategy and directed commanders in the field. Later – with the exception of Poland – its organisations in the field were responsible to the relevant commanders-in-chief.

Dalton tried to make SOE a fourth service but this was quickly squashed and the lack of sympathy and understanding with which SOE was regarded by the conventional military was as serious as any of its clashes with rival organisations, particularly when it came to the allocation of resources. For example, in early 1941 the RAF's chief of staff, Air Chief Marshal Portal, widely acknowledged as having one of the most brilliant minds, remarked of one SOE operation that 'he thought that the dropping of men dressed in civilian clothes for the purpose of attempting to kill members of the opposing forces is not an operation with which the Royal Air Force should be associated... there is a vast difference, in ethics, between the time honoured operation of the dropping of a spy from the air and this entirely new scheme for dropping what one can only call assassins'. With attitudes like that to overcome, and they were far from uncommon in the military establishment, it is not surprising that SOE had extreme difficulties in acquiring the aircraft it needed to mount its operations.

From November 1940 SOE's London headquarters were at 64 Baker Street; by the end of the war it had grown to such an extent that it occupied much of the office space between Portman Square and the Baker Street tube station as well as many flats in Berkeley, Chiltern and Orchard Courts, and in Bickenhall Mansions. Its operational organisation for Europe was based on sections each of which administered an individual country, though France, because of its proximity and political complexity, had no less than six separate ones. SOE's Cairo HQ worked on the same system for the Mediterranean, Balkans, and North Africa.

Elsewhere in the world – and there were few places SOE did not cover – it had missions, such as the Indian one, or the Oriental one based in Singapore, or it adopted a cover name, such as Force 136 which was what the India Mission was known as after 16 March 1944. It also ran and financed Special Operations Australia (see Chapter 8), though by the end of the war this had become an Australian organisation. In the Western Hemisphere SOE was represented by British Security Co-ordination in New York.

SOE also acquired various establishments outside London for training (see Chapter 2), called Special Training Schools, and stations for developing and manufacturing special weapons and devices (see Chapter 3). Its total numbers have never been officially calculated, but by mid-1944 its estimated strength was 13,200 men and women. Nearly half the men, and some of the women, served as agents in occupied or neutral countries. The casualty rate was high. For example, SOE's F Section (see Chapter 12) was one in four.

Unlike SOE, which was formed entirely for the purposes of sabotage and subversion, the Office of Strategic Services (OSS) was structured more like the Abwehr, the departments of which performed different clandestine roles but were responsible to the same head. The OSS was formed in July 1942 from the Office of the Co-ordinator of Information (COI), the co-ordinator being General William J. Donovan, and by the end of the war had grown to a total of 26,000 men and women.

The COI had been created the previous July as part of the Executive Office of the President. Its official charter was to collect, analyse and correlate all information and data that might relate to national security. But its secret, unwritten agenda – simply covered by the charter as 'supplementary activities' – was, as the official OSS history expressed it, to wage unorthodox warfare in support of the armed forces. Such unorthodox warfare would include not only propaganda and intelligence but also sabotage, morale and physical subversion, guerrilla activities and development and support of underground and resistance groups.'

To give him guidance in forming the necessary branches within COI, Donovan was in close contact with the British who had had two years' start in gaining experience in clandestine warfare, and he also received advice from William Stephenson, the Canadian head of British Security Co-ordination. Donovan's first move was to form, among other branches, one for Research and Analysis.

'The functions of R & A', the official OSS history states, 'were so broad and complex as to resist precise definition', but broadly speaking it was responsible for the collection, interpretation, and dissemination of information, intelligence, and data. SOE had no equivalent organisation. It proved to be of great assistance not only to the operational branches of OSS when they came into being, but to agencies of the Joint Chiefs of Staff, the State Department, and others.

Another early COI branch was the Foreign Information Service (FIS) which was responsible for disseminating propaganda in the Eastern Hemisphere. After the USA entered the war the FIS successfully fought against being put under military supervision. Instead, its functions became part of a civilian agency, the Office of War Information, when this was formed in June 1942.

It was part of Donovan's policy to form branches which could work closely with their British counterparts, the PWE, MI6 and SOE (the Federal Bureau of Investigation, or FBI, was approximately the US equivalent of MI5, but it was not part of Donovan's remit). However, while the USA remained neutral it was not politically possible to form such branches openly though on 10 October 1941 a section designated 'Special Activities – K and L Funds' was established in the Co-ordinator's Office which was responsible for espionage, sabotage and subversion, and guerrilla formations. Soon after the USA entered the war in December 1941, this section was divided into two: the Secret Intelligence Branch under David K. E. Bruce, known by the initials SA/B (Special Activities/Bruce), and the Special Operations Branch which was known by the initials SA/G when Colonel M. Preston Goodfellow became its head in January 1942. When OSS was formed from the COI these sections became the Secret Intelligence (SI) and Special Operations (SO) branches which were roughly the equivalents of MI6 and SOE respectively.

In 1943 the West European sections of SO and SOE became a joint organisation, based in London, but SI never had the same close links with MI6. As SO, and the other OSS branches mentioned below, were the principal OSS branches involved in sabotage and subversion only their operations are covered in this book.

An agreement between SOE and OSS to co-operate in the field was concluded in June 1942 just as OSS was being formed from its predecessor, the COI. This agreement, confirmed in September 1942, allotted each organisation certain geographic spheres within which all operations were the responsibility of either SOE or OSS. (Incidentally, where military operations were in progress or were being planned, both organisations always worked under the overall control of the local theatre commander.) Initially, SOE was the responsible agency for France, the Low Countries, Poland, Czechoslovakia, most of Norway, and the Balkans, and OSS was responsible for Finland and, later, Bulgaria, Roumania, and the northern tip of Norway.

During 1943 the two organisations worked towards forming a joint headquarters to support and direct resistance groups in the occupied countries of western Europe. Between March and September 1943 SOE's Planning Section held a series of meetings with OSS SO Free French personnel to draw up plans for the use of the French resistance before, on and after D-Day. Eight separate plans were originally conceived, but these were later boiled down to three, all of which were successfully implemented.

'Vert' covered the destruction of all railway communications to isolate areas and prevent all German movement to, from or through them. As many key German personnel as possible were to be killed at the more important rail centres. 'Tortue' covered the laying of ambushes on all roads that would prevent, or at least delay, German armoured and infantry reinforcements reaching the beachhead. It was to be supplemented by other sabotage activities such as misdirecting traffic. 'Violet' dealt with the severing of Wehrmacht telecommunications system so as to isolate certain areas from the remainder of France, and from Germany.

In January 1944 SOE and SO in London were formally integrated with the title SOE/SO, and SO personnel became part of many of SOE's country sections, though the shortage of suitable OSS agents meant that SOE always predominated in the field. Nevertheless, 523 members of the SO and OG branches of OSS fought behind German lines in France during the course of 1944, 85 of whom were SO agents and radio operators working with SOE's F, RF and DF Sections, 83 were Jedburgh (see Chapter 15), and 355 made up 22 Operational Groups (see Chapter 14). Their casualties were 18 dead, 17 missing in action or made prisoner, and 51 wounded.

In preparation for the invasion of north-west Europe Eisenhower's Supreme Headquarters Allied Expeditionary Force (SHAEF) delegated its responsibility for the control and supply of all resistance forces in France, to SOE/SO which on 1 May 1944 was designated Special Forces Headquarters (SFHQ). The same month a joint SOE/SO headquarters, Special Project Operations Center (SPOC), was established at Algiers, to conduct operations on behalf of SFHQ into southern France. It was these two organisations which were responsible for dropping the different groups of special forces into France on and after the D-Day landings on 6 June 1944 to implement 'Vert', 'Tortue', and 'Violet' and to help supply, train, and co-operate with, the French resistance. (Although separate chapters of this book have been devoted to the sabotage activities of the OGs and the Jedburghs, and to those of SOE's F Section, they all co-ordinated their operations with one another – or at least attempted to do so – and with the Inter-Allied Missions and the teams of SAS which were also parachuted into France.) From 1 July 1944 all Allied clandestine forces working into France came under the overall command of the staff of de Gaulle's French Forces of the Interior (FFI) commanded by General Koenig.

Outside Europe SOE was responsible for the Middle East, India, and West and East Africa, and OSS was responsible for North Africa, China, Manchuria, Korea, the South and South-West Pacific and the Atlantic islands. Responsibility for Burma, Thailand, Malaya, Sumatra, Germany, Italy, Sweden, Switzerland, Portugal and Spain was shared.

In the Far East, which posed entirely different problems from those in Europe, there was often a lack of co-operation between OSS and the various offshoots of SOE; and sometimes, as in Thailand where the two Allies had conflicting political aims, outright rivalry, as indeed there was in China.

Nor was opposition to the presence of the OSS in the Far East confined to the British, for both Admiral Nimitz, commanding the vast Pacific Ocean Areas, and General MacArthur, who commanded the South-West Pacific Area, banned or severely limited the presence of the OSS in their theatres. In China the OSS were equally frustrated by General Tai Li, the Chinese Nationalist government's head of internal security and counter-intelligence, when it tried to operate independently. Eventually, in 1944, it managed to enter the field by forming a unit within the Fourteenth US Army Air Force based in China.

The agreement to combine the two organisations in some theatres worked well in some places, not so well in others. For example, they worked amicably together in the Balkans and both organisations provided members for the three-man Jedburgh teams and Inter-Allied missions which were dropped into France on and after D-Day. But even when co-operation was the norm relations were not universally smooth and Bickham Sweet-Escott mentions at least two awkward moments that occurred.

The first arose from a report written by an OSS colonel who proposed setting up an underground OSS network in the Middle East to gain the Allies Arab support. There was no reference to working with the British who, he said, were completely discredited in the region, and made no mention of the fact that the British already had large organisations, both covert and overt, working towards the same end.

Apart from the dangers inherent in having two secret organisations working separately in the same area, it was obvious to Sweet-Escott and his colleagues that the colonel could hardly achieve what he sought without denigrating British policy in the Middle East. 'This hardly seemed to be furthering our common effort,' Sweet-Escott commented dryly, though he thought 'there was a good deal of force' in the colonel's contention. SOE protested, but the document already had White House approval, and it was not until the British Embassy took up the matter with the State Department that the colonel's proposal was diluted and then abandoned.

The second incident was more serious and illustrates how difficult it was to achieve co-ordination within a secret organisation, much less with another one. It arose out of talks in Washington between SOE and OSS representatives about setting up a joint training school and operational base in Algeria if the Allied landings (code-named 'Torch') in North Africa proved successful. Complete agreement on a joint establishment was reached and a telegram was sent to let SOE in London know the successful outcome of the talks. Soon afterwards, however, Sweet-Escott was summoned to meet a furious Donovan. Unbeknown to anyone in Washington, parallel talks on the same subject had been taking place in London, and these had come to the opposite conclusion. Donovan commented angrily that if this was how the British behaved SOE and OSS would have to go their separate ways, and nothing Sweet-Escott said could persuade him to believe other than that he had been double-crossed.

Sweet-Escott then asked London what explanation he should give Donovan. To his astonishment he received the reply that the SOE representative sent from London to take part in the talks had had no authority to conclude them and that anyway London had had no prior knowledge of them! Sweet-Escott refused to pass this on to Donovan and reminded London of the telegram he had sent. London then told him to apologise to Donovan but to tell him that the decision in London had to stand. 'The incident was one which OSS never forgot,' Sweet-Escott wrote. 'I was never quite clear whether they suspected our integrity or doubted our competence. Whichever it was it did not help us.'

SOE, or SO2 as it was then known, attempted to land its first agents in France in August 1940 and another attempt was made in October. Both failed, and the first agent it attempted to drop by parachute (on 14 November 1940) refused to jump. Later the same month, however, a successful, though atypical, operation was mounted with men provided by the Free French's London headquarters. SOE's war diary described it as follows: 'Five agents under the direction of Lt. Minshull, RN, were conveyed by submarine to the Gironde. In the Estuary, they seized a French tunny fishing smack, impressed half the crew, and placed the remainder on the submarine. After a successful reconnaissance to observe the procedure followed by U-boats in entering and leaving the river, they sailed the fishing boat back to Falmouth without incident. The information procured by personal observation and by the interrogation of the French fishermen proved of great value to the Navy and RAF and it is understood that successful operations based on this information were shortly afterwards undertaken.'

From this modest beginning SOE grew to become a powerful sabotage force in nearly all the Axis-occupied countries. It also delivered large quantities of arms, ammunition and explosives to the local resistance organisations it helped. There were serious setbacks and disasters. Some of these must be attributed to bad luck or the fortunes of war, but others – such as the well-known *Englandspiel* operation which led to the capture and death of so many SOE (and MI6) agents in the Netherlands – must be put down, to a greater or lesser degree, to carelessness or inefficiency, or because Baker Street was simply outwitted by the Gestapo and the Abwehr.

But overall the record of SOE is an impressive one. Its record in just one occupied country, Denmark, will have to suffice here to show the range of its operations. The extract comes from an outline history of SOE which is in the organisation's files in the Public Record Office at Kew.

'Operations included the attack (1943) on the power station of Burmeister and Wain (Copenhagen) which was engaged on U-Boat production and which was put out of action for nine months: the destruction (1944) by 20 men of 30 German aircraft, the aero mechanised workshop, and special tools at the Aalborg West aerodrome: the destruction (1945) of all the material and much machinery of the Torotor factory (Copenhagen) which was engaged on V1 and V2 manufacture: the destruction, by 33 men, with 800lb of explosive, of the only armament factory (the Rifle Syndicate) in Denmark, with final cessation of production; the destruction (1944) of the Always Radio factory, when working on U-Boat production: and its final destruction (1945) when rebuilt.

'To these examples of major destruction of the German war potential must be added much widespread minor sabotage and, above all, the incessant attacks of the Jutland "Special Forces" [i.e., SOE] against railway traffic. The early months of 1945 saw a steady increase of the flow of troops from Norway to the Western Front via Denmark, and these attacks are described as having "resulted in a reduction of the rate of movement from Norway from four divisions to less than one division a month". For instance, during the week 4th–11th February, 1945, the transport of the German 233 Panzer Division and 166 Infantry Division was attacked successfully over 100 times: by the end of the week, more than half their 44 trains were immobilised in Denmark, and 6 derailed.'

The OSS became operational much later than SOE, but its record is also an impressive one. The first SO London agent to enter the field was E. F. Floege, code-named 'Alfred', who, with his wireless operator, an SO officer called André Bouchardon, was first parachuted into France on 13 June 1943 to organise a sabotage circuit in the area of Le Mans–Nantes–Laval. Their story is told in the chapter on F Section.

When SO was formed it was Donovan's intention that it should handle black propaganda and similar methods of subversion. But SOE and PWE, which handled British political warfare, had different political heads which made it difficult for PWE to liaise with SO satisfactorily. Therefore, in January 1943, Donovan created the Morale Operations (MO) Branch to mount black propaganda operations of all varieties into enemy territory. 'Persuasion, penetration and intimidation', he said of this type of warfare, 'are the modern counterpart of sapping and mining in the siege warfare of former days.'

MO had a slow start, caused by administrative problems and disagreement with the OWI over their respective areas of responsibility. Once these had been ironed out MO expanded rapidly and eventually became an effective organisation, though the nature of its operations always made it difficult to quantify its successes. However, Elizabeth P. MacDonald, one of OSS's few female operatives, described an MO operation which was initiated by another female OSS operative, Barbara Lauwers, which did have discernible results. Lauwers, based with OSS in Rome, decided to undermine the morale of Czech troops being forced to fight for the Germans in northern Italy. 'She wrote five "speeches" from "fellow Czechs" who had allegedly defected and joined the Czech Army of National Liberation, fighting with the Allies in Italy. The "speeches" were broadcast over the BBC to Czech garrisons in northern Italy. At the same time Lauwers designed surrender passes which were infiltrated behind enemy lines by German prisoners of war working for OSS. Six hundred Czechs defected and the passes were honored by their liberation army. Lauwers won the Bronze Star for her part in this action.'

But perhaps MO's greatest contribution was, as the OSS official history states, 'that it brought to the attention of American authorities a weapon which the United States had not theretofore systematically and effectively employed'. Nowadays it is called disinformation.

In January 1943 OSS was reorganised and the post of Deputy Director, Psychological Warfare Operations (later Strategic Services Operations), was established to supervise and direct the activities of SO and MO. In May 1943, after approval by the Joint Chiefs of Staff, the Operational Group Command (OG) became a third branch, though it constituted a separate military command and only came under the Deputy Director for over-all planning. This was authorised to 'organise, train and employ operational nuclei for guerrilla warfare'. In November 1944 it was made a separate military unit within OSS so that its commanding officer reported directly to Donovan. This decision was taken as it was felt these groups, despite being in uniform, might not be treated according to the Geneva Convention if captured and that the further removed they were from any connection with OSS the better their chances of survival. In the European and Mediterranean theatres the Operational Groups normally consisted of four officers and 30 men who were divided into combat sections comprising two officers, thirteen men, a radio operator and a medic. They were all volunteers from the US Army and normally spoke the language of the country in which they were to operate.

In the Far East, Detachment 101 (see Chapter 9) worked with local Kachin guerrillas in Burma and supplied valuable intelligence to the US Army and US Army Air Forces. Its numbers fluctuated but by 1944 it comprised 5–600 men, and about 9,000 tribesmen.

Finally, in June 1943, the Maritime Unit (MU), which evolved from the training of SO and SI agents in the techniques of clandestine landings from the sea, was also given branch status which enabled it to put personnel into the field. It had four main functions: 1, landing agents from the sea; 2, supply of resistance groups and others from the sea; 3, maritime sabotage; 4, development of special equipment and devices for maritime sabotage. MU personnel were active in Europe and the Far East.

By the end of the war OSS was as ubiquitous as SOE. It, or rather its COI predecessor, was operational in North Africa as early as January 1942; and after the Allied invasion there that November it established a headquarters at Algiers. Others were also established in Cairo, Chungking, London and Corsica, and numerous SO, MO, and OG operations were organised from them.

A typical SO mission was one where a four-man team crossed into the Evros region of Greece from Turkey on 29 March 1944 with orders to cut the flow of chrome ore, a valuable strategic raw material, from Turkey to Germany by destroying two important railway bridges. They made contact with the local communist guerrilla headquarters and spent the next two months training and equipping a force of 220 guerrillas for the operation. At the end of May two targets were selected: the Svilengrad bridge in Bulgaria, which was 210 feet long and twelve feet high, and the Alexandroupolis bridge in Greece, which was 100 feet long and 45 feet high. Two SO officers and 170 guerrillas with 1,400lb of plastic explosives were sent to dispose of the former and two SO non-commissioned officers, fifty guerrillas, and 550lb of plastic explosives were sent to destroy the latter.

'Our plan was', wrote the leader of the team attacking the Svilengrad bridge, in his after-action report, '(1) to place sufficient guards to eliminate any interference from the German guard post of ten men and the Bulgarian post of 21 men; (2) to prevent any reinforcements from reaching there in time; (3) cut all telephonic communications; (4) carry out the demolition of the bridge.

'The first step was very easy because the Germans were caught napping and did not interfere until the last five minutes of the operation. They fired a flare and opened up with a machine-gun and submachine-guns in the general direction of the bridge. Luckily the bridge was already mined and we were making the connections with prima-cord. Steps two and three were easily carried out... After the demolition of the bridge we began our forced march, crossing the Arda river at 0400 hours. There a German post noticed us and notified the reconnaissance battalion.

'The next evening the reconnaissance battalion was hot on our trail... Captain —, Lt. — and the sabotage crew broke away from the main body and proceeded south to get the news of the southern bridge leaving a Greek officer in charge. This young officer after three days of maneuvering finally ambushed the CO of the German battalion and his staff and killed them all.'

The Alexandroupolis bridge was also destroyed. A total of 25 SO agents entered Greece between September 1943 and November 1944, most of whom were attached to guerrilla bands that carried out numerous sabotage attacks.

President Truman issued the Executive Order which terminated OSS on 1 October 1945, though many of its functions were subsequently taken over by the Central Intelligence Agency which was formed in September 1947. SOE officially ceased to exist on 30 June 1946.

2
Recruiting and Training for Sabotage and Subversion

Recruiting for SOE and OSS was often by word of mouth, though one would-be SOE agent was recruited in a bar and another joined by answering an advertisement for a bilingual secretary. So discreet was her induction that even after completing the preliminary training course she was still in the dark as to what organisation had accepted her, though it was always stressed to recruits that they were volunteers and could withdraw at any time.

Staff officers and agents working in the field often came from the armed forces of the two countries, and the latter were drawn from the armed forces of the governments-in-exile, from the large immigrant communities which abound in North America, and, of course, from the nationalities of those countries to be penetrated.

For operations in Europe and the Balkans, recruitment at all levels posed few problems, but in the Far East both OSS and SOE faced many difficulties. There were few Americans or Europeans with the necessary skills to fill staff positions, and as any white person was instantly recognisable they could only be used in the field on a very limited basis. Therefore recruiting was from the Asiatic communities – altogether 1,500 were trained – though by the end of the war SOE had sent 450 British officers and NCOs into the field to lead guerrilla operations such as 'Character' (see Chapter 16) and OSS had about 600 American officers and enlisted men working with its Detachment 101 (see Chapter 9).

On a world-wide basis SOE agents included, as M. R. D. Foot wrote in his outline history of SOE, 'several score Spaniards, Germans and Austrians, and several hundred Italians and Frenchmen. Their social range reached from a head of state – the regent of Siam – through an Indian princess (born in the Kremlin), several exiled Russian grandees, a prince and a duke of Napoleonic creation and some still more splendid French and Belgian families, through the whole range of the upper and lower European and east Asiatic bourgeoisie, to railwaymen, telephonists, clerks, labourers, peasants, prostitutes and coolies.'

Generally speaking they lacked, as the historian, Hugh Seton-Watson, put it, 'the habit of subordination to a regular hierarchy; were disciplined by no mandarin ethos; and were impatient or even contemptuous of the bureaucratic conventions of the diplomatic service and its auxiliaries. To the diplomats they often appeared brash, ignorant of things which diplomats were trained to regard as important, and at times a positive menace.' OSS personnel were equally heterogeneous, and those recruited within the United States included 'a noted anthropologist, a businessman, an explorer, a high-pressure salesman, a professional football player, a former Treasury agent, and an adventurer-author'.

Both SOE and OSS recruited women. SOE dispatched 50 into France during the course of the war, two of them American citizens, but few of the 4,000 female OSS recruits reached the field. One who did, Aline Griffith, an SI agent in Spain from January 1944 to August 1945, records that the training she received was the same for men and women and that though her fellow students were mostly Americans there were also 'Yugoslavs, a Belgian, several Frenchmen, and a German or two'. Three of SOE's country sections had women as their operations officers and the intelligence officer of F Section (see Chapter 12) – assessed by a female colleague as being 'really the most powerful personality in SOE' – was also a woman. But, as with OSS, the majority of female SOE recruits – who came mostly from the armed forces or the all-volunteer First Aid Nursing Yeomanry (FANY) – were used in non-combatant roles.

Another invaluable source for SOE personnel was the underworld. One of its most successful agents owned a chain of brothels and it relied on professional forgers to manufacture the right papers for those entering the field. One retired burglar ran SOE's lock-picking course and a second was such an outstanding agent that he was awarded the DSO. One British general, sacked by Eisenhower (unjustly as it turned out later), was immediately made a member of SOE's Council. Small wonder that one historian has commented that SOE sometimes enjoyed appearing disreputable.

SOE's staff officers were drawn from a much tighter social group. They were often businessmen from the City, or were lawyers, journalists or academics, professions where everyone knew everyone else, or at least knew them by reputation. This might be regarded as élitism, but where man management, total trustworthiness, and a high intelligence were essential prerequisites, it had to be. On the whole this 'old boy network' worked, though it was not infallible: the traitor 'Kim' Philby started his intelligence career in SOE before transferring to MI6.

The training system for SOE personnel has been likened to a series of sieves, each having a finer mesh than the previous one, and OSS, at least at first, tended to follow SOE's example. In Britain volunteers passed through the SOE system of numbered Special Training Schools (STS) which were nearly all isolated country mansions taken over for the duration. Many were so grand that SOE came to stand for 'Stately 'omes of England'.

These training schools not only had instructors but conducting officers. These were experienced individuals who, ideally, had been in the field themselves, and they acted as a student's adviser, father-confessor and friend. Conducting officers were consulted by the Commandant of the training school before a student's final assessment for they sometimes had a greater insight into a student's potential than the instructors.

The first hurdle for any volunteer was to pass his initial interviews which probed his commitment, linguistic ability, background, and temperament. SOE volunteers went through a series of one-to-one interviews, often without having the least idea what it was all about (though the interviewer stressed throughout that the candidate was under no obligation to proceed once he did know).

George Langelaan described his interviews and training for SOE vividly. He had joined the British Army at a recruitment office in Paris where he was working as a journalist. After Dunkirk he wrote a report on how to extract information about occupied France and how to feed information and propaganda to its people. He sent it to the War Office, but being then only a corporal, never expected to hear about it again. One day early in 1941, however, he was summoned to the War Office and was escorted by an armed policeman to room 108. There he was interviewed, informally, by Colonel Gielgud – brother of the actor, John Gielgud – who had, as a captain, recruited Langelaan into the Army in Paris. Gielgud asked if he would be prepared to return to France. Langelaan queried how this could be done and when Gielgud said by parachute Langelaan protested that he would be too terrified to jump:

'"I understand you have been proposed for OCTU... Sandhurst," said the colonel, glancing at some papers on his desk... "Drop in and see me when you get through in about three months' time."

'"But, sir... if I cannot... "

'"Please don't worry about that for the moment. To tell you the truth, I rather like your fear of being parachuted – I prefer that to people who think they are afraid of nothing."

'"But, sir. Won't I have to ask for an appointment, or something?"

'"No, just drop in one morning. I'll be here."'

When Langelaan saw the colonel again he was issued with a travel warrant for an isolated part of Scotland where his training as an agent began.

This casual, one might say amateur, approach seems to have worked remarkably well, but by mid-1943 the war had become more professional and it was replaced by an assessment board of psychologists. OSS followed the same route, and though the two organisations developed their own psychological evaluation programmes independently the end results were, according to the official OSS history, 'remarkably similar... Immediately upon arrival each candidate was subjected to routine paper and pencil intelligence tests which provided a general index of his intellectual capabilities and aptitudes.

'A variety of tests were evolved which were designed to produce not only material for a psychological analysis of the candidate but also a job analysis, namely what he could do best and whether he was capable of performing the task for which he was employed.'

The tests included ones for general initiative which, besides revealing his ingenuity, indicated the candidate's ability to 'withstand frustration, to persevere, to think clearly'. There were also more precise exercises to test a candidate's ability to memorise maps, faces, and so on, and his aptitude to process propaganda material and to speak extemporaneously before an audience.

Next came what was called a 'clinical' interview, a personal discussion between the candidate and a staff member designated as the candidate's mentor. This played a decisive role in assessing a candidate. If the results of the interview clashed with those of the tests, a rare occurrence, the interview usually carried more weight.

These assessments took 3½ days and were held at Station S, a country estate in Fairfax, Virginia. Too great an administrative burden was put on the Station when, in March 1944, all OSS personnel going overseas were sent to be tested there, so Station W, a house in Washington, was opened which ran a one-day assessment course. In June 1944 another assessment centre for personnel going to the Far East was opened on the West Coast as Station WS and in November 1944 Area F, which had previously been used for training Operational Groups (see Chapter 14), became a centre for assessing the fitness for further operations of agents returning from Europe. From January 1944 to July 1945 5,300 candidates passed through OSS assessment schools.

In Britain if an SOE candidate passed his interview he was normally sent on a two- or three-week introduction course where the prospective agent was put through a rigorous fitness programme and taught the basics of reading maps and weapons training. Personal idiosyncrasies – such as succumbing to the attractions of a well-stocked bar – were watched and noted.

If an individual passed this first test he was dispatched to a Group A, or paramilitary training, school in a particularly wild part of the Scottish Highlands, near Arisaig on the western coast. Here, during a course which lasted three or five weeks, students were taught not only how to fire, strip and re-assemble British weapons, but foreign ones as well. Living off the land, demolition work with plastic explosives, unarmed combat, and silent killing were also part of the course.

Langelaan was taught unarmed combat by a 'strange, smiling pagan statuette', a diminutive Japanese who spoke in clipped English with an American accent, but silent killing was William Ewart Fairbairn's area of expertise. Fairbairn was a retired ex-Assistant Commissioner of the Shanghai Municipal Police who held the rank of major. Another instructor teaching the same skills was Eric Anthony Sykes, a one-time reserve Shanghai policeman.

According to one source Fairbairn was the first white man to be awarded a *ju-jitsu* Black Belt and he was also an expert in other forms of martial arts. He and

Sykes emphasised that silent killing was as much an attitude of mind as a technique. 'This is *war*, not sport,' students were told. 'Your aim is to kill your opponent as soon as possible... forget the term "foul methods"... "foul methods" so-called, help you to kill quickly. Attack your opponent's weakest points.' One SOE staff officer, Bickham Sweet-Escott, remembers Sykes' instructions as being 'long, complicated and hard to remember, but each of them ended with the phrase: "and then kick him in the testicles".'

A student was taught how to use his head and each limb as a weapon of attack and that he must never stop just because an opponent was crippled. 'If you've broken his arm,' they were told, 'it's of value only because it makes it easier to kill him.' As one Canadian recruit commented, 'it turned our values upside down', and an OSS member who was taught by Fairbairn summed up his instructor's attitude succinctly: 'All of us who were taught by Major Fairbairn soon realised that he had an honest dislike of anything that smacked of decency in fighting.'

Using a knife was an essential part of silent killing and Fairbairn taught exactly which areas of the body were the most vulnerable to attack. He was an expert in knife-fighting and he and Sykes invented the double-edged commando knife named after them.

'There are several schools of thought pertaining to knife fighting technique,' an OSS manual stated, 'and perhaps the most widely known and accepted today is the Fairbairn system which embodies various slashing operations. These slashing operations are directed at vital spots on the body, arms and neck, and the penetrating technique which is most usually used is a thrusting proposition directed at the most vital spots of the body. It can be accomplished from either the front or the rear.'

Aaron Bank, a member of one of the Jedburgh teams to go into France (see Chapter 15), noted how thorough Fairbairn was in training his students with a knife. 'He waited for a really dark, moonless night and had us called out for sentry elimination training. We had been taught how to approach a sentry from the rear, snap an arm around his neck in a choke hold, and thrust a stiletto of Fairbairn design between his upper ribs while bending him backward. When it came to my turn, I approached the dummy, grasped it, and bent it back as I plunged my knife into, of all things, a knapsack instead of the ribs. Had this been for keeps, the sentry would not have been eliminated. All our previous practice had been on dummies without a knapsack. Fairbairn drove his point home. We never forgot. You had to determine before the attack whether a knapsack was being worn. A two-man elimination team was the safest and quietest, since one man effected the assault while the other grasped the sentry's rifle before it dropped, clattering, to the ground.'

Fairbairn and Sykes also taught new methods for firing weapons which had been honed by Fairbairn during his career with the Shanghai police between the wars. The loss of nine policemen shot by armed criminals led to Fairbairn's recommending new methods for using a pistol or revolver. 'Although I was responsible for the training of the Police in shooting,' he wrote later, 'I was compelled to teach only the methods as laid down in Army textbooks. Anything that savoured of being original was not permitted. The methods of loading and the use of the so-called safety catches had to be as per the book.

'I pointed out that one of our men had his safety catch on SAFE when he was killed and advanced the theory that the only man who gained the advantages of the safety catch was the criminal. I explained that I had a method of instruction based on the principle of "shooting to live" in which men would be trained to fire instinctively in bursts of two shots without even bringing their pistols to the line-of-sight: practice in the dark when all one would see of their opponents would be a shadow: firing up and down a staircase at moving objects, with off-stage noises to make the practice as near as possible to the conditions one would have to contend with in actual combat. I asked for and obtained permission to pin down all safety catches.'

The time-honoured way to fire a pistol had been standing straight, side-on to the target with the weapon fired once it had been swung up to eye level by an outstretched arm. Now Fairbairn and Sykes taught the crouching stance square on to the target with a two-handed grip on the pistol which was fired at waist level; and instead of firing a shot at a time they taught what is known as the 'double tap': two shots fired in quick succession. It was this kind of training which was of inestimable value to the hundreds of SOE and OSS agents who went into the field. As Langelaan pointed out it gave him and his fellow students a 'sense of physical power and superiority that few men ever acquire. By the time we finished our training, I would have willingly enough tackled any man, whatever his strength, size or ability.'

Once through this particular sieve, prospective SOE agents were sent from the Group A schools to the Group B finishing schools. These were country houses in southern England around Beaulieu in the New Forest. As at Arisaig, each country section had its own residence for its students; the instructors and conducting officers lived in Beaulieu Manor. The course lasted three or four weeks.

Whereas Arisaig had emphasised the aggressive techniques of subversive warfare, the Group B schools primarily taught the equally essential defensive ones to survive in a hostile environment. It required quite a different set of skills and a different temperament, and students who had done outstandingly well at Arisaig, did not always manage to make the necessary adjustment.

Students were made familiar with police methods and techniques in the countries they were eventually going to enter, were shown how to detect, and throw off someone shadowing them, and were given detailed instruction on how to appear and behave as inconspicuously as possible. The school also drummed into their students how to avoid making the smallest mistake in behaviour which might give them away: like looking the wrong way when crossing a road or not knowing the local culinary preferences when eating in a restaurant.

Students were also made to act out situations that occurred in occupied territories. These varied from the casual routine search, or scrutiny of identity papers at a control point, to the intensive interrogation which started with a shake on the shoulder in the middle of the night. They were also instructed on how to compile concise reports and to use the simplest codes to transmit them (Morse code had already been taught at Arisaig), and advice was given on basic propaganda, and how to recruit sub-agents in occupied territories.

Above all, students had to learn how to submerge themselves in their cover, just as an actor has to absorb himself in his part so completely that he assumes the *persona* of the character he is playing. With this an essential requirement for survival it is little wonder that one of the best-remembered instructors was Paul Dehn, who came from the film industry and who also, during the course of his wartime career, served as chief instructor at Camp X (see below).

The course ended in an exercise which lasted several days. It tested to the full everything the students had learned before they passed on to more advanced technical courses such as clandestine printing, lock-picking, industrial sabotage, and using advanced ciphers and operating a wireless (the wireless school was at Thame Park, east of Oxford). Industrial sabotage was taught by George Rheam at Brickendonbury Manor (Station XVII), situated between Hertford and Hoddesdon. Rheam was, wrote M. R. D. Foot in his outline history of SOE, 'the inventor of many industrial sabotage techniques and an instructor of genius... Anyone trained by him could look at a factory with quite new eyes, spot the few essential machines in it, and understand how to stop them with a few well-placed ounces of explosive; to stop them, moreover, in such a way that some of them could not be restarted promptly by removing undamaged parts from comparable machines nearby.' Later, many of these techniques became part of the training of OSS personnel and of those passing through SOE schools abroad.

Parachuting, taught at the Parachute Training School at Manchester's Ringway airport, was one of the technical courses most students were required to pass. The school's primary function was to train members of the armed forces for British airborne divisions, but it also taught SOE personnel whom the school's commanding officer called 'specials'. These 'specials' arrived in groups of 30 or so and undertook a very abbreviated training – four days compared to the standard course of two weeks. They were not allowed to mingle with those taking the standard course, either on or off duty, and were kept in safe houses.

Early training took place on static apparatus at one of the safe houses. 'The little window in the left hand gable of the west front was removed,' one trainee recalled. 'Outside was a staging with a hole resembling the hole in the floor of a Whitley bomber [the standard aircraft used for parachuting agents into the field].

On the ground below this staging was a coconut mat. In the room there was a drum to which was attached a fan. The victim having been dressed in parachute harness attached to a rope around the drum, stepped out on to the staging, dropped through the hole, and landed on the mat below. His speed was controlled by the fan attached to the drum.'

Training on static apparatus was followed by two parachute drops from a static balloon floating 700 feet above Tatton Park, before trainees made two daylight drops from a Whitley into the park. A night drop, and sometimes one into water – using techniques developed by SOE instructors – were also undertaken. Once a student had passed through the necessary training courses he was posted to an operational holding school. There he could wait for only a matter of hours before being dispatched abroad; but sometimes it could be months.

'I knew that I could fight far more intelligently and efficiently than the majority of men', Langelaan summarised his training, 'and that, single-handed, I was capable of blowing up a bridge, of sinking a ship, of putting a railway engine out of action in a matter of seconds with a mere spanner, or of derailing an express train with my overcoat. I had been taught to drive a locomotive, how to kill an enraged dog with my bare hands, to jump from a fast-moving train, how to throw a horse, to decode a message, to make invisible ink, to receive and transmit Morse.'

By the time the USA entered the war in December 1941 SOE's system of training schools in the UK was well established. Other training establishments were also started in the Middle East and Far East along the same lines, and altogether about 60 SOE establishments were formed world-wide. One of the most important was STS 103 (three digits meant it was situated outside Britain).

STS 103 is now universally known as Camp X, though there is no contemporary documentary evidence to show it was called this at the time. However, as David Stafford, the establishment's historian, and the plaque commemorating it, call it Camp X, that is what it is called here. It was an important school because it helped to cement intelligence relations between Britain and the United States and showed the latter – which had had no previous experience of clandestine warfare – SOE's techniques of sabotage and subversion.

Situated outside Oshawa, a small town in Ontario, Canada, Camp X came under the aegis of William Stephenson, a Canadian First World War fighter ace. Stephenson was head of British Security Co-ordination (BSC), the British intelligence office in New York which represented MI5, MI6 and SOE in the western hemisphere. Despite lurid tales to the contrary, Stephenson had no influence on the war outside the western hemisphere, but the work he did in establishing a first-rate intelligence liaison with the Americans eventually earned him a well merited knighthood.

In February 1941 BSC was directed to establish an SOE network in Latin America, 'to recruit likely SOE agents in the United States and other American countries, to help influence public opinion in the United States in a pro-Allied direction, to make contact with various European refugee and exile movements in the New World, and to help create secret communications channels for SOE networks'.

Following this directive the decision was made in September 1941 to open a preliminary training camp to train SOE agents for South America and other SOE agents for work in Europe drawn from volunteers in the United States and Canada. It was also the thinking of Stephenson and SOE that such a school would be the ideal showcase to display to the Americans the merits of subversive warfare, and the best methods of going about it.

At that time the United States was still delicately balanced between furthering the Allied cause while not actually being a participant in the hostilities (though in the Atlantic an undeclared war was already being waged between the US and German navies). President Roosevelt walked a tightrope, for American isolationism was still a formidable force even while public realisation grew that a clash with Germany, and probably Japan, too, was unavoidable. The momentum was towards war yet any overt sign of preparing for it was liable to cause a public outcry.

In these circumstances, to which might legitimately be added the natural aversion the American public and their politicians had to illicit warfare, it was impossible for the Office of Co-ordinator of Information (COI), the forerunner of the OSS, to set up openly the necessary organisations for covert operations or to establish any training bases for sabotage and subversion on United States territory. As the history of the OSS's Schools and Training Branch expressed it: 'What type of training was required to make an American un-American enough to stick the enemy in the back? No longer was there interest in the old tenet of standing up and fighting like a man. Now the accent must be laid on brutal, cruel, underhanded action, as definite as it must be deadly.'

Having Camp X on his doorstep to inculcate this new attitude into potential COI instructors was just what the head of the COI, General William J. Donovan, needed; and for it to be made available to him reinforced the close liaison he had already established with Stephenson and SOE. Several members of COI were also trained in Britain.

Camp X was organised so secretly that not even the Canadian prime minister, or his war cabinet, were informed that it was being constructed. Its first staff consisted of the commandant and eight instructors. It opened on 9 December 1941, two days after the Japanese attacked the US Fleet in Pearl Harbor. The course it offered lasted three or four weeks and was therefore only a preliminary one. But it did also include certain aspects of the advanced Group B schools at Beaulieu – enemy identification and the recruiting of sub-agents, for instance – and all three of Camp X's chief instructors came from Beaulieu. The second

Commandant, Major Bill Brooker, likened the syllabus to an *à la carte* menu. The instructors picked what they chose to teach according to which organisation their students came from. For members of the Federal Bureau of Investigation (FBI), for example, the emphasis was on security, while those who were destined to be dropped into occupied Europe were given a basic course in sabotage and subversion before being passed to Beaulieu.

Camp X maintained its other role, as the base for the highly secret transatlantic radio network and as a station for intercepting enemy radio communications, until the end of the war and beyond. But as a training school it closed in mid-1944. By that time 273 students had graduated from it, including the founding members of the US Army's first clandestine unit, Detachment 101.

The entry of the USA into the war opened the way for Donovan to form, officially, branches for intelligence (headed by David Bruce) and sabotage and subversion (headed by Preston Goodfellow), and to acquire training grounds for them. By the spring of 1942 the first four were up and running. The intelligence branch, called Special Activities/Bruce, or SA/B, bought a 100-acre estate about 20 miles from Washington (officially known as RTU-11, less officially as 'The Farm') and SA/Goodfellow, or SA/G, four separate training grounds near Quantico, Virginia. Area A, 5,000 acres of woods, became the advanced training school with a two-week training course; Area B, 9,000 acres of mountainous terrain, was where the two-week basic course was held after pupils had passed a preliminary one; Area C, 4,000 acres of woods, was used to train students in communications; and Area D, 1,400 acres alongside the Potomac River, became the training ground for a maritime unit specialising in clandestine operations.

Later that year, in November, Area E, which included three country houses situated 30 miles north of Baltimore, was also opened for basic training and in April 1943 Area F, located at the Congressional Country Club on the edge of Washington, became the training base of the Operational Groups. Finally, in October 1943 Area M, a former Signal Corps camp in Indiana, was opened for training as another communications camp. After mid-1944 most training was undertaken on the West Coast, where six areas – on Catalina Island, California, and elsewhere – had a monthly turnover of 100 students. The schools in the eastern part of the United States were gradually closed or converted to holding camps where returning personnel from Europe were debriefed or screened for possible further use in the field.

To set up these early training grounds Donovan urgently needed experienced instructors and practical advice. The British, and particularly Camp X's training directorate, provided both. The COI's chief training officer, Lieutenant Colonel Garland Williams, who had been the director of the New York Bureau of Narcotics, was an early graduate of Camp X; both Fairbairn and the camp's chief instructor (and later Commandant), Major Bill Brooker, lectured regularly at the

COI training schools, and both of them were later seconded to OSS; the Admiralty lent a British naval officer, experienced in the infiltration and exfiltration of agents from the sea, to run COI's maritime school; and once the agreement between SOE and OSS came into force in June 1942 more than 60 OSS officers were dispatched to the UK for training in SOE schools.

Brooker, a former chief instructor at the Beaulieu group of schools after being recruited into SOE in March 1941, had a colourful method of imparting the basics of clandestine warfare. Sweet-Escott called him a born salesman, and 'a brilliant and convincing lecturer', so convincing that Sweet-Escott was asked by 'one of his more intelligent American colleagues' if Brooker was the head of the British secret service. He certainly left his mark on COI/OSS as the following extract from OSS files reveals. '...he was very aggressive and sometimes not too diplomatic, and he gained many supporters as well as many detractors within OSS. It was not beneath him to employ bluff in "getting across" his lecture material by casting himself in the role of leading character in his spy thriller stories borrowed, probably, from many sources. *He* was the one responsible for the capture of this German agent in Canada. *He* was the one who interrogated this recalcitrant German prisoner. *He* was the one who briefed and dispatched this British agent to Germany – and the story would be complete with touching and intimate details. He himself would no doubt have been the first to admit that he was a big bluff (for he actually had little, if any, operational experience) but his argument would have been that any method was justified if it conveyed the necessary lesson to the students. This, however, did not make him any better loved in some quarters of OSS.'

Both OSS and SOE also set up training schools in the Far East. The first was SOE's No. 101 Special Training School which was opened in Singapore by its Oriental Mission in July 1941. The earliest OSS school was set up in India in the autumn of 1942 to train volunteers for its Detachment 101 which operated behind Japanese lines in Burma.

No. 101 Special Training School trained a number of British and foreign civilians as well as members of the British armed forces. Some of these were formed into 'left-behind parties' which operated from jungle hide-outs in Malaya against the occupying Japanese forces. At the end of January 1942 it was moved to Rangoon, and when Burma fell the School's instructors moved to the Guerrilla Training Unit (later known as the Eastern Warfare School) formed by SOE's India Mission at Kharakvasla near Poona. Initially this trained 150 communists to work in India if it were occupied by the Japanese, but when the threat to India subsided it gave its students offensive training for work in Japanese-occupied countries.

At first SOE found native recruitment for their Far East operations almost impossible. In 1942 the head of the India Mission warned London of the difficulties, saying there was little patriotism from which to recruit. Of 300 Burmese interviewed in India only four were selected, and even these were later discarded. No volunteers from the Malayan population in Britain could be found at all, suitable or not. Later in the war recruiting did improve and some 370 volunteers came from India, and the same number from Burma. However, only 30 Indians made it into the field compared to the 270 Burmese, half of whom came from the plains, the other half from the various hill tribes, most notably the Kachins and the Karens.

The Americans, on the other hand, had few problems recruiting for Detachment 101, even in 1942 when the outcome of the war was far from certain. 'Our recruiting for new teams had flourished', wrote one of its commanders, Colonel William R. Peers, after the war, 'largely because of the retreat from Burma. The people who had fled their homes were in refugee camps in India, and it was there we found men willing to undertake the dangerous activities we had in mind. We narrowed the initial list down to fifty people; some of these had been engaged in smuggling and illegal trading, work which seemed to fit naturally into what we expected them to do in war; others were college professors, merchants of various commodities, or managers of teak forests who had had their holdings taken over by the Japanese. For some, the reason was the money we were prepared to pay; for others it was what they felt about the war.'

For the British the Thais proved the best source early on. Thailand was in an anomalous position. Japanese troops had entered the country at the start of their Malayan campaign in December 1941 and under Japanese pressure the collaborationist Thai government had declared war on Britain and the United States in early 1942. For the British, therefore, Thailand was an enemy state. But the United States did not retaliate by declaring war on Thailand and chose to regard it as neutral, and an anti-Japanese movement, encouraged by both SOE and OSS, soon developed within the country.

In August 1942 thirty-five of the 100 or so Thai nationals in Britain volunteered to join the Pioneer Corps on the understanding that they would have, in due course, duties more appropriate to their academic qualifications. Twenty-three of these were eventually accepted, and used, as agents. Known by the code-name 'white elephants' they proved to be SOE's most successful agents in the Far East and eventually a further 54 were recruited from Thailand.

China provided 223 recruits for SOE and these were trained in India; 107 of them spoke Thai. Some, especially the first batch, were excellent – 46 went on operations and proved their worth – but others were useless. One group, code-named the 'red elephants', were described as suffering from what was quaintly known as 'Chungking taint', an admiration for all things American balanced by outright scorn for anything British. They and succeeding groups proved difficult to manage and impossible to train. The few volunteers from French Indo-China and Sumatra were equally unsuitable.

3
Equipping the Saboteurs

Successful sabotage operations needed highly specialised equipment, and the men performing it not only had to be properly trained but well armed and well equipped. Another essential ingredient for success was the arming of those who worked with OSS and SOE personnel behind enemy lines. This was a major undertaking which stretched to the limit the resources of the Special Duty Squadrons whose responsibility it was to drop supplies accurately and on schedule.

The great majority of weapons supplied by OSS and SOE to guerrilla units were identical with those used by the regular Allied armies. There are no statistics of the total numbers of firearms supplied world-wide for clandestine warfare, but, for example, in the Far East 25,000 small arms were dispatched by SOE into the field in Burma, Malaya, French Indo-China and Thailand, as well as 1,300 Bren guns, PIATs and mortars, 30 tons of explosive, and 60,000 grenades. And of the 418,083 weapons delivered to the resistance in France during the war, approximately 47 per cent were submachine-guns, 30 per cent were rifles, 14 per cent were hand guns, 5 per cent were light machine-guns, 2 per cent were carbines, and 1 per cent were anti-tank weapons.

Rifles were mostly the standard British infantryman's weapon, the .303 Lee Enfield; the carbine was the American .30 calibre M-1 Winchester semi-automatic. The most common automatic weapons were the British Bren light machine-gun and the Sten Gun. The principal anti-tank weapon was the PIAT, of which more than 1,200 were dispatched to the resistance in France, but the outdated Boys rifle and some bazookas were also supplied.

Requests from the field for heavier weapons were turned down – though a 6-pounder anti-tank gun was, on one occasion, dropped to an SAS team who used it successfully against a German armoured car – because SOE's policy was not to supply weapons that could hinder the mobility of their forces in the field. Anyway, supplying ammunition for heavier weapons would have been beyond SOE's capability. The OSS did drop some 37mm guns to an Operational Group (see Chapter 14) in southern France. These were all damaged when they were dropped by parachute, but two were put into working order and caused German casualties before they were captured.

Most of the 57,849 hand guns sent to France were British service revolvers (British Enfield and Webleys, both .380 calibre) or the American Smith & Wesson .380 revolver. Pistols such as the American Colt and the Canadian Browning were in great demand but were in short supply. The latter was almost always reserved for British commando and airborne troops, though they were available to the leaders of SOE sabotage circuits if they requested them.

When OSS was formed it found it impossible to find an adequate supply of hand guns and it therefore had to resort to the second-hand market, and its inventory of these weapons reveals it issued to its agents a motley collection, many of which were models dating back to before the First World War. By 1944, however, a wide variety of hand guns was available to OSS operatives, including the .32 Colt hammerless automatic which was easy to conceal in a shoulder holster or a pocket.

OSS also acquired the cheaply produced Liberator or Woolworth Gun (also called a flare projector for security reasons) specially designed for resistance workers in occupied countries. It was a smooth-bored, single-shot pistol which was less than six inches in length and weighed only 1lb. It fired a .45 calibre cartridge and was accurate up to about ten yards. It was a very primitive weapon – the spent cartridge case had to be extracted with a small stick before it could be reloaded – but huge numbers were manufactured in 1942. But the Free French and the governments-in-exile of other occupied countries asked for them not to be distributed in Europe as there was concern that such a weapon could cause problems after the war. Large numbers were distributed in China and the South-West Pacific Area but there is no record of their ever being used operationally.

Even smaller (3.3 inches) was an OSS design called the Stinger. This was no more than a barrel into which a .22 cartridge was fitted during manufacture. It was fired by depressing a lever while the weapon was concealed in the palm of the hand, and was then thrown away because it could not be reloaded. About 32,000 were made available to OSS and it was reported by the deputy director of the Research and Development Department in July 1944 as being 'a very popular item and is in widespread use. I have been told that it has accounted for several "Krauts" [Germans] in the crowded cities and further supply is needed.' But while there's no hard evidence that they killed any enemy personnel, it is known that three Americans were injured while handling them.

SOE's equivalent of the Stinger was the Welpen, a .22in weapon disguised as a pen. It was developed but never put into production; the more realistic-looking Enpen was – from 1944 by the British ordnance factory at Enfield. Both these weapons worked on a similar principle to the Stinger, and the Enpen was, according to one source, carried by at least one agent in the field – who preferred to carry three of them in preference to a pistol. The most popular submachine-gun (SMG) used by SOE agents and members of the resistance was the

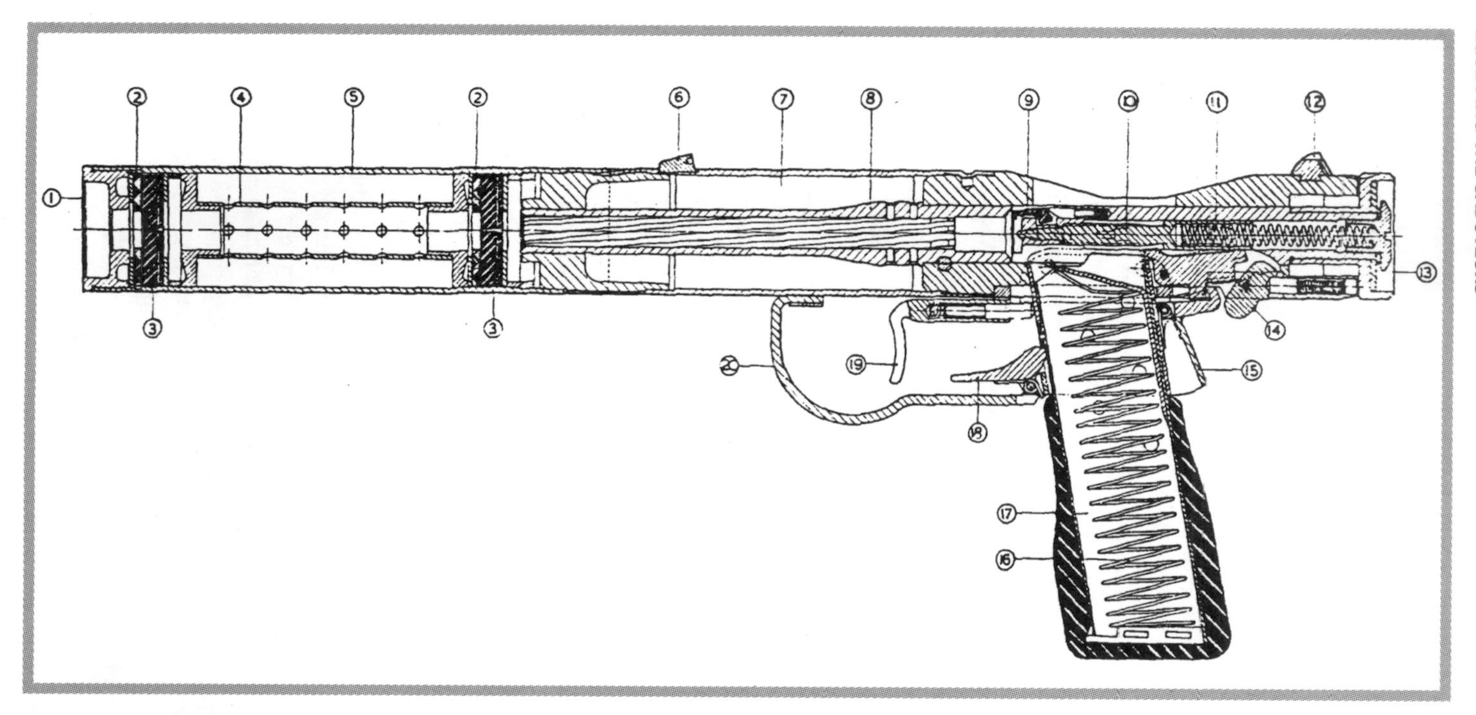

The Welrod 9mm Mk I.
1 Silencer tube end cap
2 Steel baffle plate
3 Rubber baffle (self-closing)
4 Forward silencer unit
5 Silencer tube
6 Fore sight
7 Bursting chamber
8 Barrel
9 Extractor
10 Striker pin
11 Striker pin spring
12 Back sight
13 Breech operating handle
14 Positive safety catch
15 Hand-operated safety catch
16 Magazine spring
17 Magazine and pistol grip
18 Magazine retaining catch
19 Trigger
20 Trigger guard

Sten, which could fire single shots as well as automatically. A British invention, it was robust, relatively easy to conceal as it could be broken down into two or three parts, cheap to manufacture (£1.50 in today's currency), and fired 9mm ammunition which could be procured more easily because it was also used in some German weapons.

The American equivalent of the Sten gun – though it could not fire single shots – was the M3. This fired .45 ammunition though a later version was modified to take 9mm cartridges. Another OSS SMG was the 9mm Marlin submachine-gun (UD-42). It was shaped not unlike a Thompson and was easily recognisable by its unique double magazines. Many thousands of these weapons were distributed in north-west Europe, the Mediterranean and in the Far East and they were, for instance, widely used by Detachment 101 (see Chapter 9). Although more M3s were acquired than the Marlin, the latter is generally acknowledged as being the OSS's standard SMG.

As might be expected of clandestine organisations a number of silenced weapons were developed or acquired from other sources. The OSS produced the HiStandard pistol – High Standard was the manufacturing company – which fired .22 ammunition. It was just under 14 inches long with the silencer attached, weighed almost 3lb, and its 90 per cent reduction in noise was better than that accomplished by any other silencer. The OSS ordered about 2,500 of them. One of the OSS Weapons catalogues described it as being 'excellent for use in a closed room and for eliminating sentries', and reports from the field verified this. A larger calibre pistol was being developed when the war ended.

SOE also produced silenced pistols. The most successful was the eight-shot Welrod which had a silencer built into it. It was fired with two hands, one gripped the butt the other steadied the weapon by holding the silencer barrel. According to one source, Charles Cruickshank's official history, *SOE in the Far East*, when fired it could not be recognised as a firearm at 50 yards. However, according to OSS tests, it was noisier than their .22 HiStandard, but had the advantage of firing larger calibre ammunition (.32in and later 9mm). It was 11.75 inches long and had a detachable butt so that the two pieces could be concealed under loose-fitting trousers by dangling them on loops.

Two versions of the Sten gun had a silencer, but only single shots could be fired with them, and special low-velocity 9mm ammunition was needed for maximum efficiency. A silenced Sten made a distinct hissing sound when fired. In his book, *Secret Warfare*, Pierre Lorain writes that the De Lisle Silent Commando Carbine was also 'widely employed by the many British secret services, especially in defence of Intelligence Service bases or clandestine radio stations', though another source says only 150 were manufactured. Completely silent, and accurate up to 150 yards, the De Lisle was something of a mongrel. It was modelled on the .303 Lee Enfield rifle but had a shortened Thompson SMG barrel fitted with a silencer. Its breech had been modified so that it could fire .45 calibre ammunition fed into it by a Colt magazine holding seven cartridges.

The OSS developed a silenced M3 which, when fired, made what has been described as a 'mild clap'. In the OSS Weapons catalogue issued by the organisation's Research and Development Department, the M3 was called 'an extremely effective weapon for wiping out groups of enemy personnel at close quarters, especially indoors. The appreciable noise reduction makes general alarm less immediate and widespread. The report of the silenced M3 submachine-gun becomes inaudible at 200 to 800 yards, depending upon the terrain. This is slightly less than half of the audible range of the unsilenced weapon. Experienced operators prefer the feel of the silenced M3 because the slight extra weight helps keep the muzzle from rising during automatic fire.'

Given such a laudatory write-up it is perhaps surprising that such a very limited number of silenced M3s were issued, though the initial response had been enthusiastic and thousands of silencers were produced. Only a handful were issued in the European and Mediterranean Theatres of Operations. Most went to the Far East where they were not well received by the Chinese who apparently preferred 'plenty of noise'. Attempts were made to design a satisfactory silencer for the 9mm version of the M3, and for the Thompson SMG, but these never reached the production stage.

OSS and SOE sabotage personnel normally took the field armed with a hand gun, and with a rifle, carbine, or SMG, and perhaps with a knife of some sort. But a mass of other weapons were developed by the two organisations including spring coshes, crossbows, spigot mortars, dart guns, and tear gas guns. None, except the coshes, reached agents in the field. These were produced in some quantity for OSS and a number were shipped to the UK. But an ex-OSS member, John Brunner, recalls that they were not 'much in demand' and that the only comment he heard about them in the field was that they 'didn't work'.

Special weapons and devices were developed for OSS by its Research and Development Branch and by Division 19 of the National Defense Research Committee (the predecessor, and then one of the advisory committees, of the Office of Scientific Research and Development), the laboratory work being carried out by the Maryland Research Laboratory. Initially, SOE provided special weapons and devices for OSS. But later OSS either improved on these or developed and manufactured similar ones, and it also arranged for the manufacture for SOE of a number of SOE devices. It was not uncommon for OSS personnel in the European Theatre of Operations to be supplied by SOE with devices and equipment which had been manufactured in the USA for OSS which had then shipped them to the UK for SOE use.

The OSS's Procurement and Supply Branch was responsible for seeing that the weapon or device was manufactured in the correct quantities while project engineers of the Technical Division, a sub-division of the Research and Development Branch, oversaw development to ensure that scientific research did not go beyond the bounds of practicability. The project engineer also arranged for any weapon or device to be demonstrated before representatives of the operational branches and the User Trial Committee which consisted of representatives from the National Defense Research Committee, the research laboratory, the British Liaison Mission, and the OSS's Procurement and Supply Branch. If successful the project engineer arranged for plans and specifications to be assembled and for the weapon or device to be manufactured in the appropriate quantities, and he was then in touch with those who used the finished product in the field for evaluation purposes. All equipment issued to the Special Operations Branch, the OSS's equivalent of SOE, were co-ordinated with SOE to ensure that as many as possible were interchangeable in the field.

The development of special weapons and devices used by SOE took place at The Firs, a large house in Whitchurch near Aylesbury in Buckinghamshire; at SOE's Station IX, set up in The Frythe, a small private hotel in Welwyn Garden City and where, from August 1940, SOE's wireless research was based; and at SOE's Station XII at Aston House near Stevenage. The Firs, not an SOE establishment but one with which SOE was closely associated, was run by Major Millis Jefferis under the powerful protection of Professor Lindemann (Lord Cherwell), the prime minister's scientific adviser, who ensured that Jefferis' organisation (called MD1) maintained its independence.

In May 1941 Station XII was given a new cover name, Experimental Station 6 (War Department) or ES6(WD) for short. However, when the chemical engineer, D. M. Newitt, became SOE's director of scientific research the following month he moved the Station's development laboratory to Station IX at The Frythe, but it continued to produce weapons and equipment from Station IX's designs.

Station IX was also known as the Welwyn Experimental Laboratory, hence the names given to such exotic weaponry and equipment as the Welrod silent pistol described above, the Welbike (portable motorcycle), Welfag (.22 calibre firing device concealed in a cigarette), Welman submarine (one-man submersible), Welpen (device concealed in a fountain pen which fired either a projectile or tear gas), and the Welpipe (.22 calibre device concealed within a tobacco pipe). Only the Welrod and the Welman were ever used operationally, though the Welbike proved popular among Chinese officials who were bribed with them.

Of much more use to the saboteur were the multitude of explosive and non-explosive devices, such as the tiny metal four-spiked tyre bursters, which enabled them to go about their work efficiently, reliably, and – if necessary – discreetly.

Into this last category fell various contaminants used to sabotage lubricants and fuel. When it was found that neither sand nor sugar did this satisfactorily (sugar, in any case, was almost unobtainable in occupied territories) both organisations developed and manufactured special compounds. The OSS called theirs caccolube – a bilingualism for 'bad lubricant' – or Turtle Eggs. It came in small rubber packets which could easily be concealed in the palm of the hand and slipped into the oil aperture of a vehicle. Once the engine oil was hot the rubber sac deteriorated and released its contents so that after about 30–50 miles the vehicle's engine simply seized up. The special 'grease' produced by SOE had the same effect on engine bearings, and on the axles of rolling stock, and was used with great effect by French railway workers. Both types had the enormous advantage of not being traceable to the user, as it was almost impossible to detect that sabotage had been the cause of breakdown.

However, non-detectable sabotage was a tiny percentage of the total carried out during the course of the war. By far the largest number of sabotage operations relied on explosive devices activated by various mechanisms.

The most effective explosive for sabotage was the plastic variety (PE), developed in the Royal Arsenal at Woolwich. Typically, it consisted of an explosive such as cyclotrimethylene-trinitrame – called RDX (Research Department Explosive) by the British, cyclonite by the Americans, T4 by the Italians and hexogen by the Germans – which was mixed, roughly in a ratio of 85 per cent to 15 per cent, with oil or beeswax, or even axle grease. This mixture turned it into the consistency of Plasticine which could be moulded into any convenient shape to fit against the object being sabotaged.

PE had an important advantage over dynamite or gelignite, or similar commercial explosives, because it was extremely stable and only a well-embedded detonator could detonate it. It was almost always used in an MD1 invention called the limpet mine. The limpet was probably both organisations' most successful demolition device. Designed for use against steel-hulled ships, it was manufactured in very large quantities, mostly in the USA. Raids against Axis shipping in the Gironde by Royal Marines and against Japanese shipping in Singapore harbour by Special Operations Australia personnel (see Chapter 8) proved their efficacy.

Six magnets, three on each side of the box holding the explosive, held the device to the side of a ship. At one end a delay fuze was activated by screwing down a butterfly nut. If necessary a sympathetic fuze could be substituted instead, or added. This was used if several limpets were to be placed on the same target so that the detonation of one before the others – time delay fuzes were never entirely accurate – caused all of them to explode.

The OSS version of the limpet was similar to the British Mk II model, but its waterproof case was plastic not brass. It measured 8¾ x 3 x 3 inches and weighed 8lb. Instead of PE, which reacted with the plastic, OSS used Torpex, a mixture of RDX (40 per cent), TNT (37 per cent), and aluminium powder (18 per cent).

Limpets, of course, only worked against steel-hulled ships, and when agents in the Far East pointed out that many of their intended targets had wooden hulls OSS devised the 'Pin-Up'. The limpet's magnets were replaced by a mechanism which when triggered fired a steel pin into the wooden hull to fix the device firmly in place.

The clam mine was a miniature limpet. The OSS version, again, an improved version of its British counterpart, measured 6 x 2¾ x 1⅜ inches into which two time pencils were inserted at one end. It contained 8oz of PE and was ideal for destroying vehicles, light tanks, and small boats. The even smaller Firefly, developed by OSS, measured 3½ x 1⅜ inches in diameter and weighed only 3oz. It could be dropped into the fuel tank of a vehicle or into open fuel cans. After a certain time, which varied between two and seven hours depending on the temperature of the fuel in which the device was immersed, the petrol swelled two rubber washers which activated the detonator.

Both organisations also developed more exotic devices, such as explosive coal. SOE, which code-named such devices 'toys', had ones which resembled cow pats, and mule and camel dung, and for use in the Far East Chinese 'stone' lanterns and Balinese 'carvings' which were either full of, or made from PE. OSS records show that it also manufactured explosive candles. These, like OSS coal, were made of pentolite, synthetic pentaerythritol tetranite mixed 50/50 with TNT.

Even more ingenious was the explosive flour developed by OSS. Code-named 'Aunt Jemima', this was a mixture of 75 per cent RDX and 25 per cent wheat flour and it could be baked so that it looked like normal bread. Tests were even made to make sure the 'bread' was edible and the instruction sheet gives recipes for making it. When mixed with water it made a dough-like substance which was almost as efficient as PE. It could also be moulded into bricks, rocks, tiles, and so on. Records show that it was distributed to OSS in the Far East, and Stanley P. Lovell, a one-time head of OSS's Research and Development Branch, asserted that it was used to destroy a Yangtse River bridge, but he was, according to some accounts, an unreliable source.

Apart from the one incident described by Lovell, there is no evidence that any of these devices were ever used against the enemy, but the efficiency of the candles was proved when some were stolen by an OSS Chinese employee. He lit one to illuminate his tent which was crowded with fellow employees. Two were killed and ten wounded.

Another device that could be more dangerous to friend than foe was the British-manufactured footshooter, a small tube which fired a bullet into the foot of anyone who stepped on it. It was withdrawn in China, but the head of Detachment 101 wrote after the war that his Kachin guerrillas used them with great success and that they caused 'untold apprehension' among the Japanese.

Any explosive which is safe to handle needs a firing device to detonate it and many ingenious types were developed by SOE and OSS. Often SOE developed a device first and it was then improved upon by OSS and manufactured in the USA, but SOE frequently provided their own model for OSS personnel working in the European Theatre of Operations.

The OSS Pressure Type Firing Device and its SOE equivalent was a small metal box into the lid of which was screwed an antenna (the OSS antenna was 2⅜ inches high); 40 to 50lb of pressure on the antenna compressed the lid and this activated a percussion cap which, in turn, activated the detonator.

They were typically used to attack railways as was an SOE device called the Fog Signal. This was clamped to a rail, where it looked like a piece of ordinary railway equipment. It was activated by the wheels of whatever rolling stock

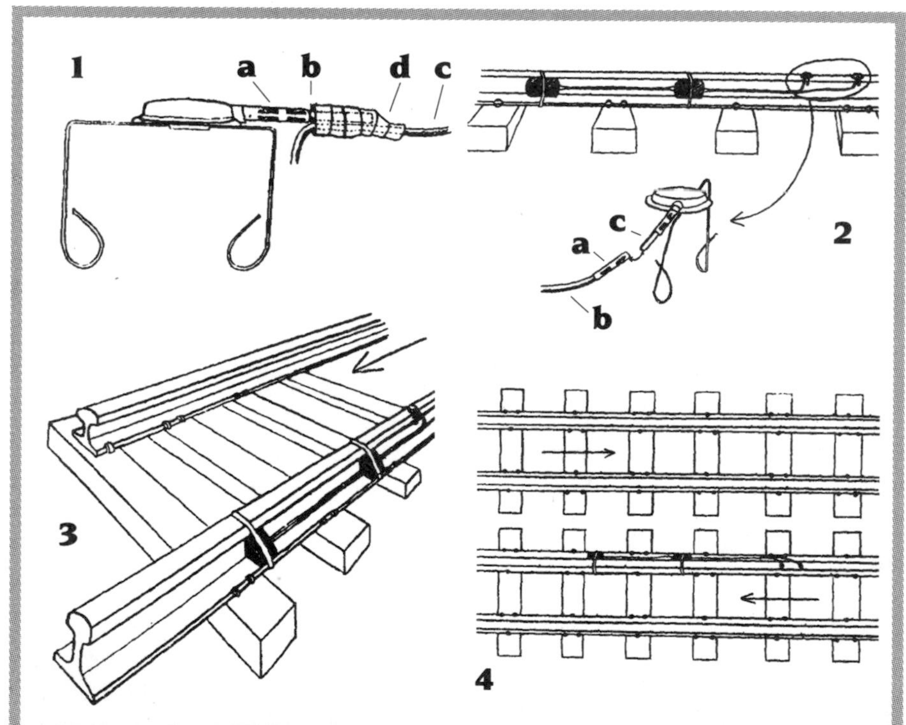

SOE's fog signal devices. Two were normally used to derail a train. The one illustrated by diagram 1 has a spring snout (a) to hold a detonator (b). The cordtex tail (c) from the charge is taped (d) to the detonator. Another type, diagram 2, had a special spring snout attachment (a) which fixed the cordtex (b) to the detonator (c), making taping unnecessary. The charges were placed on the outside of the rail with the fog signals on the side from which the train would be coming, diagram 3. With double tracks the charges were placed on one of the inner rails so that when the train derailed it blocked both tracks, diagram 4.

passed over it, and it then detonated the two or more ¾lb charges which were placed alongside the rail one metre apart. However, this 'one metre' technique, as the official OSS history called it, failed to derail its target on more than half the occasions it was used, and OSS was requested to improve it. OSS carried out tests and found that the fault lay not with the firing device but how the charges were placed – along the side of the rail instead of beneath it. This revelation came too late to be of use in France, but it was employed extensively in Yugoslavia, Italy and the Far East. The explosion not only removed about eight feet of track but also created a crater into which the engine fell.

The Release Firing Device, also made by both organisations, was employed primarily to booby-trap objects that were likely to be moved or lifted by the enemy. The OSS version weighed only 2oz and was just over 4½ inches long. It fitted into the cracks of doors or windows and could be hidden practically anywhere. The Pull Type Firing device – a metal housing that contained a spring-loaded firing pin which struck the percussion cap – could be activated by a trip wire or by someone pulling a cord attached to it.

Different types of fuze were also developed and used extensively. The sympathetic fuze, mentioned above in connection with limpet mines, was an ingenious device. It was only activated when the concussion of an explosion exceeded 9lb which was far greater than the water pressure a limpet mine would be subjected to when attached to a ship's hull. If pressure exceeding 9lb was applied to a diaphragm in the fuze it snapped shut on to a firing pin which detonated the mine. To protect the operator from a premature explosion a salt block which took between 50 and 100 minutes to dissolve was inserted between the firing pin and the diaphragm.

The most frequently used delay mechanism was the Time Pencil, an SOE invention. This, as its name implies, was a pencil-shaped device. Its striker was released when the thin wire holding the striker was eaten away by an acid. The acid was released when an ampoule in the pencil was crushed by the operator, by squeezing the thin copper tube at the appropriate place. The thicker the wire the longer the delay, and the pencils were marked with different colours to indicate the length of delay.

SOE did not have the facilities to manufacture these fuzes in sufficient quantity and in the spring of 1942 it requested OSS help; by December 1942 nearly half a million had been manufactured and shipped to Britain. OSS also worked to make the device more reliable and it produced the SRA-3 time pencil which was a great improvement.

The British also had the L-Delay time pencil which worked on the principle of a tellurium lead cylinder being stretched by a spring. This lead has the property of stretching at a uniform rate and the lead cylinder was grooved so that the thicker the groove the longer it took to break. The device was armed by simply withdrawing a pin, on which was written the time delay, and when the lead broke the striker pin was released. It was acquired by OSS in only very small numbers.

The A-C (acetone-celluloid) Delay fuze was also a British device which was commonly used in limpets. As with the time pencil, the operator broke an ampoule releasing the acetone. This dissolved a celluloid washer which held back, under spring tension, the firing pin. Different-coloured ampoules, filled with acetone of different strengths, provided delays varying from 4½ hours to 5½ days, and later others were provided that gave delays of between two and eight weeks.

The A-C Delay fuze was in great demand and the British could not manufacture enough of them. In July 1943 the first order for them was placed in the USA with the British supplying the celluloid washers as the fuze did not work properly with American celluloid. Those used by OSS and by SOE were almost identical.

The greatest drawback of all these fuzes was that their accuracy was greatly affected by temperature. For example, an SRA-3 time pencil marked white for a delay of 1hr 20m at 77°F was not activated for nearly 18 hours at 0°F, while a temperature of 125°F activated it in only 20 minutes. An electro-mechanical pencil fuze not affected by changes in temperature was eventually developed, but proved unworkable operationally.

Because of the unreliability of pencil fuzes, if the timing of an explosion were a critical factor a clockwork time delay was used. These were very accurate, were waterproof to a depth of 20 feet, and were not affected by temperature. Most were 12-hour clocks (from 15 minutes up to 11¾ hours) though a few 24-hour ones (from 15 minutes up to 23¾ hours) were manufactured. OSS also produced the Mole delayed action firing device which was activated when light was obscured from it. It was designed specifically to derail and wreck trains when they entered a tunnel.

OSS also made delayed action devices for simulating a rifle being fired and for firing a securely fixed automatic weapon such as the M3. These combined a time pencil with a device which, when the time pencil was activated, depressed and held down the weapon's trigger. There was also a type which caused the weapon to fire when it was activated by a trip wire and one which was triggered by radio transmission from a bomber aircraft. This ignited flares or signal lights, which had already been put in place, to guide bombers to their targets.

Both organisations produced pocket incendiary devices. OSS rejected SOE's version and developed one that was smaller and less noisy. Another British incendiary device improved upon by OSS was the oil-slick igniter. OSS developed at least three which were to be used to ignite oil-slicks on water or leaks from oil tanks. Both organisations developed notebooks, messenger pouches and brief cases which self-destructed when their firing devices were activated.

These were only produced in very limited quantities and were available only during the latter part of the war. They proved as dangerous to their users as did some other explosive devices, and one SOE officer, David Smiley, was badly burnt when his brief case accidentally exploded.

A brief mention must be made of the various forms of radio communications used by agents in the field. Radio sets and trained operators, were essential for any clandestine organisation and the lack, or unreliability, of equipment or personnel could have disastrous consequences. The paucity of trained wireless operators badly hampered the early work of MI9, the British escape and evasion organisation; and the fact that SOE was obliged, until June 1942, to use the radio networks of MI6 was the cause for some friction which must have lowered SOE's efficiency.

From 1 June 1942, however, SOE was allowed to construct its own sets, to use its own codes, and to have its own radio networks and home stations. F section (see Chapter 12) alone grew from just two clandestine stations in May 1941 to 53 in August 1944. These kept employed several hundred radio operators, cipher clerks and teletypewriter operators in four SOE receiving stations in the UK, at Grendon Underwood, Poundon, and Bicester in England and at Dunbar in Scotland. 'Europe was sown with transmitters hidden in woods, garages, organ-lofts of churches, and every possible hiding-place,' a draft history of SOE relates, and that at its peak SOE employed 1,500 wireless telegraphy (W/T) operators and cipher clerks in these stations who kept a round-the-clock listening watch for messages from the 496 SOE transmitters in Europe. By 1944, they were receiving and deciphering half-a-million five-letter cipher groups each week from these transmitters.

A similar expansion occurred in the OSS whose Communications Branch was formed in September 1942. When the USA entered the war in December 1941 the Office of the Co-ordinator of Information, the predecessor to OSS, had just three clerks handling signals traffic; by 1945 there were 130 with another 400 scattered world-wide.

Radio-telegraphy (Morse code) was the normal mode of communication because radio-telephony was insecure, was liable to distortion, and, where a code was employed, took longer to transmit as the phonetic alphabet had to be used for clarity. But later in the war the S-phone and its more advanced US equivalent, the Joan-Eleanor, were introduced for ground-air communications in special circumstances (see below).

To minimise an agent's transmission time it was vital that the home station knew when he was to transmit and the frequency he was going to use. It was therefore essential that his (or her) transmitter could work on an agreed fixed frequency with a high degree of reliability, and that it did not 'wander' off it. To ensure this at least three different tiny quartz crystals – which maintained highly stable vibrations the frequencies of which were determined by their thickness – were used by the agent. Depending on whether he was transmitting on his normal frequency or an emergency one – and whether he was transmitting during the day or at night – he used different thicknesses of quartz crystals, each the size of a postage stamp. These crystals could be cut with great accuracy, almost to within a kilocycle of any given frequency (1,000 kilocycles = 1 megacycle).

By 1944 there were so many clandestine networks operating that an agent going into the field was supplied with a very strict operating schedule which listed exactly when the home station would be listening for his transmission. Up to 1944 it had been normal for the home station, for three agreed days during the week, to listen in to each frequency for five minutes around the time which had been allotted to the agent for his transmission. Under no circumstances was a transmission allowed to exceed five minutes – an agent could transmit about 600 letters of the alphabet by Morse in this time – and the total length of transmissions was not allowed to exceed 20 minutes in any one day.

This system reduced the agent's transmission time because he did not need to call up the home station but could send his message in the knowledge that the home station was listening to him. But obliging the agent to stick to fixed times and frequencies was dangerous for him, and from October 1943 the system became more sophisticated and variable. For example, by 1944 the agent transmitted in the day and the home station at night, automatically between the hours of 9 p.m. and midnight.

Power was not one of the priorities for an agent's transmitter for with a single 'bounce', or ionospheric reflection, an aerial wave could cover the distances required (from about 100 miles in France to about 1,000 miles for the most distant occupied countries such as Poland). Using low power transmitters (1 to 10 watts) also had the advantage of minimising the risk of the transmitter's ground waves being picked up and homed in on by enemy radio-location units. But weight and size were critical because an agent had to have a transceiver – a combined transmitter and receiver – which could be easily carried and disguised, usually as a suitcase.

To be able to employ aerial waves a transmitter had to transmit within the frequency of 2 to 30 megacycles per second (megaHertz in today's official terminology) because beyond 30 megacycles its aerial wave would not reflect off the ionosphere. What frequency was used depended on several factors. The frequency used for transmissions from much of France was from 3 to 6 megacycles depending on whether the transmission took place at night or during the day. The most efficient frequency for daytime communication from France's Mediterranean coast was 8 megacycles.

Early sets built by MI6 and used by SOE included the cumbersome pre-war Mk XV transceiver and the much smaller and lighter Paraset. The first SOE set was the technically unsatisfactory 21 Mk I which appeared in August 1942. This was followed by the A Mk II set in October 1942. Its power output was 5 watts and its two wave bands covered 3–4.5 megacycles and 6–9 megacycles. It was a big technical improvement over the 21 Mk I and was a step towards miniaturisation. The suitcase which contained it weighed about 20lb but it could also easily be carried in three separate small parcels each measuring 11 x 4 x 3 inches.

The A Mk II remained in use until the end of the war and was copied by OSS to produce their standard set, the SSTR-1, but the most widely used set was the powerful (30 watts as opposed to 5 watts) B Mk II suitcase transceiver, commonly known as the 'B2' which was introduced in 1943. The B2 suitcase, which weighed 32lb, was divided into four compartments: an accessories box, the transmitter, the receiver, and the combined house current/battery power supply. One of the wireless operators involved in the mission to destroy the heavy water plant at Vemork (see Chapter 10) said 'it is the best W/T set I have ever used, it is very reliable and resistant to damp'. Major John Brown, who worked on radio research and development at SOE's Station IX (the Frythe, near Welwyn Garden City), was responsible for designing the B2. For the Jedburgh teams (see Chapter 15), who might find access to mains current or batteries impossible, he later incorporated a B2 transmitter, a hand generator with which to drive it, and a small receiver into one backpack unit which became known as a 'Jed-set'.

The other important transceiver was the A Mk III which because of the ever-smaller radio valves being manufactured in the USA was almost completely miniaturised. It had an output of 5 watts, weighed only 9lb, including an accessories box, and fitted into a suitcase which measured only 12 x 9 x 4 inches. Other miniature sets included the 51/1 transmitter and two receivers, the 53 Mk I, and the MCR 1 – or 'biscuit' – receiver which measured 3½ x 2 x 8½ inches and was packed into a Huntley and Palmer biscuit tin. About 10,000 of these were built, half of which were supplied to resistance organisations.

As the Allied invasion of north-west Europe approached, and power cuts became more frequent, it became more common to use batteries. The recharging of these became an increasing problem and SOE provided their agents in the field with a number of different types of rechargers. These enabled batteries to be recharged by wind, fire, bicycles, and steam as well as by the more normal manual and petrol-powered means.

Morse code communication was almost always in cipher, an esoteric subject which it is not necessary to deal with here. However, it is important to stress that enciphering and deciphering messages was a laborious and time-consuming business, and that speed and ease had to be weighed against security. Unfortunately, it was normally the case that the more secure the code the longer it took to use.

Although Morse code was the method most frequently used for transmitting messages, radio-telephony was also put to limited use in clandestine warfare. The S-phone, an ultra-high-frequency radio-telephone powered by batteries, was developed by SOE to enable intercommunication between an agent in the field and an aircraft or ship. It was a duplex receiver which meant that, like an ordinary telephone, it was not necessary to switch it from 'send' to 'receive'. The agent's set was strapped to his chest and the position of his body and the aerial tilted the wave beam skywards which lessened the extent of the ground wave, making it extremely difficult for any enemy monitoring station to detect it. It weighed 15lb and measured 7½ x 4 x 20 inches, and its range for communicating with an aircraft flying at 10,000 feet (the maximum effective height) was about 40 miles. The lower the aircraft's altitude the less the range so that at 500 feet it was only six miles. The best method of communication was for the aircraft to circle within the beam at the appropriate height so that constant communication could be maintained.

The S-phone – an ultra-high frequency secret radio-relephone, which was relatively secure as its transmissions could not be picked up by any ground monitoring station more than one mile away. It was powered by ten miniature rechargeable cadmium-nickel batteries. The set was very directional so the operator had to face the path of the aircraft with which he was communicating.

Communication by S-phone was of a very high quality so that, even though he had no need to speak above a whisper, it was easy to identify the voice of the agent and to verify that he was genuine. It could also be used as a homing beacon for aircraft dropping supplies to resistance groups.

From 1943 the Eureka-Rebecca homing device, an invention of the British Telephone Research Establishment, was also employed but it was not always popular with those in the field who had to use it because the Eureka – the part of the homing equipment deployed on the ground – was large, heavy and impossible to explain away if discovered in transit by a random search. It was used successfully by airborne forces but despite being urged, and sometimes ordered, by London to deploy it few resistance leaders – in France at least – did so. Those who did were, as M. R. D. Foot in his book, *Resistance*, has pointed out, 'delighted with the results; old mine shafts, deep river beds, old quarries hold the rest'.

Certainly, the Eureka device used to guide in the SOE 'Gunnerside' team, who were dropped to destroy the heavy water plant at Vemork, worked well, though for some unknown reason the Rebecca aboard the aircraft delivering two earlier missions into Norway was not able to home in on the Eureka's signals. The biggest problem so far as the Norwegian operation was concerned was keeping the batteries charged because the team's hand generator gave a good deal of trouble.

By the end of 1944 the OSS had developed its own ground to air radio-telephone for SI agents whose task it was to penetrate Germany. This was called the Joan-Eleanor, Joan being a major in the Women's Army Corps whom the inventor of the device much admired, Eleanor the wife of the American research engineer who developed it. It worked on the same principle as the S-phone but the part carried by the agent on the ground was much smaller – only 6½ inches long, 2¼ inches wide, 1½ inches thick, and it weighed just ¾lb. The equipment on the aircraft – the Americans used specially converted British Mosquito fighter-bombers – weighed 40lb and included an early form of tape recorder, a spool of wire on which the conversations could be recorded.

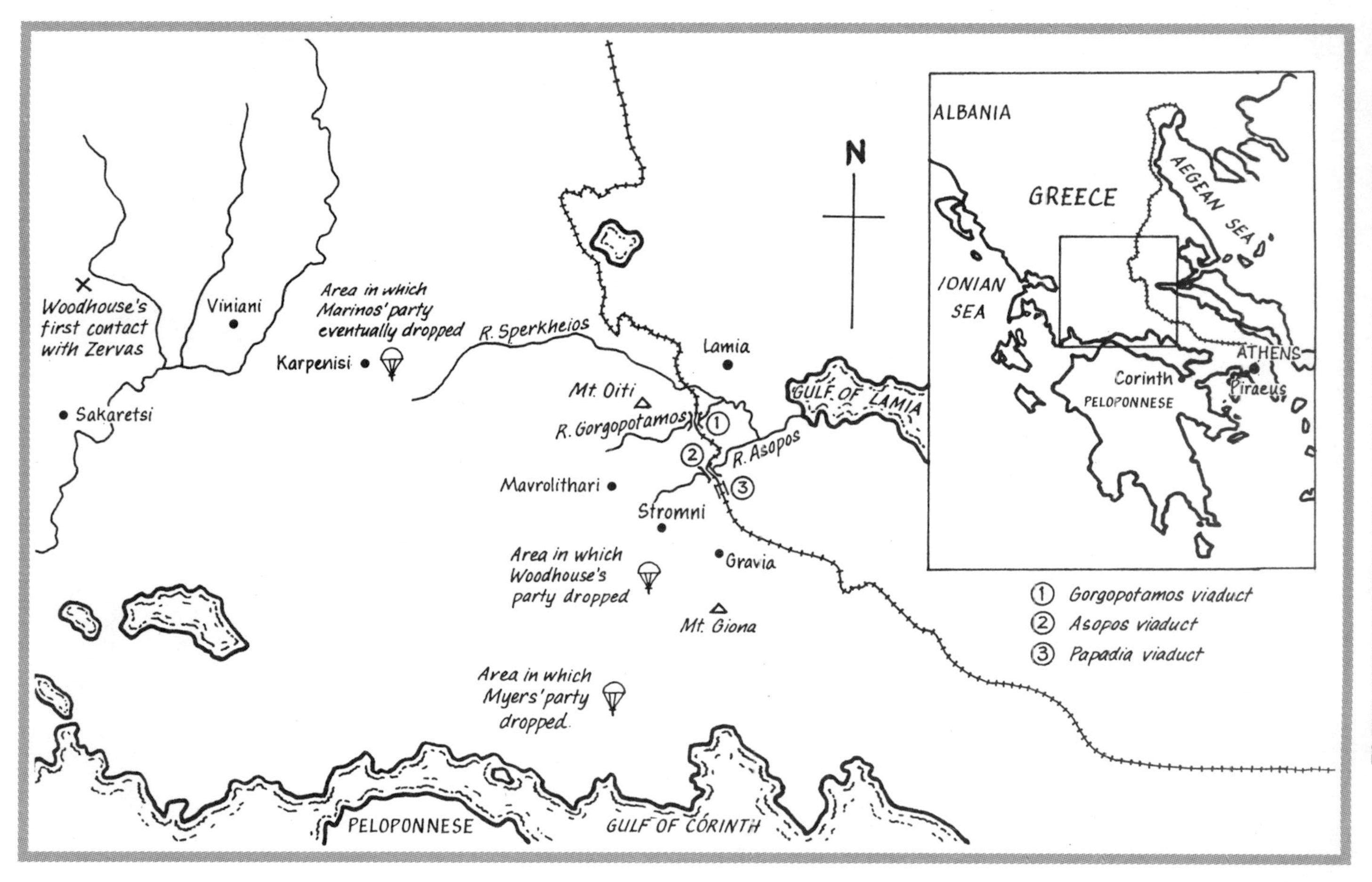
ALBANIA
GREECE
AEGEAN SEA
IONIAN SEA
ATHENS
Piraeus
Corinth
PELOPONNESE
N
① Gorgopotamos viaduct
② Asopos viaduct
③ Papadia viaduct
Woodhouse's first contact with Zervas
Viniani
Area in which Marinos' party eventually dropped
Karpenisi
R. Sperkheios
Sakaretsi
Lamia
Mt. Oiti
R. Gorgopotamos
GULF OF LAMIA
R. Asopos
Mavrolithari
Stromni
Gravia
Area in which Woodhouse's party dropped
Mt. Giona
Area in which Myers' party dropped.
PELOPONNESE
GULF OF CORINTH

4

The 'Harling' Mission and the Destruction of the Gorgopotamos Bridge

SOE's 'Harling' mission was parachuted into Greece in the autumn of 1942. Its objective was to sever the strategically important railway line which connected the rest of Europe to the Athens port of Piraeus. As many as 48 German trains packed with supplies for Rommel's troops in Libya used the line every day, and the sabotage mission, if successful, would severely hamper German operations prior to Montgomery's proposed break-out at El Alamein. The mission was a classic example of SOE's role in helping local resistance movements and of the obstacles that politics often put in the way of those whose only aim was the destruction of the common enemy.

To understand the resistance movements the 'Harling' mission was sent to work with, it is necessary to know something of the tangled politics in Greece, for they produced a number of guerrilla bands all of which subsequently spent as much time opposing one another as they did the enemy.

Since 1936 the country had been ruled by a right-wing dictatorship which by May 1941, when Greece was overrun, had crushed all overt opposition. But there were a number of underground factions of varying shades in the political spectrum waiting for the opportunity to seize power, some of whom were represented by resistance movements which began to spring up in the summer of 1941. The two main ones were the hardline Communist National Liberation Front, known by its Greek initials EAM, and the National Republican Greek League, or EDES, an anti-Royalist republican organisation. The supporters of these two groups worked with the 'Harling' mission, but later fought bitter battles against each other.

Before the British forces left Greece SOE's man there, David Pawson, recruited a left wing republican Greek Army officer, Colonel Evripidhis Bakirtzis (code-named 'Prometheus'). Bakirtzis, based in Athens, was given wireless sets but no call sign or codes, and it was not until March 1942 that there was a direct wireless link between SOE Cairo and its agents in Athens. By the time this link was established, Bakirtzis had handed over his responsibilities to a group of naval officers (code-named 'Prometheus II') and in December 1941 the head of this group, Babis Koutsoyiannopoulos, informed SOE Cairo that independent guerrilla bands were beginning to operate in certain areas, particularly on Mount

Giona. If these bands were supplied with arms they might be prepared to take stronger offensive action against the occupying forces.

Up to that time SOE Cairo had not considered waging a guerrilla war in Greece, but on 9 January 1942 it suggested that a good guerrilla target would be one of three viaducts that carried the railway line to Piraeus over a series of deep gorges south of the town of Lamia. Koutsoyiannopoulos replied that through a left wing lawyer, Alekos Seferiades, he knew of a group of Giona *andartes* (the Greek word for guerrilla) who might carry out such an operation and that summer, with Seferiades acting as the liaison, SOE began dropping supplies to them.

Seferiades, however, was a supporter of the EAM and he ensured that a communist hardliner, Aris Veloukhiotis, who led a local band belonging to EAM's military wing, the National People's Liberation Army, or ELAS, was the main recipient of these supplies. But Koutsoyiannopoulos had been ordered by SOE to arm anyone who was willing to fight and he therefore also asked that supplies be dropped to an EDES band which had begun operating in the Voltos area, in central–west Greece, under a retired republican army colonel, Napoleon Zervas.

This web of political intrigue and rivalry was mirrored to a lesser degree in Cairo. Without fully informing SOE of its purpose, the British Secret Intelligence Service (MI6), with the co-operation of the Greek government-in-exile, sent a mission to Athens in early August 1942 to co-ordinate the various resistance bands that were being formed. It was the head of this mission, a man called Tsigantes, who first suggested the destruction of the Gorgopotamos bridge, one of the railway viaducts situated south of Lamia, though apparently all SOE knew about him was that he had been dispatched to block the Corinth canal.

This lack of co-ordination between SOE and MI6 had an adverse effect on communications between the 'Harling' Mission and Athens. In the opinion of one of the mission, Themis Marinos, this played a large part in delaying the attack on the railway until after Montgomery's advance in Libya had already begun.

On 2 September 1942 SOE Cairo again asked 'Prometheus II' if it were possible to destroy one of the viaducts. On 21 September it received a positive reply but was told the local *andartes* would need the assistance of demolition experts and the necessary explosives. These would have to be parachuted into the Giona area between 28 September and 3 October where Seferiades would meet them. The landing place would be marked with a series of bonfires laid out in a cross. At the same time 'Prometheus II' asked SOE to drop an additional officer with a wireless set who would act as a liaison between Cairo and Colonel Zervas.

The search for suitable volunteers had already begun before 'Prometheus II' replied to SOE Cairo. Eddie Myers, who was to become the leader of the 'Harling' mission, was the first to be approached by SOE. An officer in the Royal Engineers, he was then a 35-year-old colonel in Combined Operations at GHQ

Cairo. A friend who worked for SOE came to see him on the evening of 20 September 1942 and asked him whom he should approach to recruit three parachute-trained sapper officers to destroy 'a bridge somewhere in the Balkans'.

Myers told him that there were none. His friend then noted that Myers was a parachutist, a regular soldier, and a trained staff officer, and urged him to take command of the force. Myers agreed and a party of nine officers and three wireless operators was then quickly recruited. With the exception of Themis Marinos, an English-speaking Greek second lieutenant who was already a trained parachutist, they were all given an abbreviated parachute course.

SOE Cairo knew nothing of the various organisations in Greece whose politics were already dividing the *andartes*, and its original plan was for the mission to rally the local *andartes* in the Giona, and those under Zervas, and to bring them together to make a combined attack on one of the viaducts. Myers and seven of the team were to be dropped by two aircraft into the Giona area. His second in command, a 24-year-old Greek-speaking major, Chris Woodhouse, and the other three members of the team, would be dropped by a third aircraft to contact Zervas. But the exact position where Woodhouse was to be dropped had been corrupted during transmission, and because there was no time to check the position with Athens he had to be dropped with Myers.

Woodhouse, who had already had experience of clandestine operations in occupied Crete, took in his aircraft Themis Marinos, one of the three wireless operators, Sergeant Mike Chittis, and a New Zealander captain in the Royal Engineers, Arthur Edmonds. After the operation it was planned that Woodhouse, Marinos and Chittis would stay behind with Zervas to act as his liaison with Cairo.

Myers' two teams comprised three Commando officers, Major John Cook, Captain Denys Hamson and Captain Nat Barker; two captains in the Royal Engineers, Inder Gill and another New Zealander, Tom Barnes; and the other two wireless operators, Sergeants Len Wilmot and Doug Phillips. Hamson and Barker were Greek speakers, Barnes and Edmonds experts at blowing up large structures. Myers took Barnes, Hamson and Wilmot in his aircraft; Cook had Gill, Barker and Phillips.

The explosives and weapons, which were to be dropped in metal cylinders with the teams, were equally divided between the three aircraft so that if necessary the teams could act independently. The explosive equipment comprised gelignite, gun cotton, fuzes, detonators, and almost the entire Middle East stock of plastic explosive, which was still a rare commodity, and there were also Sten guns, captured Italian rifles and hand-grenades to equip the *andartes*.

The personal equipment issued to the party was later described by Woodhouse as a mixture of the practical and the bizarre. It included a revolver and ammunition, a commando knife, a field-dressing ('in case the knife slipped, I suppose'), two essential pieces of escape equipment – a compass disguised as a button and a map disguised as a silk scarf – a leather belt containing gold sovereigns, a mess-tin, a water-bottle, a tin of hard rations, a torch, some coloured flares, Benzedrine pills, a poison pill (in case of capture), and two RAF badges of rank so that, if necessary, members of the mission could swap them for their army ones and pretend that they had been shot down. The team, including Marinos, wore British battledress under their parachuting kit which comprised a rubber helmet, a padded boiler suit, and rubber-soled boots. Woodhouse also insisted that everyone take metal-studded leather-soled boots as he knew that this was the only footwear that would survive for long in the harsh conditions the team would meet in the mountains.

The three Liberators with the twelve men aboard took off on the evening of 28 September from an airfield situated near the Suez Canal, but the prearranged signals for their reception were not seen and all three aircraft returned to base. Two nights later, Marinos having exchanged places with Barker, the three teams tried again. Again there was no sign of any bonfires arranged in a cross, but when Myers and Woodhouse saw three fires arranged in a triangle both decided to proceed. The third aircraft, with Cook and his team, again returned to Egypt, and as it was the last suitable moonlit night Cook could not try again for another three weeks.

Myers and his team landed in rocky and precipitous terrain some fifteen kilometres from the triangle of fires; Woodhouse and his team came down on level ground almost on top of them. Myers soon met some shepherds who took him to a young Greek officer who lived in a nearby village. He offered them food and shelter and told Myers that an *andarte* named Karalivanos was nearby and that he would take the British parachutists to him. Because he was one of the three guerrilla leaders SOE Cairo knew by name – Seferiades and Zervas being the others – Myers quickly agreed.

At dawn next morning the British encountered their first *andarte*. Myers described him as a squat little man in a dirty black uniform who 'wore three bandoliers full of ammunition, one round his waist and one over each of his shoulders. He carried a rifle at the ready. Several knives with beautifully engraved handles, protruding from various parts of his waist, completed his equipment. The smile which spread over his shaggy, uncouth face revealed an almost toothless jaw.'

The *andarte* took them to Karalivanos whom SOE Cairo had described as a regular army major commanding a large band of *andartes*, though in fact he was a bandit on the run from the police. He wore a fez and was festooned with an array of ammunition and weapons. Myers likened him to a Christmas tree because, in common with bandits of that time, he wore on his chest shining rows of sequins to impress villagers. Through Hamson Myers explained who they were and that he wished to contact the guerrilla bands in the area. Myers then asked Karalivanos where the rest of his band were and was taken aback to be told there were only five of them. Karalivanos then mentioned that there was a strong band in the area under someone called Aris Veloukhiotis, but he did not know their whereabouts.

The cylinders containing the team's stores had been scattered over a wide area but Karalivanos' men managed to retrieve most of them and hide their contents. The party, now equipped with mules obtained locally, set off to find the place where they should have been dropped so that they could keep their rendezvous with Seferiades.

In the meantime Woodhouse and his team met up with the *andarte* who had, in fact, lit the fires as a signal for supplies to be dropped to a local band supported by Tsigantes. Neither man had expected, or indeed knew about, the other, but the *andarte* said he would try to find the whereabouts of Seferiades who, it transpired, had been captured by the Italians.

Eventually, on 6 October, Woodhouse and Myers were reunited and were able, with local help, to store in caves what equipment they had managed to recover. But they did not know what had happened to the third 'Harling' team, for the mission's wireless sets were not working properly. The party began to find it extremely difficult to move in the mountains, not only because the terrain was exceptionally rough but because the local Italian garrisons had been alerted to their presence and were searching for them.

After a few days of such conditions Karalivanos left them with the excuse that he had to move his wife to safety, but luckily for the British they soon found another helper, Barba Nikos, a Greek-American who spoke a smattering of broken English. Nikos led them to a cave close to the village of Stromni on Mount Giona which they now used as their permanent headquarters, it being within striking distance of the viaducts.

Having a safe base was an important step towards accomplishing their mission, but Myers, despite sending out requests for the local *andartes* to meet him, could still not make contact with Aris Veloukhiotis. Myers, it must be remembered, knew nothing about ELAS or that Aris was its local leader. He was also unaware that Aris was avoiding him – ELAS had orders from EAM not to take the offensive – or that the other bands were in no position to help.

However, on 19 October, the same day that the mission reached the cave outside Stromni, a courier, who had been instructed by Cairo to find them, appeared from Athens. Myers gave him two notes: one to Cairo inquiring where Cook and his team were, and one to 'Prometheus II' asking to be put in touch with Zervas, who now seemed their only hope of receiving aid from the *andartes*.

While awaiting a reply to these messages Myers and Hamson, guided by a villager named Yani Pistolis, made their first reconnaissance of the viaducts. Neither the Papadia nor the Asopos appeared suitable – one was too strongly guarded, the other too difficult to attack – but the Gorgopotamos viaduct looked a possibility. 'From different view-points we could see the Italian guards as they strolled about on, and around, the bridge,' Myers later wrote of this reconnaissance. 'We could not, however, see their guard-houses, nor gauge their numbers accurately. Most of the piers were of masonry and therefore unsuitable for rapid demolition, but two of them were of steel. After examining them through my field-glasses and after a careful study of the photographs I had with me, I came to the conclusion that the four legs of each of these steel piers were "L"-shaped in cross-section.'

Pistolis now put Myers in touch with a cousin of his who obtained the intelligence Myers needed about the Italian garrison. 'He returned with most valuable information about the strength and location of the Italians, the type of their emplacements, and with details of a barbed-wire fence which surrounded the piers of the viaduct. What he told me fitted in with practically everything which I had previously discovered. My mind was made up. We would attack the Gorgopotamos.'

Soon after returning from his reconnaissance Myers was visited by another runner from Athens with a reply to his note requesting to be put in touch with Zervas. The runner told him that Zervas was still in the Voltos area, in the village of Sakaretsi, some four to six days away, and on 3 November Myers dispatched Woodhouse to find him. Woodhouse was to return with Zervas and his EDES *andartes* no later than 17 November so that the operation could be launched during the period of the next full moon. While Woodhouse was away Barnes and his demolition team prepared the explosives. Much of it had been lost during the searches mounted by the Italians, but there remained about 250kg, the minimum amount needed to destroy the viaduct's steel piers.

While the mission in Greece was making these preparations, the third 'Harling' team made a 'blind drop' – that is, no reception had been arranged for them. However, once over the area they could see in the bright moonlight that bonfires were being lit, and Marinos, who was now commanding the team with the rank of captain in the British Army, decided to jump. All four landed safely though they came under intense automatic and mortar fire from a nearby Italian camp outside the small town of Karpenisi. The wireless operator, Doug Phillips, landed in the town but was hidden by villagers and rejoined the others some days later. The other three reached a nearby village where they were sheltered by the village priest.

That night, Dimitri Dimitriou, one of the leaders of Aris' one hundred-strong ELAS band, was brought to meet them. Dimitri, who used the pseudonym Nikiphoros, told them that he had lit the bonfires when he had heard and seen the aircraft, for he had recognised it as British. But he had not seen the parachutists drop and had only been told of their presence in the village as he was passing through it.

Marinos, like the others in the mission, had not heard of ELAS, and he thought that these initials, worn on the caps of Nikiphoros' men, were a misspelling of ELLAS (Greece). When told they stood for the National People's Liberation Army he felt 'national pride swelling within me and shivers of patriotism running through my body. My thoughts did not turn to politics as I was not interested in their political beliefs... For me, those men were brothers, patriots, fighters against the occupiers.'

Nikiphoros led the squad to Aris but if they expected a friendly welcome from the ELAS leader they were quickly disillusioned. For Aris the political struggle came above every other consideration and he viewed the sabotage team with great suspicion. He even told Nikiphoros to kill Marinos as the latter was, he said, almost certainly a spy of the Greek king.

Later, Aris relented somewhat, but in a book Nikiphoros wrote many years later, he records that when he told Aris that Marinos was urging that the squad be taken to its correct destination, Aris replied: 'What destination, Nikiphoros? Do we really know what exactly is going on? Who are they? Who said they are officers? They are agents of the imperialists and capitalists who have come to work against our people. They may knock down some bridge, but they principally come to divide us, make us kill each other so that they can put us back into their harness.'

When the band reached the next village on 8 November, however, Aris was handed two notes written by Woodhouse who, while passing through the area to meet Zervas, had heard that the third 'Harling' team had landed and were with Aris and his band. One of the notes was for Aris, the other for Cook, as Woodhouse was not aware that Marinos now commanded the third team. In these notes Woodhouse said that he was on his way to meet Zervas because Myers wanted to use his band for the operation. He asked Aris for his co-operation and told Cook where Myers was hiding.

These notes changed Aris' attitude completely because he realised immediately that it would be a blow to the prestige of ELAS if EDES were allowed to take all the credit for the operation. He ordered some of his band under Nikiphoros to escort the British parachutists to Myers and said that he would follow shortly afterwards with the rest of his force; on 13 November Marinos and his squad were at last reunited with the rest of the 'Harling' mission.

Myers was naturally astonished that the third 'Harling' team had immediately managed to contact Aris with his large force of *andartes* because he had begun to think that such a force was a figment of SOE Cairo's imagination. He took Nikiphoros into his confidence and questioned him closely about the viaducts, and the Greek guerrilla confirmed Myers' decision that Gorgopotamos was the best target.

On 9 November Woodhouse was greeted by a delighted Zervas, who had been told by Athens to expect him. He hugged and kissed him and said: 'Welcome *Evangelos*' (Greek for Angel of Glad Tidings). Marinos later stated: 'In my opinion, that meeting between Zervas and Woodhouse was a crucial event in modern Greek history that saved the nation, as it checked the then real danger of submission of the country to totalitarianism and probably territorial dismemberment, which the KKE [the Greek Communist Party] was at that time discussing with Greek's northern neighbours behind the backs of all the Greeks.'

The meeting was certainly crucial to 'Harling''s sabotage mission because Zervas immediately agreed to help, chose a hundred of his *andartes* (some of whom dropped out on the way because they were so poorly clothed), and on 12 November set out with Woodhouse to join Myers. He also sent a message to Aris, and on 14 November the two leaders met at Viniani. Aris agreed to work with Zervas, and the two bands then moved to Mavrolithari which had been chosen as the base for the combined force.

Zervas agreed with Myers' operational plan but suggested Aris should also be given the opportunity to approve it. When Myers asked what would happen if Aris didn't like the plan Zervas smiled and said: 'Leave it to me, I'll pose it in such a way that, in the end, he'll consider it to be his own plan.'

Marinos later wrote that there were many conflicting opinions afterwards as to exactly who made up the final plan and how many *andartes* participated in the attack (the British estimate was 120 members of ELAS and 60 members of EDES). It was agreed that Zervas should be the commander, that Myers would act as his chief of staff, and that Aris would be consulted on any important decision before it was carried out. But the intense rivalry between EDES and ELAS ensured that subsequently each tried to grab what glory it could and this has made it difficult to assess the part each played.

The attacking force was divided into seven detachments. The two strongest, under Zervas' adjutant, were to attack the defences at each end of the bridge. Again, practically everyone writing about the operation gives different numbers, but Marinos states that the northern group comprised 23 members of EDES while the southern group, which had to attack the bulk of the Italian garrison, comprised about 70 men from both bands, the majority from ELAS. It also included Karalivanos, who had reappeared, and his four henchmen.

A third group, commanded by Cook, was to move southwards along the railway for about a kilometre to cut the telephone lines, blow up the track, and engage any Italians who might approach from that direction. A fourth group, led by Marinos, was to move northwards along the railway track. He was to derail any train bringing Italian reinforcements from the nearby town of Lamia, and to prevent those reinforcements from reaching the bridge. A fifth group was to stop any reinforcements crossing a nearby road bridge while the sixth and seventh groups comprised the demolition squad and the command post, the latter having with it a reserve force of 30 men.

Myers wanted the command post to be on the southern side where it would be sufficiently close to the demolition squad to direct and protect it. But Zervas and Aris thought the torrential river which the viaduct spanned was too dangerous to cross quickly and it was established instead on the northern slope of the ravine some 200 metres from the bridge. As will be seen, it was just as well that it was.

Further reconnaissance parties were dispatched before the entire force moved to its chosen concentration point on 24 November. Distances in the Greek mountains were always measured by the time it took to cover them and no two estimates were ever the same. This must have made it extremely difficult for a precise plan to be drawn up. The concentration point, a group of wood cutters' huts on Mount Oiti hidden in deep forest, was calculated to be about a 'six hours' walk' from the viaduct, and the following afternoon, after a last reconnaissance had been made, the force began its final approach march. It was very cold, very dark, and the air was filled with drizzle.

The two main groups were to attack the Italian defences simultaneously, at 2300, but there was a delay because the northern group had difficulty in getting into position on time while the southern had to be re-organised at the last moment. Minutes before the deadline a train packed with passengers unexpectedly appeared and was allowed to pass.

Just as Myers was beginning to think something must have gone seriously wrong the northern group attacked. 'All the small arms in Greece seemed to open up simultaneously on and around the bridge,' is how Hamson described the attack later. 'In the crackling fusillade the rifles were dominated by the quick nervous rattle of our thirty Stens and in a moment we could recognise the deeper bark of Captain Mihali's Thompson. Now the Italian machine-guns opened fire furiously, and bullets came zip-zipping past us, smacking into the hillside... The yellow flash and dull thump of grenades mingled with the pandemonium below. These were our Mills grenades; the Italians had nothing comparable – our chaps must be bombing the machine-gunners out. Now our single heavy machine-gun, below our HQ on the far side of the gorge, began to beat slowly and almost mournfully. Someone said, "they've got the old wreck going at last".'

The northern group encountered far stronger resistance than had been anticipated which included a pill-box not previously known about. The *andartes* cut a gap in the barbed wire surrounding the post, but were spotted by the Italians who opened up on them with automatic weapons. Unaccustomed to such intense fire the *andartes* retreated and sent one of their number to the command post for help. It was decided to commit the whole of the 30-man reserve, under Zervas' second in command, to help overcome the Italians' stubborn resistance, and because it was on the same side of the ravine it was able to enter the battle quickly.

The fighting intensified and as the minutes passed Zervas became increasingly nervous because he thought that the operation had been betrayed. He said that if the northern end of the bridge were not soon captured he would order a general withdrawal. But as his second in command had taken the Very pistol with him he could not implement this threat and Myers made sure, by sending Woodhouse to retrieve the pistol, that no retreat would take place without his ordering it. Woodhouse returned with the pistol and the news that the reinforcements were making progress and were in good heart.

The southern group had launched its attack soon after the northern group and from the cheering Myers gathered that it was going well. About an hour later a loud cheer went up from the southern end and a white flare was fired which indicated that the defences there were in the hands of the *andartes*. As this was the side of the ravine from which the demolition party, under Tom Barnes, had to lay its charges, Myers decided to risk ordering it in although mopping-up on the south side was still continuing. 'I ran down to a point where I could look straight across to the opposite side of the valley, where Tom and his men were lying up, waiting for my signal. I flashed my torch and shouted at the top of my voice: "Go in, Tom! The south end of the bridge is in our hands. Go in! I will join you as soon as possible."'

Barnes and his team now moved up to the girders only to find that they were U-shaped and not L-shaped as the plans had indicated, and as Myers had thought. While the demolition team worked frantically to reshape the charges a hand-grenade was dropped from the bridge. Luckily, it fell wide of the demolition party because it would have detonated their explosives and killed all of them.

Hamson raced out from under the bridge and let fly at whoever was above with the choicest epithets in Greek that he knew. 'Dungdogs,' he shouted. 'Whoresons, may I do unnameable things to your dead ancestors. Haven't I told you we are here? We have a ton of explosive with us, fools that you are.' This had the required effect and the demolition team was able to continue its work.

Meanwhile, Myers had returned to the command post and then joined the northern group to urge the *andartes* forward. At first he had no success, though he could tell that the Italians' resistance was almost at an end. He then heard, above the sounds of battle, a shrill whistle, Barnes' signal for everyone to take cover as he was about to light the fuzes. Myers described the demolition vividly: 'There was a tremendous explosion, and I saw one of the seventy-foot steel spans lift into the air and – oh, what joy! – drop into the gorge below, in a rending crash of breaking and bending steel-work.'

At the command post Zervas, Aris, and Woodhouse joined hands and danced and sang with ecstasy at seeing part of the bridge fall into the gorge. The explosion must also have put heart into the *andartes* fighting at the northern end for Myers at last succeeded in getting them to make a final charge which overran the last Italian positions.

Myers now moved back to the broken bridge to contact the demolition party, only to be told that it needed more time to sever the second steel pier and to cut and twist the two spans that had been dropped into the gorge. As this conversation was taking place – by shouting above the roar of the raging river – Myers heard a loud explosion behind him, and then heavy firing recommenced.

What had occurred was that, while the battle was raging at both ends of the bridge, the two parties assigned to cutting the telephone lines, and preventing the approach of reinforcements, had proceeded as planned. But the booby-trap which Marinos had laid on the rail – which was the explosion Myers heard behind him – did not derail a train approaching from Lamia with reinforcements because it had been travelling too slowly. But the train did stop and some of the Italian troops jumped off to return the *andartes*' fire. The rest stayed aboard the train which crawled slowly towards the bridge.

A few minutes after the booby-trap had exploded under the train, Woodhouse shouted to Myers that Zervas wanted to withdraw within the next ten minutes. Myers replied that it would take another twenty for Barnes to complete his demolition work and that on no account was the withdrawal signal to be fired before then. But he knew that ammunition must be running short and that the reinforcements could not be held back for long. Luckily, Barnes and his team were able to prepare the second charge within that time and after fifteen minutes there was another explosion which completed the demolition of the fallen spans and severed two of the legs of the second steel pier.

Immediately after the explosion the green flares for a general withdrawal were fired by Zervas. It was then 0230. Before the *andartes* withdrew Zervas' *aide-de-camp* wrote the Homeric verse, 'One omen is the best, to defend one's country', on a piece of paper, signed it Napoleon Zervas, dated it, and left it as a warning of the national struggle to come against the occupying powers.

None of the *andartes* was killed and they had only one or two wounded. It was not known how many of the 80-strong Italian garrison were killed but the estimate was about 30. One Italian prisoner was murdered in a most barbarous manner at the instigation of Aris, sixteen local Greeks were subsequently shot among the ruins of the bridge as a reprisal, and the cousin of Pistolis was arrested and executed. The bridge was out of action for nearly six weeks and the Germans took over the guarding of the viaducts.

Several months later there was an interesting sequel to the 'Harling' mission. When Myers, who had remained in Greece to try to implement SOE's policy of unifying the guerrilla bands, heard that trains were again crossing the Gorgopotamos bridge, he decided to mount a new operation, this time against the

Asopos viaduct. Although planned earlier, this operation became part of a deception plan which called for widespread sabotage in Greece in June–July 1943 to make the Germans believe that the Balkans would be invaded, not Sicily.

Although Aris initially agreed to help, *andarte* assistance was not forthcoming. Instead, on the night of 24/5 June 1943, mission members, reinforced by new personnel from Cairo, reached the bridge by descending the gorge. This approach had seemed to the Germans so impossible to negotiate that they had not bothered to guard it, though the bridge itself was heavily defended. The party laid their charges, blew up the bridge, and escaped.

This time the railway line was out of action for four months. Myers, who planned the operation but did not lead it, recommended the leader for a Victoria Cross, but was told that the officer did not qualify for it as not a shot had been fired.

SOE's 'Harling' mission accomplished the destruction of the Gorgopotamos viaduct too late to be of any help to Montgomery who, when asked about the operation after the war, said that he had never heard of it. However, it proved to be not only of enormous importance as the opening gambit in the Greek resistance movement's struggle against the Axis occupying powers, but as a stimulus to resistance movements elsewhere. 'In the military context,' Woodhouse was later to write, 'it showed for the first time in occupied Europe that guerrillas, with the support of Allied officers, could carry out a major tactical operation.'

5
Maid Honor Force

The opening chapter gave some indication of the versatility of SOE as a sabotage and subversion organisation. In March 1941 it even raised its own small force of commandos to help in the infiltration and exfiltration of agents from France. Its commander was Captain Gus March-Phillipps whom Major-General Gubbins had recently recruited from No. 7 Commando as an instructor for SOE's ever-increasing number of agents. To avoid having to rely on the Royal Navy to deliver and pick up agents, March-Phillipps suggested that his small force use a fishing smack. This was agreed and March-Phillipps requisitioned a 39-ton Brixham trawler, called *Maid Honor*, owned by a member of the Royal Yacht Squadron who had converted her to a yacht.

The Admiralty placed such severe restrictions on the trawler's use that it was never employed for its original purpose, but in August 1941 Maid Honor Force, as SOE called March-Phillipps' party, was assigned an unusual task. It was employed to search the creeks and inlets of Vichy French territories in West Africa because it was thought these were being used by U-boats for refuelling and revictualling between operations against Allied convoys.

Before *Maid Honor* set out, extensive work was carried out aboard. This included armour plating, a collapsible deckhouse beneath which was hidden a Vickers Mk 8 2pdr gun, and a pile of fishing nets in the stern concealed four depth-charges. When questioned on the use of these March-Phillipps said that 'if we can't knock a sub out any other way, we shall heave these into the ocean. The sub will proceed to perdition, closely followed by ourselves.'

After a relatively uneventful passage, *Maid Honor* reached Freetown on 20 September where they joined the rest of the force who had arrived at the end of August. March-Phillipps then began a detailed search in the Gulf of Guinea, reconnoitring the suspected areas. A typical operation was one carried out by March-Phillipps and his second-in-command, Geoffrey Appleyard, in early November, when they reconnoitred the delta of the Rio Pongo, some 40 miles north-west of Conakry. The trawler took them to within ten miles of the coastline and March-Phillipps and Appleyard went ashore in a folbot while *Maid Honor* stood out to sea with orders to return in three days. The two men hid up during the day and covered the various branches of the river at night to check if a German supply base for U-boats had been established there. Nothing was found but crocodiles, one of which, to the consternation of the canoeists, draped itself over the bows of the folbot.

While Maid Honor Force was travelling to West Africa and carrying out their search operations there, Louis Franck, head of SOE's newly formed NEUCOLS (neutral colonies) mission in West Africa, was pressing London to be allowed to attack Axis shipping sheltering in the harbours of neutral West African countries. The 7,561-ton Italian merchant ship, *Duchessa d'Aosta*, and a German tug, the 200-ton *Likomba*, were two possible targets. Both lay in the neutral Spanish port of Santa Isabel on Fernando Po, an island situated in the Gulf of Guinea. The initial suggestion was to cripple the Italian ship by destroying her propellers and to hijack *Likomba*. The tug had been used by German personnel of a British Cameroons plantation to escape shortly before war was declared and there seemed a possibility that the Germans might try to leave Fernando Po in her.

SOE files on the operation reveal that the argument to allow sabotage attacks on Axis shipping in neutral harbours was a protracted one. It was eventually settled when Louis Franck arrived in London in November 1941 and managed to persuade both the Foreign Office and the Admiralty that such operations could be carried out without compromising the British government. Formal permission was also given to seize *Duchessa d'Aosta* as well as the tug, for the merchantman's cargo, which included wool, copra, coffee and copper, was said to be valued at £200,000.

The crew of *Duchessa*, whose officers were to be lured ashore to a party on the night of the proposed raid, were not thought to be capable of putting up much opposition. One report said that they were 'debilitated and demoralised, [and] appeared to be incapable of sustained activities outside their own pleasures, but the ship's wireless which had been left unsealed by the Spanish authorities, continued to be a potential source of danger to Allied interests'.

Leonard Guise, SOE's courier between Lagos and Fernando Po, reported that the captain had returned to Europe and the ship was under the command of the chief officer. He confirmed that the crew's morale was not good, that many of them, so he said, were suffering from venereal disease, but that 'apart from two incidents when bottles were thrown at the British Consulate the crew does not seem intensely anti-British.'

The local British chaplain also managed to carry out a survey of the crew. He obtained an invitation to a party aboard *Duchessa*, the ship's chief officer having been duped into believing that the chaplain was a Spaniard. He had to leave in a hurry when it was discovered that he was not, but was aboard long enough to be able to confirm that morale was poor and that the crew had even removed and sold some of the ship's brass fittings.

In the meantime *Maid Honor* had been ordered to Lagos so that March-Phillipps and his team could be the nucleus for a raiding-party. She arrived at Lagos on 14 December and once Franck had won his argument March-Phillipps' force of eleven men was enlarged to 32 by adding several members from the SOE mission and local volunteers from the colonial administration in Lagos (the GOC West African Command having refused to allow troops to be used).

But Franck had doubts about March-Phillipps being given charge of 'Postmaster', as the operation was now code-named. He stated that though he considered Maid Honor Force admirable in its way, 'it did perhaps not have the necessary qualifications of leadership for the successful conduct of an operation of this kind which required a good deal of planning and special leadership... although recognising that W.O.1 (March-Phillipps) has qualities of courage and enterprise, [Franck] considered him lacking in common sense and therefore not a suitable leader for this job.'

However, Major V. Laversuch, Franck's deputy at Lagos, sent a telegram on 28 December urging that March-Phillipps' 'sea-faring and general experience' were most valuable in an operation of this kind and that the personnel of Maid Honor Force who were the 'backbone of whole party' had the 'utmost confidence and trust in him'. This was enough to ensure that March-Phillipps remained in charge. A tug, *Vulcan*, and a launch *Nuneaton*, together with their civilian crews, were lent by the Nigerian governor-general whose co-operation never wavered (which, according to the SOE files, is more than could be said for the Foreign Office). The Royal Navy, after initial Admiralty indifference and opposition by the C in C South Atlantic, played its part by ensuring that a corvette, HMS *Violet*, was on hand to 'intercept' the Axis ships once they were on the high seas.

The story of 'Postmaster' from the raiders' point of view has been told before, though until the relevant SOE files were released there was very little documentary evidence to support these eye-witness accounts. Now it is possible not only to confirm (or correct) these accounts, but to piece together for the first time the preparations made by SOE on the ground, and the subsequent fall-out from the operation.

While the plans for 'Postmaster' were being drawn up in Lagos, one of SOE's men in Santa Isabel, a 45-year-old Royal Engineers' officer named Richard Lippett (code-named W.25), was making arrangements to help March-Phillipps and his men carry them out. Lippett, who was ostensibly employed on Fernando Po by the Liverpool shipping firm of John Holt, used one of his sub-agents, an anti-Falangist Spaniard who worked in a local hardware shop, to arrange two dinner-parties for the officers and some of the men of the two Axis vessels. The first was a blind, but the second was arranged for the night on which the cutting-out raid was to be mounted.

Lippett wrote in his report on the operation that at about 2335 (local time: one hour behind Lagos time) there was a loud explosion followed by a smaller one which, according to the British Acting Vice Consul in Santa Isabel, an SOE officer, were violent enough to bring down the glass candelabra in the dining-room of a nearby resident. Lippett said that the Acting Vice Consul and another SOE officer of the British Consulate were waiting for the bang. 'After the first one they heard a very Oxford voice saying: "I... am... laying... another... charge." That was all that was heard. Thank God it was only heard by them as really no one was aware of anything between the time of the bangs and the time the ships were well out, and no one could say anything definite until the news came over the radio that the Navy had encountered the ships in difficulties in the Atlantic, and were taken to a British port, and quite 50 per cent really now believe this to be true.'

The other 50 per cent were not quite so naïve, however, and suspicion immediately fell on Lippett for being involved in this splendid act of piracy. He had arranged a game of badminton early the next morning, but the court was surrounded by soldiers who refused to allow him to play. 'They said that two ships had been taken the night before from the harbour, by a fleet of battleships... Mrs Montilla [Lippett's badminton opponent] said well done, the English are very smart. I said no the English would never do a thing like that especially in a Spanish port. She said just wait and we shall see, it's a good thing they are away I do not like them either.'

Lippett's report – its grammatical and spelling errors obviously symptomatic of the strain he was under – then described an extraordinary scene. An hour or so after the operation had been completed the German captain of *Likomba*, a man named Specht, entered the British Consulate very drunk and demanded to know where his ship had gone. He attacked one of the SOE members of the consulate staff forcing the other to come to his aid. 'W.51 rushed to the affray and put some heavy North of Scotland stuff on him, and literally knocked the s—t out of him,' Lippett wrote. 'When he saw W.51's revolver he collapsed in a heap, split his pants and emptied his bowells on the floor. The police then came up and took him away but he was up and doing the next day at liberty.'

Lippett was not so lucky for his liberty was soon curtailed when he was summoned before the local police chief and the head of the Colonial Guard. He was interrogated closely, and virtually put under open arrest. 'I do not like the Falangist HQ, it is very Gestapo like,' Lippett concluded his description of his ordeal, 'and no one is allowed any legal help therein.' His passport was taken from him and he was told that he would have to be a witness at the courts-martial of two Spaniards thought to have been caught up in the affair (Lippett's sub-agent had already wisely decamped).

The pressure of all this took its toll and in early March Lippett, who was by that time reported by Laversuch as being 'in a highly nervous state', left Fernando Po in a native canoe, having knocked out two policemen to secure his freedom.

But what exactly had happened in the harbour? *Vulcan* and *Nuneaton*, with the two raiding-parties aboard, had sailed from Lagos at dawn on 11 January. On the night of the 13th they thoroughly rehearsed their plan which was to cut out the two vessels soon after the lights of the town had been extinguished. There was to be no fighting if it could possibly be avoided.

The following night, after hanging about outside Santa Isabel harbour because they had arrived early, the two vessels had begun moving towards the entrance when a rather untoward incident occurred which underlined that perhaps Franck had been right to voice his doubts about the courageous but impetuous March-Phillipps.

'As arranged *Nuneaton* moved ahead and very slowly crept nearer to the harbour,' wrote Leonard Guise, who was in the launch. 'Some dismay was felt aboard her when an excited and well-known voice came bellowing through the darkness, "Will you get a b-b-bloody move on or g-g-get out. I'm coming in." As zero hour was 12 p.m. (Lagos time) and the whole scheme swung on the extinction of the town lights which it was known would occur at that hour, this demand was resented. *Nuneaton*'s skipper responded by swinging across *Vulcan*'s bows and stopping dead. After some furious comments from each ship common sense prevailed and *Vulcan* sheered off into the darkness to wait.'

Thirty years later Guise said in a radio programme that 'there was for one moment a rather sticky little scene when we on *Nuneaton* could hear Gus quite loudly disclaiming that he'd every intention of going in and to hell with it. Gus himself struck me as completely intrepid, almost to the point of overdoing it, because... this was not really a military operation. It was a burglar's operation and burglars don't go in shooting. But Gus gave the impression that he much preferred to do a job when he did go in shooting.'

At the correct time *Nuneaton*, as arranged, approached the harbour first to drop two folbots whose crews were to board *Likomba*. *Vulcan* then joined her and together they moved towards their targets. As they did so Lieutenant Graham Hayes, one of Maid Honor Force and the leader of the *Nuneaton* party, saw from his folbot, in the centre of the harbour above the darkened town, 'a lighted window in which the light was dipping and flashing, mixed with which we read the repeated signal OK OK.' Although he assumed that this was the work of SOE agents ashore, it may just have been his imagination for none of the British agents on the island reported making such a signal.

As *Nuneaton*'s engine had proved to be temperamental, it was arranged that her target, *Likomba*, should be cut loose first and taken in tow. The first folbot crew landed on a 70-ton lighter *Bibundi* which was unexpectedly found to be tied up alongside the German tug. The crew were challenged by the night-watchman aboard the tug, but they managed to persuade him that they had come with a letter for the captain. However, when the second folboat crew appeared on deck armed to the teeth the night-watchman, and a local native who was also aboard, took fright and jumped into the water and swam ashore. Charges were then laid on *Likomba*'s mooring chains and once these had been severed *Nuneaton* took both vessels in tow and headed towards the harbour entrance.

While the party in *Nuneaton* were dealing with the Axis vessels, March-Phillipps and his party had boarded *Duchessa*, covered by two Bren guns set up on the roof of *Vulcan*'s bridge. Only Appleyard managed to get aboard at the first attempt, jumping a gap of six feet to do so, and when the second charge did not explode he rushed forward and replaced it (it must have been his voice that Lippett heard). The crew offered no resistance, but one managed to jump overboard and swim ashore.

'By this time', March-Phillipps wrote in his report, 'bugles were sounding on the shore and there was much activity near the pier head, which ceased very suddenly at the sound of the explosions. Shouts of "*Alerta!*" could be heard and it is presumed that those on shore believed an air raid to be in progress.'

'The boarders', wrote one of the March-Phillipps' party, 'were armed with "coshes" – 12-inch bolts covered with rubber, and strictest orders were given to avoid the use of firearms. Once aboard, the raiders, about twenty in all, split into small parties to carry out their allotted tasks. Gus, followed closely by his diminutive bodyguard "Haggis", led his party quickly through the ship and captured the bewildered crew without a shot being fired... From the bridge Gus was able to see Apple and André fix their charges to the heavy anchor chains forward, and Andy [a Danish seaman, Anders Lassen] and his party heave aboard the heavy hawser and make it fast to the bollards.'

Immediately *Duchessa* was freed from her mooring chains, *Vulcan* took her in tow. '*Vulcan*'s performance was almost miraculous,' March-Phillipps recorded. 'She gave the *Duchessa* two slews, one to starboard, one to port, like drawing a cork out of a bottle, and then without the slightest hesitation, and at a speed of at least three knots, went straight between the flashing buoys to the open sea, passing *Nuneaton* and *Likomba* a few cable lengths from the entrance. This operation, the most difficult in my view, was performed with amazing power and precision.'

The whole operation from boarding the ships to towing them out of the harbour had taken no more than 35 minutes.

So far the plan had worked to perfection, but now it began to go slightly awry. As arranged, HMS *Violet* had been alerted to intercept the tug and its larger prize and escort it to Lagos, but unfortunately she ran aground and missed the rendezvous. To make matters worse *Nuneaton*, with the two smaller vessels, broke down only ten miles from Santa Isabel. *Vulcan*, with March-Phillipps aboard, cast off from *Duchessa* and returned to *Nuneaton*, but after reprovisioning the launch as best he could, March-Phillipps decided that *Duchessa* was the most important prize and that the tug had to return to her as quickly as possible and again take her in tow.

Eventually, at 1430 on 18 January *Violet* hove in sight and sent a boarding-party to *Duchessa* to investigate. The young sub-lieutenant leading it apparently knew nothing of the subterfuge being perpetrated and thought he really had captured a genuine prize. When March-Phillipps tried to disabuse him of this notion, and demanded to speak to the corvette's skipper, the sub signalled to the corvette that 'the captain of the Italian ship wishes to speak to the captain of *Violet*. Italian captain speaks good English.'

March-Phillipps, after establishing his bona fides, persuaded the corvette's captain to go and search for *Nuneaton* while *Vulcan* continued to tow *Duchessa* to Lagos. This the captain agreed to do, but by now *Nuneaton* and her two prizes had been sighted by a British merchantman, the SS *Ajassa*, which proceeded to tow the three vessels to Lagos at such a speed that they arrived there before *Duchessa*.

These few hiccups aside, 'Postmaster' was rightly regarded by all involved as a resounding success which did SOE's reputation no harm at all. 'We hope', one SOE staff officer wrote tartly after the event, 'that SOE will be permitted to demonstrate that what was possible in Fernando Po is possible elsewhere: perhaps on the next occasion it will not be found necessary to preface twenty-five minutes [of] compact and decisive action by over four months of prolonged and desultory negotiation.'

In fact, similar operations were planned for Angola, where two German ships were to be captured from Lobito Bay, and Goa. The Angolan operation was never mounted and the one against four German ships in Goa, which relied on bribing the crews, was bungled.

The aftermath proved to be as long-drawn-out as the operation had been brief. The first reaction came the day after it had been mounted when Berlin-controlled Paris Radio repeated an official German news agency report from Madrid that a Free French destroyer had entered Santa Isabel and had captured the three Axis vessels. This curious rumour gave SOE exactly the cover it needed, and on 21 January a local Lagos newspaper reported that the Admiralty had issued a communiqué which stated: 'In view of German allegations that Allied naval forces have executed a cutting-out operation against Axis ships in the Spanish port of Santa Isabel, Fernando Po, the British Admiralty consider it necessary to state that no British or Allied warship was in the vicinity of Fernando Po at the time of the alleged incident. As a result, however, of information obtained from a German broadcast, the British C-in-C has dispatched reconnaissance patrols to cover the area. A report has now been received that a large unidentified vessel has been sighted and British naval vessels are proceeding to the spot to make investigations.'

On the diplomatic front all hell broke loose, and rumbled on for the next year and a half, but the Spaniards could prove nothing. They complained bitterly and often, the final act taking place between the Foreign Secretary, Anthony Eden, and the Spanish ambassador in London. The latter wrote to Eden on 26 October 1943, again accusing the British of being responsible for the incident 'against the official view set forth by the British government that the act was not instigated by British naval forces but by those of General de Gaulle'. He went on to say that the 'Spanish government reiterate their desire to obtain satisfaction for the act of aggression committed at Santa Isabel and the violations of international law involved.'

Eden, in his rejection of the ambassador's complaints, which he did not deign to send until 22 December, denied that the British government had ever suggested that the forces of de Gaulle had been responsible and that it had never denied that the vessels in question had been captured by the Royal Navy – but on the high seas so that no violation of international law had taken place.

The immediate postscript to 'Postmaster' was that a month later Vice-Admiral Mountbatten, the Chief of Combined Operations, proposed to the Chiefs of Staff, that a small élite raiding force of about 50 men be formed under him. This was approved and March-Phillipps and his men became the nucleus of it. But even after they came under the operational command of Combined Operations, when they were called the Small Scale Raiding Force, they continued to be administered by SOE. Their headquarters was Anderson Manor near Bere Regis in Dorset which was known as Station 62, and they were given the cover name of No. 62 Commando. However, *Maid Honor* did not return. She was sold to the Sierra Leone government but became the victim of teredo worms.

Considering the Admiralty's total indifference towards the *Duchessa d'Aosta* before the operation – they thought that she would be unseaworthy after lying idle for so long – it is interesting to note that she was sailed to Britain in July 1942, was renamed *Empire Yukon*, and did sterling work for the Allied war effort for the remainder of the war.

For his part in 'Postmaster' March-Phillipps was awarded the DSO; Laversuch and two of the civilian crew of the tugs the OBE; Lippett, Guise, and a member of the Nigerian Maritime department, the MBE; Hayes was awarded the MC and Appleyard a bar to his. For his part in the operation Lassen was given an immediate commission. He later rose to the rank of major – and was possibly the only officer in the British army on active service during the Second World War never to have had any formal military training – before being killed at Comacchio in

Italy in an operation which earned him a posthumous VC. March-Phillipps, Hayes, and Appleyard were all subsequently killed while still serving with SOE, the first two on a cross-Channel raid, Appleyard in an air crash.

'Postmaster' was one of the SOE's earliest successes and of vital importance for its future because, at the time, its stock in London was low, especially with the Foreign Office. The operation had, Laversuch was told by Baker Street, 'done SOE a great deal of good with the FO (this is very important), the Admiralty, War Office, MEW, Ministry of War Transport, etc. etc. and the success of this neat little business is enhancing our reputation and prestige considerably.'

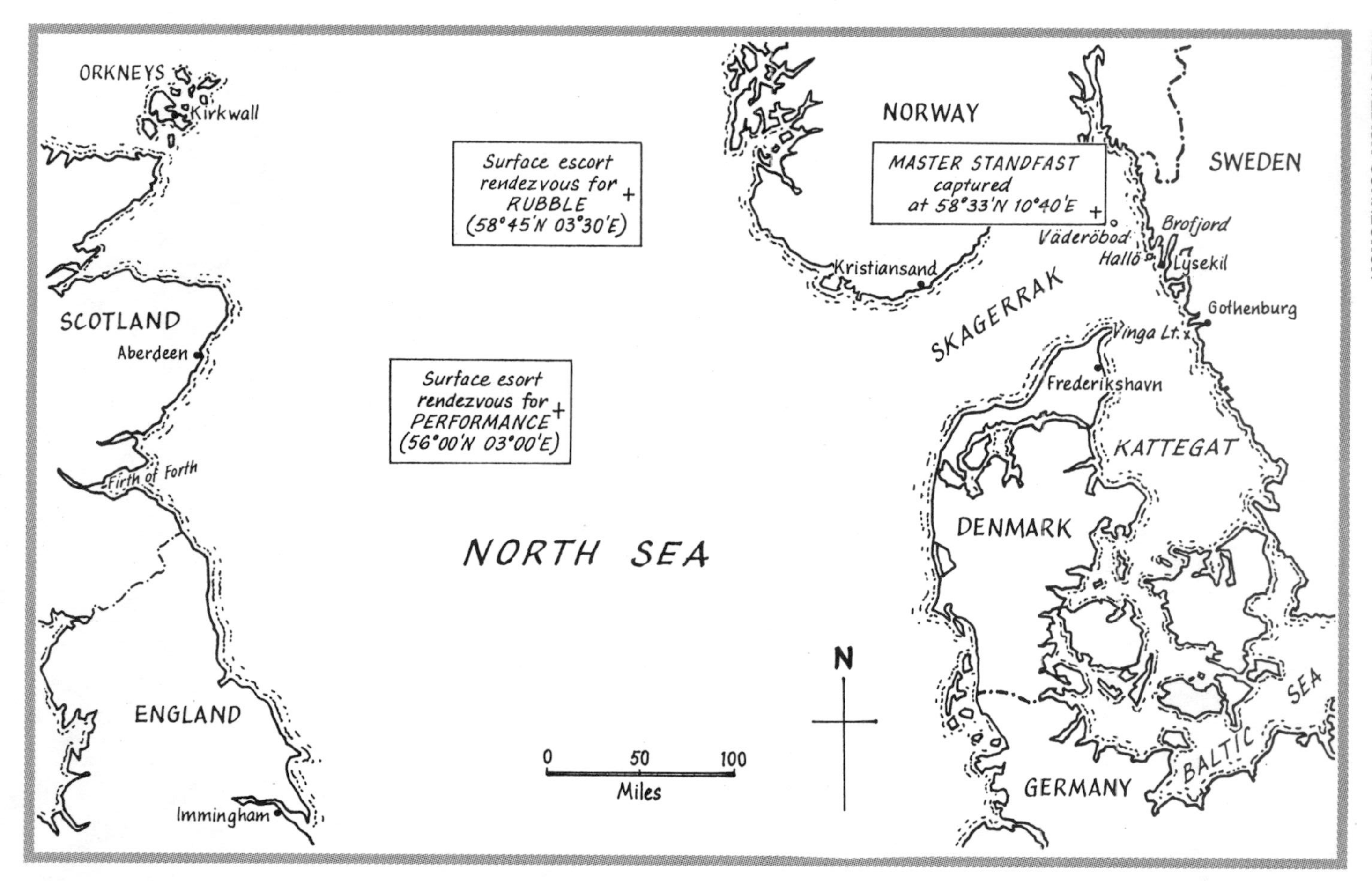
ORKNEYS
Kirkwall
Surface escort
rendezvous for
RUBBLE
(58°45'N 03°30'E)
NORWAY
MASTER STANDFAST
captured
at 58°33'N 10°40'E
SWEDEN
Brofjord
Väderöbod
Hallö
Lysekil
Kristiansand
SKAGERRAK
Gothenburg
Vinga Lt.
Frederikshavn
SCOTLAND
Aberdeen
Surface esort
rendezvous for
PERFORMANCE
(56°00'N 03°00'E)
Firth of Forth
KATTEGAT
DENMARK
NORTH SEA
N
ENGLAND
0
50
100
Miles
GERMANY
BALTIC SEA
Immingham

6
The Swedish Connection

SOE was part of the Ministry of Economic Warfare whose task it was to deny the Axis the raw materials they needed to wage war. In Europe this proved almost impossible to achieve once the Germans had overrun much of the continent, but the sabotage of factories and rail communications in occupied countries, and the subversion of manufacturing companies in neutral countries which traded with the Nazis, were all part of the effort to slow the flow of essential goods into the Third Reich.

Occasionally clandestine operations were mounted that not only denied essential materials to the enemy but also acquired them for the Allied war effort. Those carried out by George Binney are outstanding examples of such operations. The fact that one of them meant a serious breach of Sweden's neutrality, which could have involved her in war with Germany, worried Binney not at all, nor, it seems, the British government. Desperate times called for desperate deeds.

After the Germans had invaded the neutral countries of Norway and Denmark in April 1940 the British no longer had access to the special steels which Sweden produced because the Germans were blockading the Skaggerak, the waters that connect the North Sea with the Kattegat and the Baltic Sea. At that time George Binney was the British Iron and Steel Control representative in Scandinavia. He used his position as cover for intelligence work on behalf of the Ministry of Economic Warfare. His contacts there were Charles Hambro and Harry Sporborg who, in November 1940, became, respectively, Controller and Head of SOE's Scandinavian section. Later Hambro became SOE's CD (executive head).

Binney was in Norway when the Germans invaded the country. He escaped to Sweden, and on 4 May warned that if the British government did not take over payment for all the goods ordered at the start of the war under the Anglo-Swedish War Trade Agreement, those goods, and indeed the Swedish economy as a whole, would fall prey to the Germans. The British Treasury concurred and it was also agreed that the goods should be stored until a means could be found to get them to Britain. An especially urgent consignment consisted of roller-bearings manufactured by a Swedish firm for a new strip mill in Wales which had the largest rolled steel capacity in the British Isles.

While Binney was negotiating with the Swedish government the war situation quickly deteriorated further for the British. On 10 May 1940 the Germans invaded the Low Countries and then overran France. Sweden was now quite as isolated as her British trading partner. But the Swedes were happy to continue trading with the British, and were no doubt grateful when Binney arranged for the British government to take up all the French orders which had been nullified by the fall of France. But they feared that the long-term storage of any goods ordered by the British would attract adverse German attention. Binney managed to get some of the goods out – one load went via Petsamo, another by rail through Russia to the Persian Gulf – but neither of these routes proved a long-term solution.

On 9 June 1940 Binney received a directive from the chairman of the British Iron and Steel Federation for whom he worked. 'It is of paramount importance that we receive all the war stores on order in Sweden (ball-bearings, machine-tools, special steels, Swedish iron, etc. etc.). You must repeat must at all costs get them to England.'

There remained only one way: to run the blockade of the Skaggerak. The previous month *Nora*, a Swedish merchant ship loaded with timber, had in fact made the 500-mile passage to Britain, so Binney and Hambro knew that breaking the blockade was not impossible. Binney studied the charts of the Skaggerak and came to the conclusion that though both sides claimed to have mined it the main channel was too deep, and the current was too strong, for mines to have been effectively laid in it. If this risk were accepted it only remained to find suitable ships and to wait for a suitable time when the nights were longer and visibility was poor.

As it happened there were 26 Norwegian merchant ships lying in Swedish ports which had been stranded when the Germans overran Norway, and for legal reasons the Swedes had subsequently resisted German efforts to have them returned there. One of the last acts of the Norwegian government before it went into exile in London had been to decree that all Norwegian ships in foreign ports owned by anyone residing in an occupied country automatically came under a Norwegian marine directorate in London called Nortraship (Norwegian Trading and Shipping Mission). These ships, at least theoretically, were therefore available to the Allies and if they did not solve Binney's problems in one way they would do so in another. For even if it proved impossible to sail them through the Skaggerak they could be used for storing the goods ordered from Swedish manufacturers so that, technically speaking, they were not on Swedish territory. And if the Germans invaded Sweden the goods could be denied them by scuttling the ships.

Binney was a forthright individualist whose 'pugnacious and piratical spirit', as one writer has described him, was very much in the tradition of the kind of character SOE liked to employ. (His status was, in fact, somewhat ambiguous because the government's Steel Control Board had lent him to SOE, having borrowed him from his firm which was still paying his salary.) With a wide circle of contacts to draw on, Binney's arguments certainly won over any doubters in London, though the British Legation in Stockholm, where Binney was based – and whose head, Victor Mallet, Binney had christened 'windy Vic' – continued to be horrified by his activities. He was given permission to make a trial run of attempting to break the blockade and chartered a Finnish ship to transport 300 tons of steel and spare ball-bearings for the Welsh steel mill. It was a valuable cargo but not irreplaceable. The ship, the *Lahti*, left Gothenburg on 5 July, a moonless period of the month, and managed to reach the outer limits of the Skaggerak before being spotted by a German aircraft and ordered into Kristiansand. Binney reckoned that a more determined captain would have faked an engine breakdown and might have escaped once night fell, but he was satisfied with the results for it showed that the minefields were, if not a total myth, not that much of an obstacle.

But Binney did not under-estimate the difficulties involved. 'We are left with two alternatives,' he cabled Hambro on 9 July 1940, just under two weeks before the War Cabinet approved the charter for the newly formed SOE. 'Either on the grounds of *force majeure* to leave everything in the hands of the Swedish steelmakers for them to dispose of as best they can, i.e., to Germany, or alternatively to settle with the Swedes on a reasonable basis and to stock that portion of the material at the bottom of the North Sea which we are unable to ship successfully to England.'

In other words, Binney knew that some, perhaps most, of the ships would be lost or that they might all have to be scuttled. But, he added, ever the pragmatist, even if the stockpiled goods never reached Britain it was probable that the Swedes would delay switching over entirely to manufacturing for the Germans while the British continued to provide orders for Swedish industry.

In August the Ministry of Shipping appointed Binney their representative in the negotiations to charter some of the Norwegian ships, and subsequently the British government secured the charter of five from Nortraship, ostensibly for storing goods ordered from Swedish manufacturers. The next problem was to man the ships. The captains declined to help and a cable from one of them to his owners in Norway was intercepted by the Gestapo. In the uproar that followed the operation was suspended and even when Binney was given permission to proceed the problem of crewing the ships remained.

Eventually, Binney's enthusiastic personality won over enough volunteers, not only from the original Norwegian crews, but from British crews stranded by the invasion of Norway, including the survivors of two destroyers sunk at Narvik who had managed to escape to Sweden. Of those who sailed, 58 were British,

57 were Norwegians, 31 were Swedes, and there was also one Latvian. Three of the captains were British and two were Norwegians. A £1,500 bonus was guaranteed to the crew of each ship that arrived safely in Britain, this being in addition to their normal salaries and war risk allowance.

Binney's next move was to ensure that the four vessels could be scuttled quickly so that their precious cargoes would not be captured at sea. Explosives, the most obvious means, were ruled out for the Swedes had the strictest rules about allowing explosives and weapons into the country. Binney consulted a British Lloyd's surveyor resident in Gothenburg as to the best alternative and the surveyor came up with an ingenious idea. Four holes were cut into each side of each hull before loading commenced and remote-control valves were fitted. Once the ship was loaded the holes were below the waterline, and provided the remote control levers for opening the valves were thrown overboard after the valves were opened there would be no way of stopping the inrush of water. The surveyor calculated that it would take only an hour for a ship to sink, making any salvage of it impossible. 'This must be the first time Lloyd's have been consulted', he said, 'on how to scuttle a ship.' Other alterations included adding to the ships' bridges blocks of concrete six inches thick designed to protect their occupants from bullets and splinters.

By the end of November preparations were nearly complete. Although crew defections and recruiting continued until the last moment, the ships began loading at Gothenburg. But the objections of the British Legation, the subversion of the Norwegian crews by Gestapo agents, the rising chorus of doubters about the entire operation, now reached a new intensity. It seemed to Binney that everyone opposed him and he accused Mallet in particular of fighting a different war. 'Do you realise', he told one of his few supporters, 'that I spend 75 per cent of my time stopping other people from trying to stop me doing what has to be done?'

SOE, however, continued to back the operation to the hilt, and to insist that it should be mounted, and if there were any serious doubters in Whitehall they were quickly won over by the argument that it was survival that mattered. British industry desperately needed whatever Binney could provide.

The chief of the harbour police at Gothenburg, Captain Ivar Blucker, also proved a vital ally for Binney. The Germans, of course, knew what was going on – though they were subsequently, and uncharacteristically, caught off guard – but Blucker stopped Nazi sympathisers being planted in the crews and arrested two Swedish officers for feeding information to the Germans about the ships. Even more vital for the success of 'Rubble', the operation's code-name, was that when the ships finally sailed he arranged for the disruption of all telephone communications so that, unless the ships were spotted by a German vessel on the high seas, they would have many hours' start before their departure was reported to the German air and naval authorities in Norway.

By New Year's Eve all four cargo ships had been moved to their point of departure, a small fishing port called Lysekil some 45 miles north of Gothenburg, where they were to await the right weather conditions before making their dash for freedom. The fifth, a tanker in ballast which Binney had thought useful to bring along, arrived on 8 January. The ships, all painted battleship grey, were now ready to sail but unfortunately for Binney the weather remained fine and clear, and it was not until the afternoon of 23 January that, with snow falling, they were able to leave the fiord.

The tanker in ballast sailed first, at 1500, because she was the slowest and if there were a U-boat waiting for them in international waters Binney preferred to lose an empty ship. The 6,900-ton *Tai Shan*, in which Binney sailed, left at 1630. Each ship sailed an independent course with orders to make top speed for the pre-arranged rendezvous with the Royal Navy in the North Sea. Radio silence was to be maintained unless a ship was attacked or mined. No ship was to go to the aid of another; getting the cargoes to their destination had the first priority.

The snow gave the ships the protection they needed from German sea patrols, but by dawn, as the fastest ships passed Kristiansand, the snow had petered out and the sky cleared. But luckily for the blockade-busters it was still snowing on shore which delayed German air patrols from taking off. The British Coastal Command aircraft which were to escort the ships and protect the naval forces sent to meet them were also delayed by early morning fog, but at 0950 on 24 January the cruiser *Naiad* sighted the fastest merchantman, the 5,400-ton *Elizabeth Bakke*, which signalled that she was making 19 knots and was being followed by the other four ships. As she was making such good speed she was allowed to proceed independently while the British naval force concentrated on locating the others.

Throughout the morning the luck of the remaining four ships held, but shortly after midday a German reconnaissance aircraft appeared and began shadowing *Tai Shan*, but was later chased away by two Blenheims. At about the same time the two slowest ships at last emerged from the Skaggerak, still apparently undetected. Their luck held even when German aircraft appeared overhead. The German pilots, seeing the Norwegian flags both ships were flying, mistook them for friendly vessels, and actually began to escort them! Even when British naval forces appeared to escort the blockade-busters the Germans remained confused; the German naval commander thought the British warships were laying mines to prevent the break-out into the North Sea of two German battle-cruisers. Eventually the penny dropped, and the empty tanker, the straggler of the fleet, was bombed and machine-gunned, and its Swedish First Officer was fatally wounded. But the air attacks never really developed, night fell, and by early next morning all five ships had safely reached Kirkwall Roads in the Orkney Islands.

'Rubble', in bringing safely to Britain 25,000 tons of essential cargo valued at £1,000,000 as well as five precious merchant ships whose replacement value was put at £200,000 each, could be counted an unqualified success for SOE, though the Deputy Prime Minister, Clement Attlee, told Dalton that there were differences of opinion as to who had played the major part in the operation, the Ministry of Supply having made no mention of SOE in its report. 'But this is much to our credit', Dalton wrote to Attlee on 2 February 1941, 'since it shows we are pretty good at covering our tracks! In fact, as explained in a note which I asked Nelson to send to Morton for the P. M., Charles Hambro was principally responsible both for conceiving the plan and organising its execution both from this end and during a visit to Sweden. He was ably assisted by Sporborg, his no. 2. Much credit, of course, was also due to others, especially to Binney... It was a good piece of team work.'

It was soon recognised as such for Hambro and Binney were knighted, each of the ships' captains received the OBE, and some other members of the crews were also awarded civil decorations. The most difficult decision was how to award Ivar Blucker. He could hardly be given a British award, but some show of gratitude was needed and a pair of gold cufflinks with the royal crest on them were sent to him from the King's Private Secretary via the Foreign Office. In due course he was sacked from his post for aiding Binney, and moved to London to become part of Binney's organisation for mounting future blockade-running operations.

Dalton told Binney that with SOE help he hoped Binney would continue to break the blockade. 'The prime minister is delighted with the results of the operation,' he told him. 'Are you returning to Sweden to bring over further cargoes?' After some hesitation by the government – for the Germans had reacted strongly, the Norwegian government-in-exile had started to dither, and the Foreign Office had continued to do so – Binney returned in April 1941 with orders to purchase 15,000 tons of special steels and, in due course, when the nights grew longer, to launch 'Rubble II' (later renamed 'Performance') with other Norwegian merchant ships still lying in Swedish ports. The Germans, now thoroughly alert, put intense pressure on the Swedish government not to co-operate in any way with another blockade-running operation. For their part the Swedes put just about every legal obstacle they could in the way of Binney's plans.

These plans were based on manning and loading ten more Norwegian ships, and then making a break-out similar to that of 'Rubble'. But this time Binney was adamant that, despite the absolute and total Swedish ban on importing weapons and explosives, each vessel would be armed with Lewis machine-guns and that they could be quickly and easily scuttled by attaching limpet mines to the interior of their hulls.

To organise the arming of the ships by smuggling the weapons aboard, and to train the machine-gun crews, Binney appointed Brian Reynolds, a Briton who had found himself stranded in Sweden after volunteering to fight for Finland during the recent Russo-Finnish war. Reynolds' background was described as 'colourful'. His motto, 'anything for an unquiet life', reflected his adventurous personality, and his physique and thinning red hair earned him the nickname of 'The Lion'. He became so useful and was so adaptable that Binney soon made him his deputy for the operation.

Once they got wind of what was going on the Germans increased their pressure on the Swedes not to allow the ships to sail. But various legal manoeuvres had given the British the right to use the Norwegian ships and the Swedes refused either to seize them themselves or to allow the Germans to do so until the Swedish courts had pronounced on which country had the greatest legal right to them. But the German threats, which included stopping shipping leaving and entering Gothenburg, eventually pressured the Swedes into changing their legal procedures. This tipped the immediate balance in favour of the Germans – and delayed the ships from sailing – but the eventual ruling of the Supreme Court, which was not given until March 1942, was in favour of the British. Binney, who had only been prevented from mounting a cut-and-run operation because all the ships were ice-bound for two months, now made the decision to sail, and on the evening of Tuesday 31 March 1942 the ships left Gothenburg.

This time they were not allowed by the Swedish authorities to shelter elsewhere along the coast prior to making the dash through the Skaggerak, though they were permitted to remain within Swedish territorial waters so long as they did not stop. Binney knew that these restrictions, plus the shorter hours of darkness, the clear weather with a full moon, and the strength and preparedness of German patrols, would make the operation especially hazardous. Nevertheless, he issued a stirring Order of the Day, and he and the 400 British and Norwegian crew members were in good heart as the ships left the harbour at five-minute intervals.

At first everything went according to plan, though the expected fog did not arrive; but later, when they were forced out of Swedish waters by coastal pack ice, the ships were shadowed and fired upon by German armed trawlers. When they tried to return to Swedish waters the Swedish Navy forced them out again and during the next 36 hours five of the ships were sunk and two, *Dicto* and *Lionel*, were forced to return to port.

Four of the five ships which were lost scuttled themselves to avoid capture, and the Germans took 211 crewmen from them prisoner. But *Storsten*, a 5,353-ton tanker, although she, too, was scuttled, was really lost to enemy action. She hit a mine, was attacked by a German bomber, and was then fired on by a German patrol boat. With his ship severely damaged, the captain had no alternative but to detonate the scuttling charges and abandon ship. In the poor visibility prevailing the tanker's boats, with 45 men and two women in them, managed to evade the German patrol boat and it was then decided to try and reach the rendezvous with the Royal Navy instead of making for the Norwegian coast. It proved to be the wrong move and though subsequently one of the boats reached Norway, where most of the survivors were rounded up by the Germans, the other was lost without trace. Tragically, the 150 Norwegians captured from the sunken ships eventually fell into the hands of the Gestapo and 43 of them died, 31 of them in the Sonnenberg concentration camp.

By the Thursday morning only three of the ships were continuing their passage. The 10,324-ton tanker, BP *Newton*, had reached the middle of the North Sea and was on the look-out for the expected Royal Navy escort; the 6,305-ton *Rigmor*, another tanker, was 100 miles astern, and within reach of British air cover; and the tiny 461-ton tanker, *Lind*, was at the mouth of the Skaggerak. All three ships had been attacked the previous afternoon by German patrol bombers but had managed to escape serious damage. The Lewis gunners aboard BP *Newton* had even managed to shoot down one of them. BP *Newton* and *Lind* were eventually found by friendly air and sea forces, and were escorted into the Firth of Forth, but *Rigmor* was hit by German bombs and later had to be sunk by her naval escorts.

'Performance' lost half the ships that had sailed and, though it was not known until after the war, eventually cost more than 50 lives. Of the tonnage 20 per cent arrived in Britain, 45 per cent was still safe aboard the two cargo ships which had been forced to return to port, and 34 per cent had been lost. 'Not as bad as I feared,' the foreign secretary, Anthony Eden, noted on 4 April.

The Swedish government was none too pleased and orchestrated a press campaign which expressed outrage that the British had flouted the country's neutrality laws by smuggling the Lewis guns aboard the ships. But when the masters of the two blockade-runners that had returned were arraigned for arms smuggling they were only given nominal fines, showing that the Swedish authorities were still trying to perform their almost impossible juggling act of satisfying both combatant powers. But not unnaturally they remained inclined to the combatant most likely to win the war. 'If only we could occasionally win a battle,' Mallet wrote despairingly to Hambro later in the year, 'we might find the Swedes more ready to be cheeky to Adolf.'

The question now was how to extract the two remaining cargo ships and their valuable cargoes, and to give them adequate protection. The Admiralty dismissed as impossible early plans for 'Cabaret', as the next blockade-running operation was code-named, but SOE insisted that it had to be mounted and the Minister of Supply wrote to the First Lord of the Admiralty that unless the two cargoes could be brought to Britain a new factory in Scotland might not be able to start production.

'One of the chief bottlenecks in the production of war stores in all countries alike is ball bearings,' the Minister stated. 'My department has for some time past found the greatest difficulty in maintaining a large enough flow of suitable ball bearings to meet all requirements, and particularly requirements in connection with tanks and aircraft. We had hoped and expected that our supplies would be supplemented from the United States but now that they are so well advanced on their own production programme they realise that they, too, are faced with difficulties in this category, and far from being able to help us they want us to help them.'

Eventually the Admiralty agreed that the best chance of getting the ships through the Skaggerak was to use Motor Gun Boats (MGBs) as escorts. They were fast and heavily armed, and were more expendable than larger units of the Royal Navy. They could rendezvous with the two ships off the Hallo Islands, just outside Swedish waters, where trained gunners and anti-aircraft armaments could be transferred to the two blockade-runners.

But the problem of getting the two ships to the rendezvous was more difficult to solve because the Swedes had given the Germans to understand that everything possible would be done to prevent them leaving Gothenburg. Although the Swedes had no legal right to restrain the ships, they refused to give them clearance and put chains and other obstacles in their way to stop them leaving harbour quickly.

The story of 'Cabaret' was full of diplomatic twists and turns and was further complicated by the negotiations which were under way for an increase in Sweden's oil quota from the Allies. A measure of the urgent need Britain had for the ships' cargoes is that she was prepared to interfere in these negotiations in order to obtain them. In November 1942 Roosevelt's adviser, Harry Hopkins, drafted a personal message for Churchill to send to the President on the subject – which was regarded as 'a very hot potato'. Indeed, it roused as big a diplomatic furore in Washington as it did in Stockholm.

'I recognise that your advisers had intended to use the oil quotas to obtain other concessions from the Swedes,' Churchill wrote, 'and will be reluctant to see this weapon used for my immediate purpose. I am however afraid that our need for the materials is so urgent that I am obliged to ask you to play this card now.'

Eventually, and reluctantly, the Americans agreed to play it. This, and the fact that by the end of 1942 the course of the war had begun to change in the Allies' favour, made the Swedes rethink their policy towards the two ships, for though they were not yet ready to be cheeky to Adolf they now knew the Allies would probably win the war. On 13 January 1943 they announced that on 17 January they would give clearance for the ships to sail from Gothenburg and to lie-up in a fiord near Vinga.

When they heard of these preparations to escape, the Germans reacted swiftly by making preparations of their own which included the suspension of the Gothenburg shipping traffic and the dispatch of three destroyers to Kristiansand, a force too formidable for the MGBs to counter. But on 4 February the destroyers left Kristiansand and that evening the MGBs, one of them with Binney aboard, sailed from Aberdeen. But 70 miles from the Skaggerak they were ordered to return because a powerful German naval force was moving into the same area (it transpired that the cruiser *Köln* and the heavy cruiser, *Admiral Hipper*, were being transferred from Norway to the Baltic) and the return of the destroyers to Kristiansand and the lengthening hours of daylight then dictated that 'Cabaret' must be cancelled.

By the time this decision was made Binney was already planning another operation ('Bridford'). This entailed using the MGBs themselves as cargo carriers which, stripped of all internal fittings, and with a skeleton crew, would be able to transport 40 tons of vital supplies. It hardly compared with what *Dicto* and *Lionel* had in their holds, but there was still such a desperate shortage of some types of ball bearings that tiny quantities were even being flown in from Stockholm.

Binney's plan was well received. At first it was envisaged that the MGBs would be crewed by naval personnel and fly the white ensign. But the Swedes pointed out that, unless in distress, no belligerent warship was allowed to remain in Swedish ports for more than 24 hours. It was decided, therefore, to recruit and train selected merchant seamen for the role and for the MGBs to fly the red ensign of the Merchant Navy which allowed them, as with all merchant ships, access to Swedish ports, the right to anchor in Swedish waters, and to carry defensive armaments. Additionally, each vessel would carry an SOE representative responsible for security and welfare.

Binney's orders were to run between 400 and 500 tons of supplies through the blockade during the winter of 1943/4 and five specially converted 117-foot MGBs, armed with Oerlikons and machine-guns, and with a theoretical - and it was theoretical – top speed of 23 knots, were provided for this purpose. The MGBs, named by Binney *Hopewell*, *Nonsuch*, *Gay Corsair*, *Gay Viking* and *Master Standfast*, would pick up their cargo from the small fishing port of Lysekil while *Dicto* and *Lionel* would give the necessary logistical support from nearby Brofiord. All this took time to arrange and negotiate with the Swedes, and it was given to SOE and Binney to organise. Binney, in case he was captured, was given the rank of commander in the RNVR.

No sooner had *Dicto* and *Lionel* moved to Brofiord, which they did on 7 September, the Germans moved destroyers back to Kristiansand. But they were anticipating the break-out of the ships not the arrival of the MGBs. The MGBs' departure was delayed by engine trouble – a recurring problem – but at 1645 on Tuesday 16 October the five MGBs, with Binney aboard *Nonsuch* and Reynolds aboard *Gay Viking*, left Immingham on the Humber and started their crossing of the North Sea. But the MGBs continued to be plagued with engine problems. *Gay Viking* was affected first and she soon lost contact with the other four. When two of the others developed problems Binney ordered all four to return to Immingham. However, *Gay Viking* knew nothing of this order and carried on as planned, picked up her cargo, and arrived back at Immingham on 31 October.

The same day Binney in *Hopewell* set off again with two of the other MGBs. One soon had to return to port – gearbox problems this time – and the third MGB, *Master Standfast*, lost contact with *Hopewell* in the Skaggerak in the middle of the night. The captain subsequently lost his bearings and eventually stopped his engines for fear of running aground. As the MGB lay motionless in the water off Vaderobod an unknown vessel approached her from astern. The MGB's after gunner spotted her first. He had seen hundreds of German trawlers and ice-breakers in his time and her long undercut bow left him in no doubt as to her origin. 'She's a Jerry,' he said. 'A Bremen-built bastard.'

The captain replied that he thought it was more likely to be the Swedish pilot boat. 'I think not,' said the after gunner. A recognition signal was flashed but was not answered. The unknown vessel swung across the MGB's stern and ran parallel with her starboard side at a distance of about 300 yards. The captain, still sure she was the pilot boat, hailed her; but when he received no reply he put the MGB's engines full ahead. The unknown vessel – she was in fact V*p* 1606 of the German 16th Patrol Vessel Flotilla – now fired a warning shot ahead of *Master Standfast* and turned on a searchlight which blinded those aboard the MGB and made any further identification of the unknown vessel impossible. The captain – whose first trip it was in charge – then stopped his engines again.

'For God's sake don't let her come alongside,' said the SOE representative, suspecting the worst. He wanted the MGB to escape by heading off south-east at top speed, but the captain knew that, among the islands and rocks abounding in the area, this was impossible. Instead he turned on his navigation lights to show that he was friendly and then, in case the unknown vessel was not, began preparations to scuttle the MGB. The unknown vessel soon revealed that she was not friendly by firing bursts from her Oerlikon into the MGB at point-blank range. These shattered the wireless mast, mortally wounded the captain, and severed the steering. In the chaos which followed the Germans boarded the MGB and took her into Frederikshaven where the wounded were attended to.

Hopewell reached Lysekil, loaded 41 tons of ball bearings, and moved on to Bofiord to await the right opportunity to escape. Favourable weather was forecast on 10 November but the MGB received a battering in the open sea and soon had to return because of a seized-up gearbox. A new one was flown out and on 30 November *Hopewell* made a second, and successful, attempt to return, though two of her three engines malfunctioned. While she was at sea the other three MGBs set out for Sweden again. Two were forced to return, but *Gay Cor-*

sair arrived at Lysekil and after a delay which lasted three weeks began her return voyage with 40 tons of ball bearings on Christmas Eve.

The delay had allowed her crew to do some Christmas shopping and they noticed the change of mood in Sweden. Even the toy aeroplanes were now British not German. Just as *Gay Corsair* arrived Binney set out in *Hopewell* accompanied by *Gay Viking* and, after the usual mechanical trouble which by now had become endemic, arrived at Lysekil on the morning of 28 December. Bad weather delayed their departure, but on 16 January *Gay Viking*, loaded with ball bearings, began the return passage alone as repairs had to be made to *Hopewell*. More by luck than good judgement she avoided the German patrols, but was then badly damaged in a collision in the Humber. The next day, 19 January, *Gay Corsair* sailed for Sweden and arrived safely but it was not until 16 February that she and the repaired *Hopewell* were able to start the return passage which the two skippers decided to make in consort.

'All went well', wrote the skipper of *Hopewell* afterwards, 'until a searchlight was sighted very fine on our starboard bow. At this time we had fishing vessels on either side. We turned about on a 90 degrees course until the beam was extinguished, and then headed north, through the line of vessels extending between the searchlight and our course.' Persistent echoes on their radar warned him that the MGB was being trailed by German sea patrols so he deliberately took his craft right into the minefields off the Danish coast, knowing that the Germans would not dare follow them and that the MGB's draught was too shallow to detonate any of the mines. Nevertheless, it was a high risk option to take; an MGB with Brian Reynolds aboard was sunk by a mine in the Skaggerak shortly after the war ended and Reynolds and all but two of the crew were lost.

The MGBs had now completed six round trips and had brought out more than 240 tons of ball bearings and special machinery. But the nights were beginning to shorten and they were still way below their target of 400 tons. *Nonsuch* made the next passage, the only successful one she accomplished, and at the beginning of March *Gay Corsair* and *Gay Viking* succeeded in returning with a further 67½ tons of ball bearings. The operation was now suspended because of the lengthening hours of daylight, but in addition to ball and roller bearings 'Bridford' had managed to bring from Sweden machine tools, high-speed steels, spare parts, and electrical and measuring equipment. In total 347 tons had been transported as against 88 tons brought in by air, an achievement for which Binney, who had personally completed four round trips, was awarded the DSO.

Only one operation remained for the 'Grey Ladies' as the Germans called the MGBs. In the weeks preceding and following the Normandy landings of 6 June 1944 the resistance networks in the occupied countries had begun, under SOE direction, an intense campaign of sabotage to disrupt German communications and hamper and pin down their forces. So active was the Danish resistance movement that it was in danger of running out of arms and ammunition, and though some were dropped by air it was not only inadequate in quantity but was unacceptably hazardous for the aircrews involved. It was therefore decided to use three of the MGBs to run in supplies to Sweden which would then be smuggled into Denmark.

Binney was recovering from a heart attack so Brian Reynolds took command of the operation, code-named 'Moonshine', and was commissioned as a lieutenant-commander in the Royal Naval Reserve. The first attempt took place in September 1944, but bad weather and other factors prevented it and no less than nineteen other attempts from reaching Sweden and it was not until mid-January 1945 that the MGBs successfully unloaded their first cargo – 44 tons of arms and ammunition – at Lysekil for onward transmission to Denmark. Two of the MGBs returned with 63 tons of cargo which included conveyor band steel which was badly needed in Britain, but the third was damaged in a collision and had to be abandoned. So ended one of the most unusual and vital operations in which SOE was involved during the course of the war.

7
Black Radio

Both SOE and OSS used Black radio for subversive purposes and one of its most effective manipulators, Sefton Delmer, began his career in SO1. Black radio was as distinct from the white variety as Commandos were from the Boy Scouts. It had 'various shades of nigritude' as one analyst – and practitioner – of this type of warfare, Ellic Howe, has pointed out. They ranged, he wrote, 'from dense black to grey according to the target and objectives, but subversion – the disruption of the enemy's will and power to fight on – was the common factor in all the output intended for German ears or eyes. Furthermore, nothing perpetrated by the Black specialists could possibly be acknowledged by HM government as being of British origin. Indeed, the Black operators could do a great many things that would have been absolutely impossible for white propagandists.'

Department EH (Electra House) took over Black propaganda (see Chapter 11) from Section D, one of SOE's predecessors, on the outbreak of war in September 1939 and established itself in the stables at Woburn Abbey, the ancestral home of the Duke of Bedford. After Germany invaded France in May 1940 this department began using an anti-Nazi German civil servant who broadcast subversive propaganda to Germany. But otherwise EH achieved little before its Black radio output became the responsibility of SO1 when SOE was formed in July 1940.

In their first directive to SOE, dated 25 November 1940, the Chiefs of Staff ordered that 'subversive activities should be given preference over the [organisation of] secret armies in the occupied territories'. As a result of this directive, twenty Black broadcasting stations, or Research Units (RU) as they were called, came on the air between November 1940 and November 1941, aimed at audiences in Axis or Axis-occupied countries.

These first twenty stations were followed by another nine in 1942 and a further sixteen in 1943, though many were replacements for stations that had become outdated. In Ellic Howe's opinion, and he was in a position to know, the transmissions of the early stations were 'a waste of human effort and the electricity required to transmit them'. There was an exception, an RU called *Gustav Siegfried Eins* (GS1) which, he said, attracted 'a modest (and sometimes even appreciative) audience in Germany by the end of 1941'.

Gustav Siegfried Eins – the German signallers' equivalent of George Sugar One – was the invention of a talented journalist, Denis Sefton Delmer. Born in Berlin in 1904, he was the son of Austrian parents who registered him as a British citizen but had him educated in England. Bilingual to the extent of being able to imitate the accent of a Prussian aristocrat or a Berlin dustman, Delmer joined the *Daily Express* in 1927 and by 1937 he was its Chief European Correspondent. In early 1941 he was recruited by Leonard Ingrams into SO1 where the Socialist politician, Richard Crossman, was already overseeing an RU, *Sender der Europäischen Revolution* (Radio of the European Revolution), operated by a group of European Marxists. But Crossman's RU, which was directed at revolutionary socialists in Germany and the 'good' anti-Nazi Germans there, was not the appropriate medium to counter a new left-wing radio station the Germans had recently started and which was aimed at British workers.

'Old ladies in Eastbourne and Torquay are listening to it avidly,' said Ingrams to Delmer, 'because it is using the foulest language ever. They enjoy counting the Fs and Bs. Well, my minister [Dalton] thinks we should reply in kind, and as he is a Socialist, he thinks a right-wing station would be the appropriate one to carry the filth.'

Delmer agreed with alacrity and GS1 was born. Unlike Crossman's RU, where the German running it had a free editorial hand, Delmer's recruits had to follow Delmer's rules and editorial policy. This policy was much more pragmatic than Crossman's in that Delmer was not politically motivated but was prepared to corrupt or suborn the loyalty of any German who happened to listen – and there were soon plenty of them.

'We want to spread disruptive and disturbing news among the Germans which will induce them to distrust their government and disobey it,' Delmer stated. 'Not so much from high-minded political motives as from ordinary human weakness... Our listeners are intended to feel they are eavesdropping on the private wireless of a secret organisation, whose members presumably know what the programme of the organisation is. What the listener learns of this programme he picks up by studying the news that we put over. He finds that we are anti-communists who once thought Hitler pretty good, fought alongside him in fact, but are now appalled at the corruption, godlessness, profiteering, place-hunting, selfishness, clique rivalries and Party-above-the-law system which the Party has.'

Delmer decided to call the head of this secret organisation, *der Chef*, because he had heard Hitler being called this when, as a journalist in the early 1930s, he had travelled with the Führer's entourage. But he left it to the imagination of his German listeners to decide what the station's call-sign, GS1, stood for. To broadcast as *der Chef* Delmer found a German journalist named Peter Seckelmann. He had come to London in 1937, and when war broke out had joined the Pioneer Corps. 'His voice seemed to me just right for *der Chef* as I envisaged him,'

Delmer later wrote, 'virile and resonant with just that slight trace of a German drawl which I had found so often in the speech of Junker officers of the Kaiser's guards regiments.'

Der Chef's first broadcast took place on 23 May 1941 and was centred on the extraordinary event which had taken place earlier that month when Hitler's deputy, Rudolf Hess, had parachuted into Scotland with the apparent aim of negotiating peace between Germany and Britain. 'First, let's get this straight,' rasped *der Chef*. 'This fellow is by no means the worst of the lot. He was a good comrade of ours in the days of the Free Corps. But like the rest of this clique of cranks, megalomaniacs, string-pullers and parlour Bolsheviks who call themselves our leaders, he simply has no nerves for a crisis. As soon as he learns a little of the darker side of the developments that lie ahead, what happens? He loses his head completely, packs himself a satchel full of hormone pills and a white flag, and flies off to throw himself and us on the mercy of that flat-footed bastard of a drunken old Jew Churchill. And he overlooks completely that he is the bearer of the Reich's most precious secrets, all of which the f——g British will now suck out of him as easily as if he were a bottle of Berlin White-Beer.'

This was mild stuff compared with what was to come and when the Lord Privy Seal, Sir Stafford Cripps, was sent a GS1 script by Crossman's left-wing supporters at Woburn, which gave a lurid account of a German Admiral's orgy with his mistress and four seamen, he was horrified. He apparently went straight to the Foreign Secretary, Anthony Eden, to complain. 'If this is the sort of thing that's needed to win the war,' he stammered in fury, 'w-w-why I'd rather lose it.'

He called those at Woburn 'that beastly pornographic organisation' and demanded to know to what possible audience it was appealing. 'Only to the thug section of the Nazi Party,' he suggested, 'who are no use to us anyway.' He, like Crossman, wanted the RUs to be used to broadcast messages of hope and sympathy to the 'good' Germans.

Eden was as shocked as Cripps; and Bruce Lockhart, the head of PWE, agreed that the programme had gone too far. But Rex Leeper, who was in charge of Black propaganda at Woburn, successfully defended GS1 and Delmer. 'I am not pornographic myself,' he wrote to Bruce Lockhart. 'It bores me and for that reason disgusts me perhaps less than it would otherwise, provided I can see a purpose behind it in the fight against "evil things". If in the Secret Service we were to be too squeamish, the Secret Service could not operate... This is war with the gloves off, and when I was asked to deal with Black propaganda I did not try to restrain my people more than "C" [the head of MI6] would restrain his, because if you are told to fight you must fight all out. I dislike the baser sides of human life as much as Sir Stafford Cripps does, but in this case moral indignation does not seem to be called for. Delmer is a rare artist and a good fellow. I want to back him in the work he is doing...'

Gustav Siegfried Eins was saved. It may have been toned down slightly when the Political Warfare Executive (PWE) took over the functions of SO1 in August 1941, but in the autumn of that year the American embassy in Berlin, which assumed Delmer's station was broadcasting within the Reich, was reporting back to Washington, then still neutral, that the station was 'using violent and unbelievably obscene language' to criticise Nazi officialdom, especially the SS. 'Superficially it is violently patriotic and is supposed by many German officers to be supported by the *Wehrmacht* in secret. A very large number of Germans listen to this station, and often names, dates and addresses are given in such detail that it may be assumed that the statements could be quickly discredited if no background existed.'

So effective was GS1 that the following year an SOE agent in Sweden also reported that it was being transmitted from within Germany and claimed that it had more listeners there than any other station. It was, he said, destroying the people's faith in the Nazis who were being fed credible stories of 'scandal, corruption, tyranny of the Nazi bigwigs, crying injustices'.

Delmer's sources for these stories were various. Initially *der Chef*'s spicy tales were fictitious, though they contained just enough facts – which Delmer supplied from his own intimate knowledge of Germany, from German newspapers, and from information gleaned from German refugees – to make them acceptable to their audience. Later, after he was able to make use of the information extracted by the Combined Services Detailed Interrogation Centre where prisoners of war, wittingly and unwittingly, gave much useful information about their home backgrounds and the latest forces' jargon, as well as their military roles. Prisoners were also extremely useful in confirming that the rumours spread by *der Chef* were being believed by the German population.

Delmer also soon established links with the intelligence divisions of the three services, and he worked particularly closely with the Naval Intelligence Division in which his friend Ian Fleming was working. Another source were the letters that were intercepted from Germany to neutral states. An example of the information extracted from these were the 'splendid gossip-rich letters' written by the young American-born wife of a German industrialist to her girl friend in Nevada. As she mixed socially with Cologne's Nazi burgomaster and his circle, *der Chef* constructed some convincing stories about the dissolute lives of Nazi party members in that city. In one letter the woman described to her confidante a magnificent sugar cake made in the shape of Cologne cathedral. It had been baked for the burgomaster and his friends just after the sugar ration had been severely reduced for ordinary Germans, and *der Chef* made sure that everyone who was listening to GS1 in Germany knew the full details about this extravagant gift.

The fact that *der Chef* had fooled the American embassy in Berlin posed something of a dilemma for Woburn because at this time the British were striving to persuade the United States to enter the war. If Washington was allowed to assume that the *Wehrmacht* was about to rebel against the Nazi Party the American government might reasonably think that Hitler would fall without the United States having to intervene. But if the Americans were told the truth there was no guarantee that *der Chef*'s true identity would be kept secret. Eventually, it was decided that SO1's representative in Washington should tell President Roosevelt about GS1 on the understanding that it was for the President's ears only.

Roosevelt was apparently highly amused by the story, so amused that he could not keep it to himself. Soon everyone in Washington knew about *der Chef* – though it apparently never filtered through to the Germans – with the result that by the time the US entered the war in December 1941 Delmer's work was already well regarded there. Donovan, in particular, wanted to know more about the techniques of Black radio propaganda, and this eventually produced, so Delmer relates, a 'close and profitable collaboration' between his organisation and the OSS.

Der Chef continued to broadcast until 18 November 1943 when Delmer decided to use Seckelmann's talents elsewhere. It seemed that the best way of disposing of *der Chef* was to pretend that at long last the Gestapo had tracked him down and listeners in Germany heard him being gunned down to the cry of 'Got you, you swine!' However, this dramatic ending was somewhat negated by the fact that the engineer in charge, knowing no German and unaware of the programme's contents, repeated it an hour later in the usual way. So *der Chef* died twice.

The success of GS1 led the Admiralty to propose to Delmer at the end of 1942 that a Black station be started to attack the morale of U-boat crews. For one of the services to make such a request was a real breakthrough for the whole concept of Black radio, and Delmer jumped at the idea. But he said that for the new RU, *Deutscher Kurswellensender Atlantik*, to be convincing its broadcasts had to be made live which was beyond Woburn's technical capacity at that time. But this difficulty was overcome and later Delmer was allowed to use the powerful 600kW medium-wave transmitter, code-named 'Aspidistra' (after Gracie Fields' song 'The biggest aspidistra in the world'), which had been purchased from the United States and erected for PWE at Crowborough in Sussex.

Originally the idea of acquiring 'Aspidistra' had been conceived by SO1 with the idea of intruding on, and overpowering, German broadcasts and the German jamming of BBC broadcasts, and it was used very effectively for this purpose after the landings in North Africa in November 1942. It was designed to make extremely quick changes of frequency to avoid jamming, but also to take over the frequency of any German station that stopped broadcasting temporarily so that it could then broadcast as if it were that station. So efficient was it in this respect that it could take over a frequency within one two-hundredth of a second of the German station shutting down.

Delmer was determined that his new RU – called *Atlantiksender* by the Germans – would break new ground. He insisted that news items be written in colloquial German – 'none of our stuff is going to sound as though it is being read aloud from some learned periodical' he told his staff – and he employed the latest music with which to entertain his listeners between the items. This was done by purchasing the latest German hit records in such neutral cities as Stockholm, but was also provided by the members of a German dance band who had been captured in North Africa and sent to Britain.

The OSS were especially helpful with this project – which it appropriately code-named 'Muzak' – and indeed the official OSS history states that it 'became a joint Anglo-American undertaking'. The Morale Operations Branch of OSS set up a dummy corporation to handle the business side of hiring orchestras, studios, and singers to record the latest American jazz tunes – jazz, forbidden in Germany, was immensely popular with the German forces – to which German lyrics were often added. It also arranged for German-speaking singers such as the Metropolitan opera star, Grete Stueckgold, and Marlene Dietrich to make special recordings in German, and short variety shows were also recorded.

Delmer wrote that of course Marlene Dietrich was not allowed to know how her songs were being used and when she visited Europe Delmer had to stop broadcasting them in case she heard herself singing on what was ostensibly a Nazi radio programme. According to Delmer she only learned the truth when she visited Berlin after the war and had rotten tomatoes hurled at her for being a Nazi sympathiser!

Another source of popular music for the programme was the band of the Royal Marines which, in a secret session in the Albert Hall, recorded a catchy Berlin music hall song which Delmer had chosen to be *Atlantiksender*'s theme tune. He chose it because he had learned from prisoners that it was a favourite among U-boat crews who had composed some new, lewd, verses for it. The first verse began '*Ich war in Sant-Nazaire in einem Puff...*' ('I was in a brothel in Saint-Nazaire...') These new verses were sung by a member of Delmer's team who was, no less, a nephew of General Werner von Fritsch, a former commander-in-chief of the German Army. Apparently, he was not asked by the Royal Marines bandmaster for a translation.

As with GS1 Delmer acquired much of his inside information for *Atlantiksender*, and later its Army equivalent, *Soldatensender Calais*, from prisoners of war, the German newspapers, and so on. But in addition he acquired a German teleprinter (*Hellschreiber*), which the London correspondent of Goebbels' official German news agency had inadvertently left behind at the beginning of the war. To disseminate the agency's news quickly across the extensive Nazi-occupied territories, Goebbels began using a *Hellschreiber* and Delmer was able to receive the agency's bulletins at the same time as did German newspapers and radio stations. And because Delmer's staff were quicker off the mark than their German counterparts they broadcast the latest news on *Atlantiksender* before the Germans could get round to doing so. This gave the station what would nowadays be called enormous 'street cred' with those who listened to it.

Delmer also used the RAF's photographic reconnaissance flights to maximum effect when he started broadcasting over *Atlantiksender* the damage done by RAF raids on German cities, telling his anxious U-boat audience exactly which streets in their cities had been destroyed. He was able to be so accurate because copies of the photographs, taken by high-flying Mosquitos directly after a raid had finished, were rushed by Air Intelligence to his new studio at Milton Bryan where a special team analysed them with the aid of stereoscopic viewers and a library full of maps of German cities and Baedeker guides.

Not all the broadcasts of *Atlantiksender*, which began on 22 March 1943, or those of *Soldatensender Calais* – re-named *Soldatensender West* after Calais was captured in September 1944 – which began on 24 October 1943, were directed against the *Wehrmacht*, for Delmer decided that neutral firms and businessmen who continued to trade with Germany were good targets as well. In one instance he obtained the necessary details from the Ministry of Economic Warfare about a Swedish firm which was purchasing ball bearings in Sweden and smuggling them into Germany. So ribald and caustic were *Atlantiksender*'s comments about the firm and its directors that it stopped supplying its German customers – blackmail by Black propaganda as Delmer rightly called it.

Soldatensender Calais broadcast on the same wavelengths as Radio Deutschland when the latter was unable to broadcast because of Allied air raids. It was more grey than black for it was not difficult to guess its source, but it probably contributed to the 'softening up' of the German forces defending the Atlantic Wall against an Allied invasion. And when the invasion came *Soldatensender Calais* was quick to exploit its success, and both *Atlantiksender* and *Soldatensender* were employed to promote the written Black propaganda Delmer and others were also producing.

On 11 June Fritsch's nephew again went on the air, not singing dirty verses this time but speaking with the intonations of a typical aristocratic Prussian officer: 'This is a report, an epitaph, and a warning. An epitaph for the comrades of the Kremlin Division, who were cut off on the beaches of Ouistreham and Arromanches, who were left in the lurch and hammered to death. Only a few men of one regiment in this division remain. Of the 916th Grenadier Regiment, only a couple of men from it have got back to tell the tale. What these comrades have to tell us must be a warning to everyone. It is a warning to all those who may be lying in an outpost somewhere on the beaches, or are stationed somewhere up on a hill, or on the coast. And as they lie there they may get the order, "hold on, reinforcements are on their way to you." The reinforcements will not come. They cannot come because nothing is being done about sending reinforcements, because all these men have been written off – written off as dead and lost...' And so on.

If the Normandy invasion gave Delmer excellent opportunities to attack the morale of the German Army in France, he regarded the attempted assassination of Hitler in July 1944 as the culmination of all that he had been working for, and *Soldatensender Calais* worked overtime to exploit it.

'To me,' Delmer wrote, 'the most astonishing and gratifying aspect of the generals' coup was the way Hitler's Third Reich appeared to being doing its best to live up to the picture we had been presenting of it, a picture which I myself had always regarded as a propaganda caricature. But here were genuine German generals rising in rebellion against Hitler just as though *"der Chef"* of *Gustav Siegfried Eins* were directing them. And the Gestapo and the SD [*Sicherheitsdienst*, the security service of the SS] had been shown up as the fumblers we had always said they were.'

OSS's Morale Operations Branch launched its first Black broadcast from Tunisia in June 1943. The station was called '*Italo Balbo*' after the Italian Air Marshal who had been opposed to Italy's close relationship with Germany. Balbo had been shot down by his own side in Libya in 1940, but many Italians believed he was still alive and the station's purpose was, according to the official OSS history, 'to promote discord and dissension between Fascists and Nazis and between Fascists and the Italian civilian population, urging resistance against the Germans and against those Italians who had "sold out to the Nazis".'

This was very much in accord with Delmer's approach to Black radio, that its purpose was 'to corrode and erode with a steady drip of subversive news' the confidence of the German population in its leaders. But sometimes OSS's approach to Black radio broadcasts against Germany was more sensational. For on one occasion at least OSS seemed bent on trying, in one fell swoop, to alter the course of the war. This occurred in September 1944 when Howard Becker, a professor of sociology who was running OSS's Black propaganda, urgently requested the use of 'Aspidistra' for a one-shot broadcast. This was agreed and what followed was what Delmer described as being one of the most fantastic broadcasts of the war – a speech by one of the generals involved in the *putsch* against Hitler who had died by his own hand when it had failed.

'I am Colonel-General Ludwig Beck,' the speaker announced in a deep, resonant voice. 'I am not dead as has been lyingly and all too prematurely reported by the spokesmen of our traitor rulers. When on the night of July the 20th I was compelled to go through the act of shooting myself, I did not die – I was only wounded. Friends carried me away, pretending I was a corpse. They took me to a secret place where I was nursed back to health. I would have remained in hiding there until the end of the war. But the plight of my fatherland compels me to come forward and speak.'

The broadcaster then appealed to the German Army to rise against the regime in order to save Germany from total destruction and to reduce some of the German people's war guilt. Delmer described it as a beautifully written piece and beautifully spoken. But he thought it rather too far fetched for he suggested it might have been better to send out the broadcast with the claim that this was the speech Beck would have made over the official German radio if the assassination had been successful. Professor Becker, not unreasonably, preferred to do it his way. Although the BBC reported that German transmitters had jammed this broadcast more promptly than any other transmitted from Britain, it did not have the desired effect of an immediate uprising against Hitler.

Another OSS Black radio station was *Volksender Drei* which started to broadcast from Paris in August 1944. Its chief speaker purported to be the commander of an unnamed German town in the path of the Allied advance who had mutinied and taken over the town 'to end useless slaughter'.

Perhaps more effective was Operation 'Annie', an OSS Black radio station which purported to be transmitting from the Rhineland, but which in fact was sent out by Radio Luxembourg, one of the most powerful transmitters in Europe. This was a particularly effective means of transmitting the programme as Radio Luxembourg had been one of Goebbels' chief outlets for his radio propaganda when it had been in German hands. The Germans were therefore not ready to jam it and most German radios had been fixed to tune into its wavelength.

Annie's chief attraction to its listeners was the accuracy of its battlefield reports which it relayed with great detail and much local colour. It was so reliable that later interrogations revealed that some German battalion commanders listened to it to update their situation maps. But once the Americans had crossed the Moselle into the Rhineland the official OSS history states that Annie began reporting US armoured columns as being miles ahead of their real positions and telling of 'lost encounters and imaginary surrenders, thus instilling a feeling of futility within enemy ranks'.

It is impossible to assess quantitatively the success of the Black radio campaigns launched by the Allies. Some of the stories Delmer spun certainly provoked a reaction from the German government which had to issue official denials.

In his well-documented and measured appraisal of Black propaganda Professor Cruickshank says that *Soldatensender Calais* was probably the most successful of the RUs and that it was causing trouble long before the Normandy landings. He quotes a German report of March 1944 which said *Soldatensender Calais* was creating great unrest and confusion by the news it was putting out about the military situation and the home front. This included verbatim transmissions of the official German news service with a number of 'more or less tendentious items mixed in', and that its listeners were trusting it more and more because, as a rule, its reports were accurate.

Cruickshank then goes on to relate that after the landings the German High Command had to broadcast warnings about *Soldatensender Calais* which included an example of the 'ingenious false news' the Black radio station was transmitting. The example it repeated was the Black broadcast about children becoming ill in German evacuation camps. The *Soldatensender Calais* broadcaster announced that reassuring reports for parents had been received from the camps as the number of deaths from diphtheria had decreased from 548 to 372, and that 'there is reason to believe that the number of deaths will be kept at this comparatively low figure in spite of the great lack of doctors and drugs'. This statement, the German Army announcer stated, was a pack of lies, but that it 'sticks like a venomous thorn in the heart of every soldier who has taken it for true and who may have his own children in one of the evacuation camps'. Officers, the announcer ordered, must tell their men about the station and German soldiers must remain untouched by it. 'We are too pure spiritually', the broadcaster said, 'to be concerned with such dirt.'

Cruickshank points out that such 'widespread and angry reaction to the transmissions of *Soldatensender Calais* leaves no doubt that it was having its effect on morale', and that the station had a wide audience among the German armed forces. It is impossible to calculate how much, if anything, this contributed to the Allied cause, but there seems little doubt that Black radio played its part in the Allies' victory.

Valentine Killery, who started SOE's Oriental Mission in Singapore in May 1941, rejected any possibility of using Black radio broadcasts against Japan because the Japanese government had banned all short-wave receivers and this would have made the potential audience extremely small. It also seemed extremely unlikely that anyone who did hear it would believe that a dissident organisation existed in Japan – in fact, there wasn't one – and finding someone to make the broadcast in acceptable Japanese was a further drawback.

The idea of Black broadcasts to Japan was revived by SOE in May 1944, but this time it was suggested that, with the help of the Korean National Revolution Party, with which SOE had been co-operating for more than a year, the radio station should purport to be broadcasting from Korea not Japan. 'The existence of a Korean station in or near Korea with contacts with Korean revolutionaries in Japan is, in view of the Japanese suspicions of Koreans in general, perfectly plausible,' the writer of one SOE memo suggested, though he went on to admit that 'it is not considered that at this stage it would be practicable to produce even the semblance of a subversive Japanese movement'.

This idea, too, was shelved and it was eventually left to OSS's Morale Operations Branch in SEAC to start Black broadcasts in the Far East. The first ones, which began in the spring of 1945, were two radio programmes using Japanese wave lengths which purported to originate in Sumatra. Soon afterwards MO established a small staff of specialists on one of the Mariana islands, which beamed Black broadcasts to Japan daily, and to occupied countries in south-east Asia, and these continued until the end of the war.

8
Special Operations Australia and the Singapore Strike

One of SOE's most successful sabotage raids of the war was 'Jaywick', which was mounted in September 1943 by canoe specialists belonging to Special Operations Australia (SOA) against Japanese shipping in Singapore harbour. SOA originally used Inter-Allied Services Department as its cover-name but this was changed to Services Reconnaissance Department (SRD) in May 1943 when it was re-organised. In Australia it was, and is, better known as 'Z Special Unit', the department which administered the organisation's Australian personnel. In April 1943 General Blamey, MacArthur's Land Commander in the South-West Pacific Area, called SOA 'a joint British Australian organisation', but it was at that time largely financed by SOE, had at its head an SOE officer (Lieutenant-Colonel Egerton Mott and then Lieutenant-Colonel Chapman-Walker), and initial impetus for its early operations, in the case of 'Jaywick' at least, came from Colin Mackenzie's India Mission. However, its status obviously changed during the next two and a half years for in October 1945 a note from one SOE officer to another stated that 'SRD is an Australian organisation. It is not, which so many people still seem to think, an SOE mission.'

'Jaywick' was the brainchild of Ivan Lyon, a regular army captain in the Gordon Highlanders. In February 1942 he was employed by the Oriental Mission to set up an escape route from Singapore through the myriad islands that make up the Rhio Archipelago by establishing supply dumps and providing a ferry service from one of the islands to Sumatra. Lyon was the ideal person to do this because he was an experienced yachtsman who had sailed for a number of years in the area and knew it well.

One of the vessels used to evacuate army personnel and civilians along this route was a 70-foot Japanese fishing boat, the *Kofuku Maru*, which had been taken over by the Malayan authorities on the outbreak of war. Her skipper at that time was a middle-aged Australian named Reynolds who had served in the Royal Navy during the First World War. When the Dutch authorities in Sumatra decided to sink all shipping to avoid it falling into Japanese hands Reynolds decided to sail his boat to India instead. When he arrived he was paid £250 by the India Mission for his work on the escape line and *Kofuku Maru* passed into the hands of the India Mission.

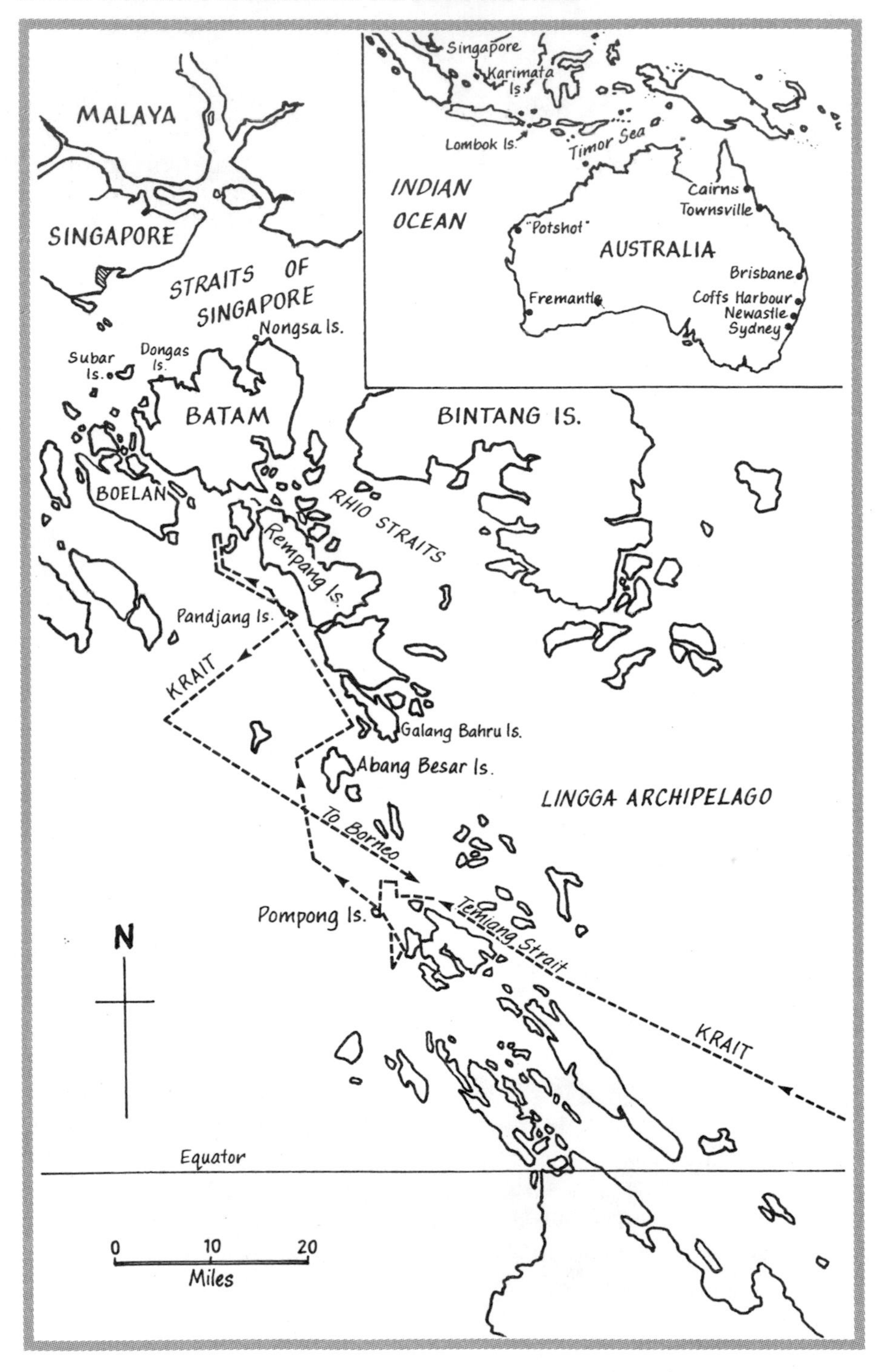

Singapore
Karimata Is.
Lombok Is.
Timor Sea
INDIAN OCEAN
"Potshot"
AUSTRALIA
Cairns
Townsville
Brisbane
Coffs Harbour
Newastle
Sydney
Fremantle
MALAYA
SINGAPORE
STRAITS OF SINGAPORE
Nongsa Is.
Subar Is.
Dongas Is.
BATAM
BINTANG IS.
BOELAN
RHIO STRAITS
Rempang Is.
Pandjang Is.
KRAIT
Galang Bahru Is.
Abang Besar Is.
LINGGA ARCHIPELAGO
To Borneo
Pompong Is.
Temiang Strait
KRAIT
N
Equator
0
10
20
Miles

Left: Jump suit and SSTR-1 suitcase wireless used by SOE personnel.

Below: OSS's silenced .22 calibre HiStandard pistol with its two instruction sheets, the spare screen roll and ammunition.

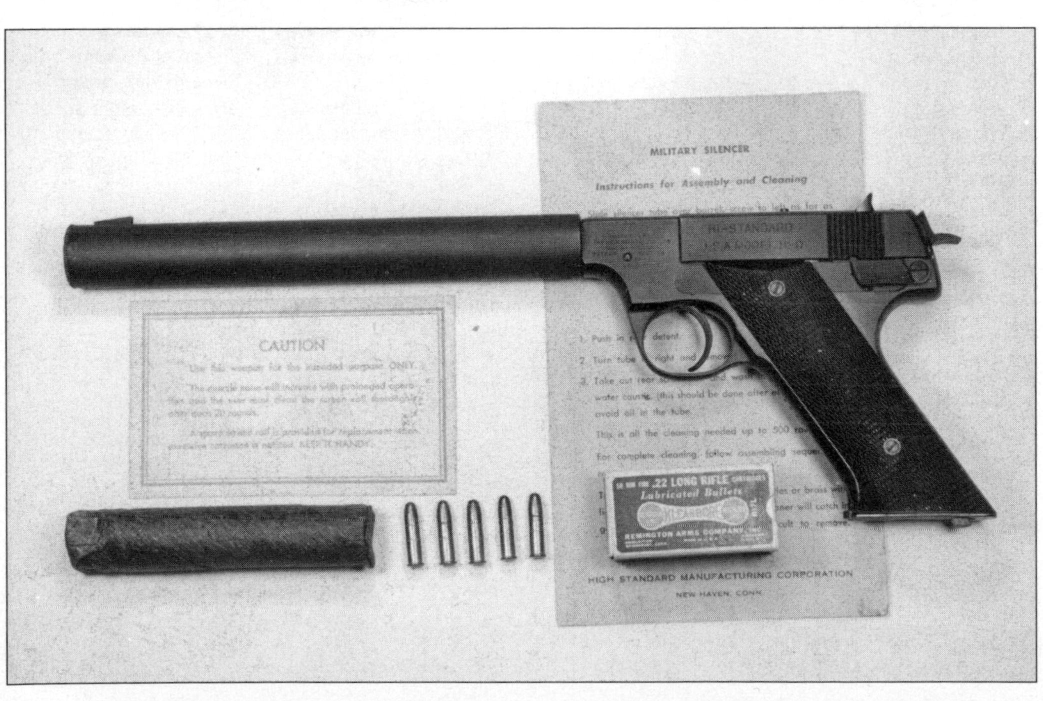

Display of OSS weapons and devices

1. Stiletto
2. Smatchet
3. Spring Cosh
4. Caccolube
5. Dog Drag
6. Firefly incendiary device
7. The Silenced M3 SMG and .22 pistol. The unsilenced barrel lies beneath it
8. Silenced .22 pistol
9. Liberator pistol
10. Stinger
11. Time Pencils. The one lying above the box is the British L-Delay pencil
12. Clam mine
13. Beano with an extra impact fuze lying to the left
14. Mole
15. Release firing device (Switch)
16. Pocket incendiary. It is on top of a boxlike device which is not identifiable
17. Adhesive paste
18. Anerometer
19. Large Thermite Well
20. Magnetic limpet mine
21. Pin-up limpet mine
22. Detonator magazine
23. Crimping pliers
24. Pull switch
25. Pressure switch
26. Two versions of Fog Signals
27. Tin containing A-C delay device
28. Small Thermite Well camouflaged as a tin of Postum
29. Oil Slick Igniter
30. Incendiary packet
31. Three fuze igniters

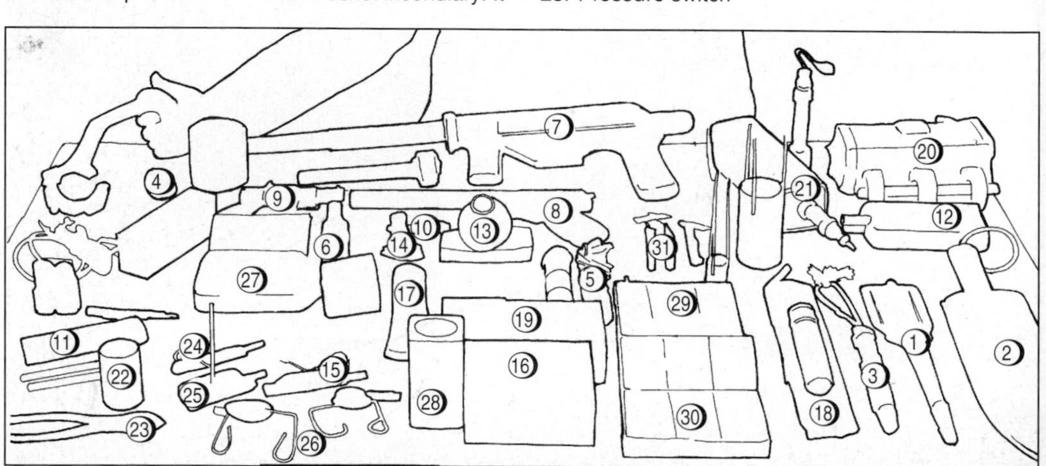

Right: 2nd Lieutenant Themis Marinos, the only Greek member of SOE's 'Harling' Mission which destroyed the Gorgopotamos bridge in Greece in November 1942.

Below: German engineers inspecting the Gorgopotamos bridge after its destruction by SOE's 'Harling' Mission in November 1942. The photograph was taken by the head of the engineers' unit which repaired it.

Right: The ELAS leader, General Napoleon Zervas (left), who co-operated with SOE's 'Harling' Mission in Greece, and his adjutant Captain Michalis Myridhakis.

Left: Captain Tom Barnes, head of SOE's 'Harling' Mission's demolition team which destroyed the Gorgopotamos bridge.

Above: The Brixham trawler *Maid Honor* which gave its name to the SOE party raiding Santa Isabel on the Spanish island of Fernando Po in January 1942.

Right: The crew aboard *Maid Honor* in Poole harbour while under training. Geoffrey Appleyard, wearing bathing trunks, is in the foreground. In the background March-Phillipps is bending over.

Above: SOE targets: *Duchessa d'Aosta* and *Likomba* taken from the British Legation at Santa Isabel on the Spanish island of Fernando Po (Public Record Office, Kew).

Below: SOE's operation 'Rubble': George Binney, pipe in mouth, with members of the crew of *Tai Shan* after breaking the German blockade of Swedish ports in January 1941.

Above: *Krait*, the vessel used by SOE members of 'Jaywick' to raid Singapore harbour in September 1943. (Australian War Memorial, 044211)

Below: Ivan Lyon, the SOE commander of 'Jaywick', observing Japanese shipping in Singapore from high ground on the northern end of Dongas Island. (Australian War Memorial, 067335)

Above: Guerrilla members of OSS's Detachment 101 standing by a bridge in Burma which they have just blown.

Below: A Detachment 101 light plane evacuating an American pilot rescued by members of the Detachment. The photograph was taken in July 1944.

Above: Group of OSS's Detachment 101 personnel, Kachins and Americans, during the siege of Myitkyina, Burma, which lasted from May to August 1944. The boy in the centre holding a submachine-gun may have been the group's mascot, but, as with the Karens, Kachins of all ages fought the Japanese.

Right: Norsk-Hydro plant at Vemork, Norway, which was attacked by SOE members of 'Gunnerside' in February 1943. (Popperfoto)

Above: Machinery destroyed at a factory at Figeac by an SOE *réseau*. (HMSO)

Below: Picking up stores dropped by the RAF for the French resistance. (HMSO)

Dramatic railway sabotage by Tony Brooks's SOE 'Pimento' circuit. (HMSO)

Above: Lieutenant-Colonel Francis Cammaerts, DSO, field name 'Roger', was one of SOE's most effective operatives in France where he was head of the highly successful 'Jockey' *réseau.*

Above right: Captain Harry Rée, DSO, OBE, field name 'César', ran SOE's 'Stockbroker' *réseau* in eastern France until he was forced to flee to Switzerland.

Below: Operational Group 'Percy Red' leaving for the Haute Vienne. This is an enlarged print of microfilm found in OSS files.

Above and below: Two targets of Operational Group 'Patrick': the dam at Eguzon in central-western France and the bridge half-a-mile below it. Microfilm of these French photographs were found in OSS files and were presumably used to brief the Group.

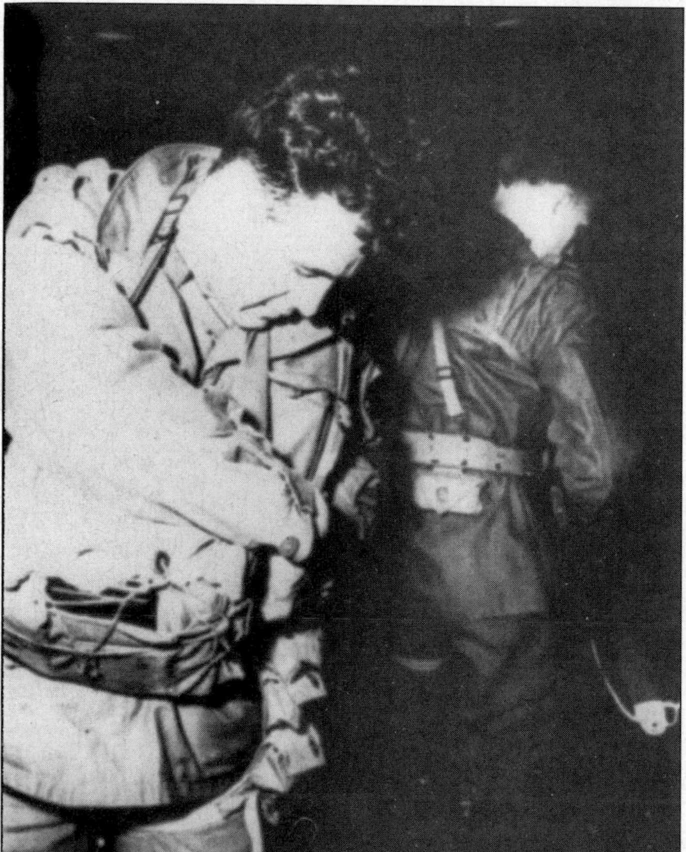

Above: Nearly all of the 4,000 women recruited by OSS had clerical or administrative jobs, and few had the opportunity to work operationally. Here, Mrs Marjorie Levenson is performing the important task of processing documents brought in from the field by Jedburgh and Operational Group teams. This photograph is an enlargement of microfilm found in OSS files.

Left: This photograph of 'Jeds' preparing to be dispatched into the field comes from microfilm found in OSS files.

Above: Jedburgh team 'Alan' after the capture of Villefranche, September 1944. Its leader, Captain Toursair, is third from right. The English member, Stanley Cannicott, is third from left.

Below: Stanley Cannicott of Jedburgh team 'Alan' instructing the Maquis in weapon-training.

Left: Lieutenant-Colonel E. H. Peacock, DSO, MC and bar. He commanded 'Otter' in Force 136's operation 'Character' in Burma in the spring of 1945 and was one of the war's great guerrilla leaders.

Below: Young and old Karens took up arms to fight the Japanese in Burma under the leadership of British officers who mounted operation 'Character' for SOE's Force 136.

Lyon's initial plans for 'Jaywick' were built around the vessel, for no sooner had he escaped from Singapore than he was thinking of ways to return to attack the Japanese. His original team included Major Campbell from the Oriental Mission, who was a Malayan planter by profession, and a South African captain named Chester who worked with the India Mission. Chester dropped out before the party embarked for the operation; Campbell was in charge of the administration of 'Jaywick'. When the project was approved by London in July 1942, Mackenzie passed it over to SOA, because Australia was the most suitable base from which to launch it.

Lyon was seconded to SOA, and arrived in Australia the same month. In due course *Kofuku Maru*, which had been renamed after a deadly East Asian snake, the krait, was shipped to Australia as deck cargo on a freighter after Reynolds had twice abandoned attempts to sail her to Fremantle because of engine failure. Reynolds came to Australia, too, and remained her captain until *Krait*, while on passage to Cairns in northern Queensland, reached Townsville.

'Jaywick' was initially considered an Army commitment but the Australian Army authorities wanted to use Lyon and his team in Timor, and were not prepared to attack Singapore. Lyon, through family connections (his father was a general), obtained a meeting with the Governor-General of Australia, who took a special interest in Special Operations, and he arranged for Lyon to meet members of the Naval Board. At this meeting it was decided that 'Jaywick' would have the complete support of the Royal Australian Navy and that it would come under the protective wing of the Director of Naval Intelligence, Commander Long, but that in all other respects it would be regarded as an SOE undertaking. Once the Navy had given its backing, the Army relented and the operation was officially mounted under its aegis.

After the politics had been disposed of Lyon recruited Lieutenant D. N. Davidson, RNVR, as his first lieutenant and eventually twelve others, all of whom – except the engineer and the medical orderly, a Welshman named Morris, who was Lyon's batman – were members of the Australian navy or army. Training commenced with a three weeks' course of physical training and unarmed combat at the Army Physical and Recreational Training School at Frankston, Victoria, and at the end of August a training camp known simply as 'X' was set up in Refuge Bay some twenty miles north of Sydney.

The training, as described in Ronald McKie's book, *The Heroes*, was very tough indeed. 'From the start Davidson, who never gave an order he could not carry out himself, made a strict rule that the men must reach the beach below [the camp] by bosun's chair and must return by swing-climbing up the cliff-face on a rope – a Commando technique they soon mastered, though after a two-or-three-day exercise with little sleep and on basic raiding rations, the climb was almost impossible.' At the camp the men concentrated on canoeing, night movement, the use of weapons and special explosives, and killing techniques.

The original date for the departure of the team from Australia had been 1 December 1942, with 15 December being the last possible date, because originally Lyon had been keen to time the raid for 15 February, the anniversary of Singapore's surrender. As it turned out none of these dates proved practicable as *Krait* did not arrive in Sydney until Christmas morning. She departed Garden Island [the navy's Sydney dockyard] on 17 January 1943 and the following day left Refuge Bay for Cairns with the 'Jaywick' party aboard. But then, as this abbreviated version of her log records, her 'engine stopped and was towed by minesweeper but tow parted in heavy swell. Hoisted sail. Put into Newcastle when engine restarted. Engine repaired with help of minesweeper personnel. Entered Coffs Harbour on 22 January as bilge pumps choked and weather rough. Then made for Brisbane where overhaul of engine and substitution of new parts was found to be necessary. Disappointing in view of the repairs carried out in India.'

Further breakdowns meant that the party did not reach Cairns for nearly two months after their departure from Sydney; and while they awaited a new diesel engine for *Krait* they undertook further training at Z Experimental Station near Cairns. Despite the delays and frustrations Lyon's team impressed itself on Chapman-Walker who reported back to London on 13 February: 'With regard to the personnel and training I do think that they have a first class team of young men, who seem tremendously keen and sensible and, as you may gather from the notes on training, they really have been put through some pretty tough work. Lyon himself, though shy and peculiar on first acquaintance, does seem to know his job, to know exactly what he means to do, and to have a real gift for leading his men... he certainly gives the impression of knowing what he is at, and seems very thorough in what he does: though I am sure no one wholly sane would conceive such a project.'

At last, on the night of 9 August 1943, *Krait* sailed northwards from Cairns for the 2,400-mile, eighteen-day passage round to Exmouth Gulf on Australia's west coast from where the operation was to be launched. The fourteen men on board were, as McKie described them, two public-school Englishmen with Scottish names and backgrounds (Lyon and Davidson), a Welsh coal miner, a northern Irish-Australian, and ten Australians, one of whom, Page (the medical officer), was descended from French Huguenots, and another, Carse (the navigator), the grandson of an English clergyman who had renounced all to search for gold. Of these fourteen, ten were naval men and four came from the army, though only four of the naval contingent – Carse, the engineer McDowell, and two Australian able seamen, Gain and Jones – were professional seamen.

Krait's armoury – a large waterproof box positioned behind the wheelhouse – included two Lewis guns for anti-aircraft defence, two Bren guns, eight Owen submachine-guns, and six .303 rifles, and in her holds were stored 45 limpet mines and 200 hand-grenades. Besides the normal basic food she also carried sealed tins containing enough food and water to sustain four men for four days – these could be buried at strategic points along the canoes' routes or even submerged off a beach – and 50,000 cigarettes and gold Dutch guilders to give to any natives who might help them. Besides anti-malarial drugs, sulpha and morphine, the list of medical supplies included a dozen bottles each of rum, whisky, gin, and lime juice. Everything aboard that could float – pencils, paper, toothbrushes – was of Japanese make so that if anything were accidentally dropped overboard in Japanese-occupied waters it would not rouse suspicion. Her fuel tanks, and the eight 44-gallon drums carried on deck, gave her a range of about 13,000 miles.

In his book McKie mentions a box of 'L' pills (cyanide capsules) which were to be served out to the canoe crews in case of capture, but this is not referred to in the files. However, there are copies in the files of specific orders that the canoe teams were not to be taken alive and how they were to ensure this. If capture was certain they were to shoot themselves; if one of the crew of the two-man canoes was wounded the other would shoot him first before shooting himself. There is nothing in the files to suggest why such drastic action was necessary, but presumably it was thought that if one man were made to talk he would reveal the whereabouts of the other members of the party.

At that time Exmouth Gulf was the location of a semi-secret US naval base code-named 'Potshot' and it was there that *Krait* lay for a number of days to refuel and restock her food and water, and to receive four new 17-foot canoes, an improved type of folboat which had been rushed out from Britain for the operation. Then at 1400 on 2 September *Krait* made her way out of Exmouth Gulf and headed north towards Lombok Strait which led into the Java Sea.

Once clear of land the fresh southerly breeze produced an unpleasant sea on the ship's port quarter. It gave Lyon his first real opportunity to gauge the seagoing qualities of the heavily loaded *Krait*, and she did not behave well. She rolled heavily and was slow to right herself; on one occasion she lay over until one of the crew standing beside the wheelhouse found himself waist deep in water. It was not an encouraging start, but by morning conditions had improved and although the pilot manual for the area predicted 'very hazy' conditions at that time of year visibility, somewhat to their consternation, remained excellent. Lyon therefore decided to head directly for the Strait as there seemed no point in trying to avoid air patrols, and all members of the party 'turned native' by changing into sarongs and staining their bodies. This worked for the more dark skinned members of the party but, according to McKie, 'Lyon never succeeded in appearing more genuine than an amateurishly stained public-school Englishman in fancy dress, and Davidson never more than a music-hall darkie who had forgotten to put on half his make-up'. But it was agreed that they were adequately disguised to pass any distant scrutiny, and that if any Japanese came close to them they would be fighting not bluffing them.

At sunset on 8 September they were at the entrance and they set a course for the middle of the Strait and gave the ship's engines maximum revolutions. However, there was a strong southerly current flowing through the Strait. At the narrowest point this was so strong that *Krait* was actually pushed backwards and it took four hours to pass a 4-mile-long island on their port side. As another clear day dawned they were still in the Strait with Bali eleven miles to port and Lombok nine miles to starboard, but there was no sign of any patrol craft though they did see some small sailing craft. 'This was the first opportunity to judge the crew under seemingly hazardous conditions,' Lyon commented in his after-action report. 'Their complete calm was most encouraging.'

Their luck held – the promised haze settled over the Strait and apart from some Macassar *prahus* crossing ahead of them they saw no ships of any kind. Lyon described the passage across the Java Sea as 'most dull. We lumbered along at 6½ knots in hazy weather, sighting nothing but an occasional sail. We wore the ensign of the Japanese Merchant Service.' They steered for Cape Sambar off the south-western coast of Borneo and then sailed along the coast through the Karimata Strait to the Karimata Group of islands where at dawn on 14 September they found themselves amongst numerous junks and fishing craft. They then steered directly for the Temiang Strait entrance in the Lingga Archipelago, intending to make landfall at dawn on 16 September.

Approaching the Strait they again encountered many native vessels as well as a large tanker which passed a quarter of a mile ahead of *Krait* heading north. Lyon estimated her to be about 10,000 tons. She was blacked out and showed no signs of having seen them. They were also surprised to see a European Bermudan rigged yacht which Lyon assumed had been looted from Singapore. Their immediate destination was the small island of Pompong on which survivors from a sunken British warship had been temporarily stranded the previous year. They had reported it uninhabited but that it had water, making it an ideal base for the party while they looked for a suitable place to hide *Krait*.

They arrived off Pompong on the afternoon of 16 September and while they were taking soundings to find a way through the coastal reef of a nearby island a Japanese flying-boat passed close overhead without paying them any attention. This incident, combined with the ease with which they had arrived at their destination, made Lyon conclude that peacetime conditions prevailed in the area and that the best way of escaping notice was for *Krait* to keep on the move, but that she should stay in isolated areas, avoid any contact with natives, and should never appear twice in the same place in daylight. He decided that the cumulative effect of gossip by natives seemed to present a far greater risk than casual enemy patrols. It was therefore decided to drop the three canoe teams (six men) at a suitable island closer to Singapore the following night and for *Krait* and her crew to return to the coast of Borneo.

The reflections of searchlights in the direction an Island fifteen miles to the south-west of them, the sound of aero engines being warmed up at dawn the next day, and then the appearance of two fighter aircraft overhead, indicated that there must be an airbase somewhere in the Lingga Group, and hurried the decision to disembark the canoe teams so that *Krait* could withdraw. Some natives in a canoe then appeared and *Krait* quickly weighed anchor and moved north.

It had been originally planned for the canoeists to launch their attack from an island closer to Singapore, but north of Galang Bahru they passed an island called Pandjang which had sandy coves and appeared to be uninhabited, and decided that when night fell the teams could be dropped there. But as they had just passed what looked like an observation tower on Galang Bahru they decided to maintain their course as if bound for Singapore in case they had been reported. By nightfall *Krait* was in the entrance to the Boelan Strait, between Boelan and Batam Islands, just 21 miles from Singapore, the lights of which could plainly be seen reflected on the clouds. They then turned back and despite a violent tropical storm found their way to Pandjang, the lights on the fishing *pagars* (inhabited fish traps), whose positions they had noted while sailing north, aiding their navigation.

A suitable anchorage was found at Pandjang and by dawn on 17 September the three teams, together with their operational gear, and food and water for one month, had been landed in a cove they called Otters' Bay. *Krait* then weighed anchor and headed for the Temiang Strait and Borneo, having been instructed by Lyon to rendezvous with the canoe teams at Pompong Island between the hours of dusk and dawn on the night of 1/2 October.

Carse, who was now in command, noted in his log: 'September 18, 1030: Steaming east-south-east and approaching the southern entrance of Temiang Strait. Sing yo! ho! for Borneo. All the crew are feeling the strain of long hours and ceaseless watching. Unless we get a quiet time soon I will have to issue Benzedrine. I have the same feeling but have now only had four hours off the wheel in about thirty-six and look like being here until we clear the Strait at least.' And the next day he noted: 'Our present job reminds me very much of the anxious father waiting outside the maternity ward for news.'

For two weeks *Krait* cruised amongst the islands off the south-west coast of Borneo. Although the crew sighted several fishing craft and junks they were never challenged. They rode out several storms and on 26 September Carse hove to in an isolated spot so that the crew could take turns in the dinghy and scrape off the worst of the weed clinging to *Krait*'s bottom. They were days of

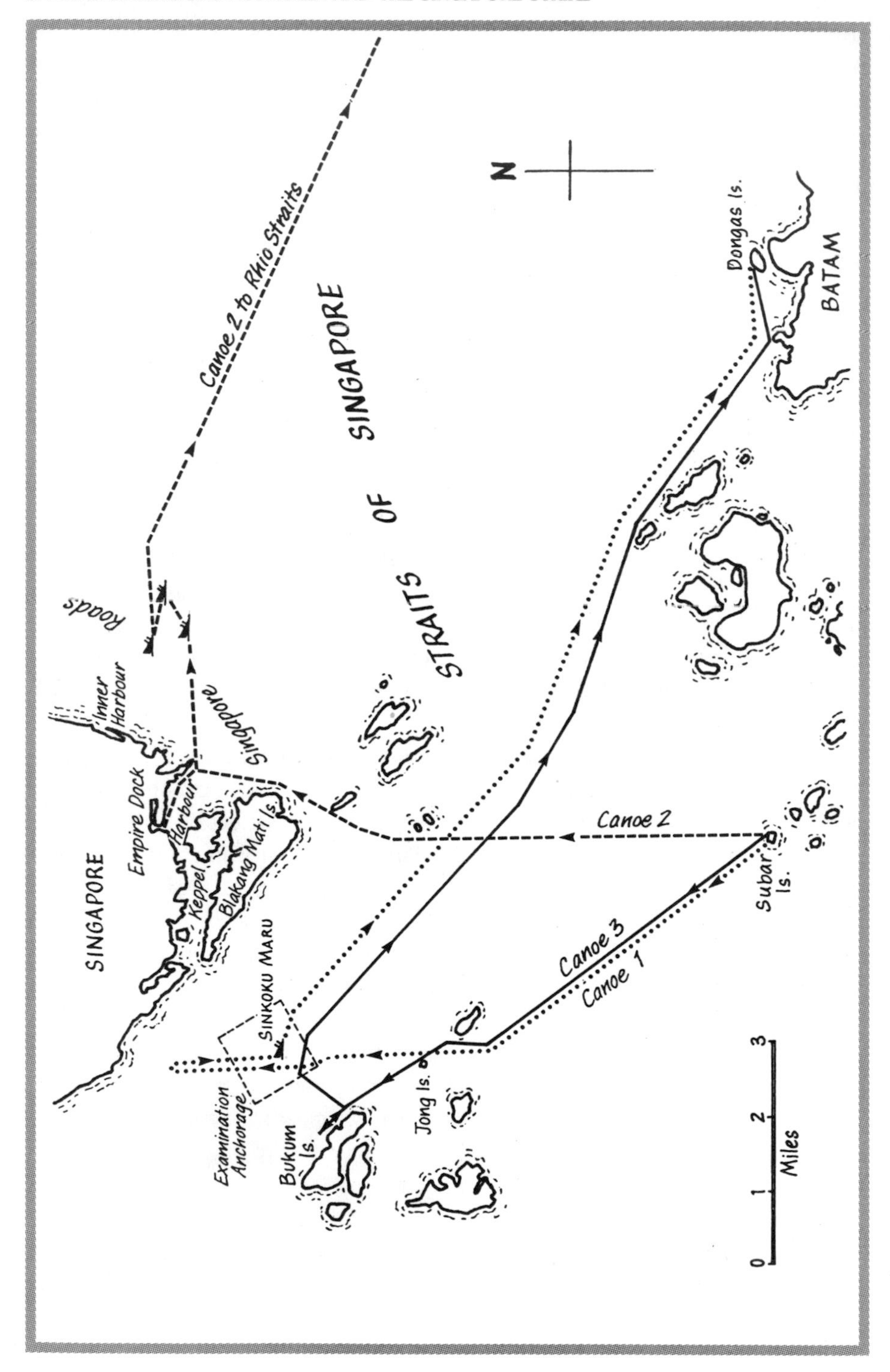
SINGAPORE
Empire Dock
Keppel Harbour
Blakang Mati Is.
Inner Harbour
Singapore Roads
STRAITS OF SINGAPORE
Canoe 2 to Rhio Straits
N
Dongas Is.
BATAM
Canoe 2
Subar Is.
Canoe 3
Canoe 1
SINKOKU MARU
Examination Anchorage
Jong Is.
Bukum Is.
0
1
2
3
Miles

anxious waiting, especially as they heard no announcement about the raid on the Japanese radio, but on 29 September the aimless wandering ceased and they began the passage back to their rendezvous. 'Well, we feel a little more cheerful now,' Carse noted, but added that there was still no news of the canoeists and, 'Anxiety remains, however, as we do not know if we are walking into a trap or not.'

After *Krait*'s departure Lyon was only able to find suitable cover for the party and to confirm that the bay was uninhabited. But a more extensive reconnaissance in the morning revealed that there was a native village on the other side of the island about a quarter of a mile from where the party had landed, but that there was no track leading from the village to the party's base. Lyon therefore decided it was safe to remain where they were and they carried their stores about twenty-five yards into the jungle from the bay where they had landed and pitched their camp beside a water hole. They then hid their reserves of food in a cliff face and posted a sentry who reported the usual activity of small junks and fishing craft, and of transport aircraft flying on regular schedules from an airfield on a nearby island.

Having set up their base camp ahead of schedule the men rested for two days, and spent another checking their equipment and stores before setting out at dusk on 20 September. 'Each man wore over a khaki shirt,' McKie wrote, 'a black two-piece suit of water-proofed japara silk, which narrowed and gripped at wrists and ankles, two pairs of black cotton socks, and black sandshoes with reinforced soles; and each man carried a black webbing belt, which could be slipped off while paddling, a .38 revolver and 100 rounds, a sheath knife (Davidson also wore a throwing stiletto), and a short loaded rubber hose, and in zipped suit pockets a small compass and a small first-aid kit containing bandages, needles and surgical thread, powdered sulpha, and morphia bottles with needles attached.'

When loaded with food and water for a week, and with all operational stores and their crews – a total weight of some 700lb – the canoes were very sluggish and were very low in the water. Nevertheless, by midnight the ten miles to the entrance of the Boelan Strait had been covered and a camping place was found on a nearby island which was so secure that the next day they all went bathing. The next night – 'owing to constant alarms at unfounded dangers' – progress was slow. Only twelve miles were covered before they had to shelter in a sandfly-infested swamp perilously close to a native village to avoid being on the water at daylight. They were undetected and the following night made good progress, arriving at their chosen observation post, Dongas Island, at midnight. Although Lyon described it as a jungle-covered hump of land with an extensive swamp on the south side, it was uninhabited, had drinking water and an excellent view of Singapore Roads from high ground on its north side, and featured a narrow inlet protected by a sand spit where they could conceal themselves in comfort.

The six men spent the next five days resting and observing likely targets. With no blackout in operation they could see the lights of cars driving down Singapore's Beach Road. In Keppel Harbour, some eight miles distant and right opposite the island, they observed a considerable movement of shipping, as there was in the nearby Roads, and Lyon calculated that there were never less than 100,000 tons of stationary shipping at the same time, and the free movement of medium-draught native craft in and out of the harbour seemed to indicate that there were no minefields. During the late afternoon of 24 September Lyon observed what he estimated as being no less than 65,000 tons of shipping assembled in the Roads alone. He knew that unfavourable tides would make an attack on these ships difficult 'but the nature of the target was such that an attempt seemed imperative'. The canoes were therefore launched that evening, but the tide was so strong that they made no progress against it and had to return.

This abortive attempt made the party realise that if they were to be successful they must move westwards to another launching place for the attack where the tides would be more favourable. The following night, therefore, all three canoes moved to the small bracken covered island of Subar which overlooked Examination Anchorage. This had no beach or fresh water but was an excellent observation post. Each team was allotted its targets and by 1900 all three canoes were loaded and ready to move. Canoes no. 1 (Major Lyon and Able Seaman Huston) and no. 3 (Lieutenant Page and Able Seaman Jones) paddled in company towards their targets in Examination Anchorage until they reached the vicinity of the small island of Jong. Page then left Lyon to attack shipping alongside the wharves on the island of Pulau Bukum, while Lyon headed for the shipping anchored in Examination Anchorage. Meanwhile, no. 2 canoe (Lieutenant Davidson and Able Seaman Falls) made for Keppel Harbour.

'I arrived at my target area about 2230,' Lyon wrote in his report, 'to find that all shipping, except tankers, were blacked out and completely invisible against the background of hills. After some searching I located a ship, but on close inspection found that it "belonged to Page". When my time limit was exhausted I decided to attack a tanker [later identified as the 10,000-ton *Sinkoku Maru*], two of which I could clearly distinguish by the red light in place of the normal white anchor light. We made a direct approach from astern and placed two limpets on the engine room and one on the propeller shaft.'

While they were doing this Huston noticed an extraordinary thing to which he drew Lyon's attention: a man was watching them intently from a porthole only ten feet above them! He continued to look at them intently as they worked and after they had left the ship's side to set off for Dongas Island twelve miles away he withdrew his head and lit his bedside lamp. Though Lyon makes no mention of their reaction to this in his report, it must have given both men a terrible shock, but the tanker crewman obviously did not report their presence for no alarm was raised.

Page and Jones reached their target area earlier than Lyon, at 2200. All the wharves were illuminated and there was a large barge with arc lights on which some unspecified type of work was being carried out amidst clouds of steam. There was also a sentry guarding a loaded tanker which was far too large to be attacked effectively. Despite these hazards Page examined the whole length of the wharves but he found only one suitable target, an old freighter, and on this he placed his limpets. By now the tide had turned and was running west to east which made it relatively simple for the canoeists to approach Examination Anchorage where they attached limpets to two more freighters. They then returned to Dongas Island where they arrived at 0515, about the same time as Lyon. Shortly afterwards they heard, to their great delight, the first explosion echoing across the water from Examination Anchorage.

With the flood tide to starboard, progress was slow for Davidson and Falls in canoe no. 2 but the passage across the Strait was uneventful except that a searchlight on the island of Blakang Mati swept the sky every so often. Then, just before they reached Keppel Harbour, a large steam ferry burning navigation lights, and bound for the south of Blakang Mati, nearly ran them down but did not spot them. They found the gate in the boom that protected the entrance to the harbour open and, with no boom patrol boat present, were able to slip through it without difficulty.

'Inside the boom against the east wharf were 2 ships,' Davidson wrote in his official report, 'but they were too small to be worthy of attack. No shipping was seen at the main wharf, and that in the Empire Docks was too brilliantly lit up and too small to warrant attack.' So they turned back, crossed the boom once more, and headed for the Roads where they found a number of excellent targets. Davidson chose three freighters, all of which were of 5,000–6,000 tons. Two of them were heavily laden, the third was in ballast. Limpets were placed on the port side of each ship, on the far side from Singapore's lights. Then at 0115 on 27 September the canoe headed for the Rhio Straits, Davidson having decided to make directly for Pompong Island and not rendezvous first with the other two canoes at Dongas.

It was not an entirely uneventful passage through the straits as Davidson later related in his report: 'We halted at a point of land 6 miles west of Pulau [island] Nongsa and left again at 1900 hrs proceeding in the direction of Pulau Tanjong Sau. Here we landed shortly before 0430 hrs on 28th and left again at 1900 hrs passing to the north of Pulau Lepang to Tanjong Piayu, thence to Pulau Anak Mati and down the channel between Pulau Rempang and Pulau Setoko. Off

Tanjong Klinking we encountered the patrol boat and had to hug the bay. Just after we landed on Pulau Pandjang at Otters' Bay a violent storm arose. We rested during the day of the 29th Sep. and set off on the last lap at 1900 hrs. When 4 miles from Pulau Abang Basar a violent storm arose, bringing with it a deluge of rain, thunder and lightning, and lashing the sea into a fury. We kept the bows of the canoe into the wind and sea and were tossed about for two hours, when the storm abated. We landed on Abang Besar and left again at 1900 hrs. on 30th Sep. Pulau Pompong, our rendezvous with "Krait", was reached at 0100 hrs 1st Oct. "Krait" appeared at 0015 on the morning of the 2nd October.'

While Davidson and Falls were battling their way down between the islands of the Rhio Archipelago the other two canoes left Dongas Island at dusk on 27 September. They expected to encounter patrols but saw none. Before dawn they found a suitable spot to lie up for the day and discovered when dawn broke that it was a Chinese graveyard. That night good progress was made and they reached Otters' Bay in the early hours of 30 September despite being buffeted by the same storm which Davidson and Falls, farther to the east, ran into when a few miles off Abang Basar.

The approach of another storm then delayed their departure from Otters' Bay that night which had serious implications as they had little time in which to reach the rendezvous. It was decided to risk making the 28-mile passage by day and the two canoes left the following morning, allowing an hour's interval between their departures. Several aircraft flew over them without showing any interest in them, and though they must have been clearly visible to the observation post they had passed on the way north in *Krait*, this did not react to them either.

After both crews had rested for a short while on an island they arrived at Pompong at 0300 on 2 October, just within the time limit. But they were so exhausted that when they circumnavigated the island in search of *Krait* they failed to see her and next morning were dismayed to see her sailing away down the Temiang Strait. Arrangements had been made for *Krait* to return if the first rendezvous failed. But, anticipating that they might have to wait some time, the crews approached some local natives who agreed to provide them with fish and vegetables.

The natives said that conditions for the local inhabitants were wretched. All local trading had stopped and they were without rice, sago, or clothing. When asked if it would be possible to smuggle rubber to Australia in return for rice – an interesting echo of 'Mickleham' (see Chapter 13) and perhaps in some way connected with that operation – the natives thought it impossible as there were Japanese restrictions on native vessels sailing east of Ambon. Luckily for the canoeists *Krait* returned 24 hours later and the whole party was reunited.

The passage across the Java Sea was again uneventful, but in the Lombok Strait one final nerve-racking incident occurred on the night of 10/11 October and is recorded in the log of the voyage kept by the navigator, Lieutenant Carse: 'As the darkness approached we increased speed to our maximum and drove her at it. A fresh south-easterly had sprung up and the sea was short and very choppy. As we neared the northern narrows we encountered tide rips with the waves breaking all over us. This went on till 2300 when we got into the Strait proper and the water was fairly calm. At 2330 the look-outs, ABs Falls and Jones, reported a sail approaching upon the Lombok side. While looking at it I saw it was a large naval patrol, with a bone in her teeth, approaching rapidly on our beam. All hands were called and armed and everything prepared to evacuate. She approached bows on to within about 100 yards, then slowed down and turned alongside on our port quarter. Seeing her beam on she appeared to be a modern type destroyer between 260 and 300 feet long. After pacing us for about five minutes she sheered off and went directly away from us, although we were undoubtedly seen she did not hail or challenge us in any way, neither did she use a searchlight. It was midnight before she was out of sight.'

The encounter took place in bright moonlight so that the destroyer could see what type of vessel *Krait* was and that she was flying the Japanese ensign. This, Carse surmised, was why they weren't challenged, but the incident left the whole crew 'in one large lump, safe and sound although many sighs of relief were heard'. Carse speculated in his log that the destroyer had sighted them just as there was about to be a change of watches and the duty officer wanted to get to his bunk. Alternatively it was possible that the local patrol boats had already got into trouble with some high-ranking official for stopping ships similar to *Krait*, and so it had been decided to leave her alone. Whatever it was the crew regarded it as a miraculous escape.

Krait arrived at Exmouth Gulf on 19 October without further incident, having covered 4,000 miles of enemy-occupied waters in 48 days without suffering one casualty. This was an outstanding achievement in itself. The fact that the 'Jaywick' team destroyed or badly damaged seven enemy ships amounting to between 36,843 and 39,111 tons turned their achievement into one of the epic sabotage operations of the Second World War.

A year later another raid, code-named 'Rimau', was mounted by Lyon on Singapore – this time using a submarine and submersible electric canoes called 'Sleeping Beauties', an SOE invention – but all the participants, several of whom had taken part in 'Jaywick', were caught or killed, and those taken prisoner were executed. *Krait*, after being used on further clandestine operations, survived the war and was employed for a number of years in Borneo as a timber carrier.

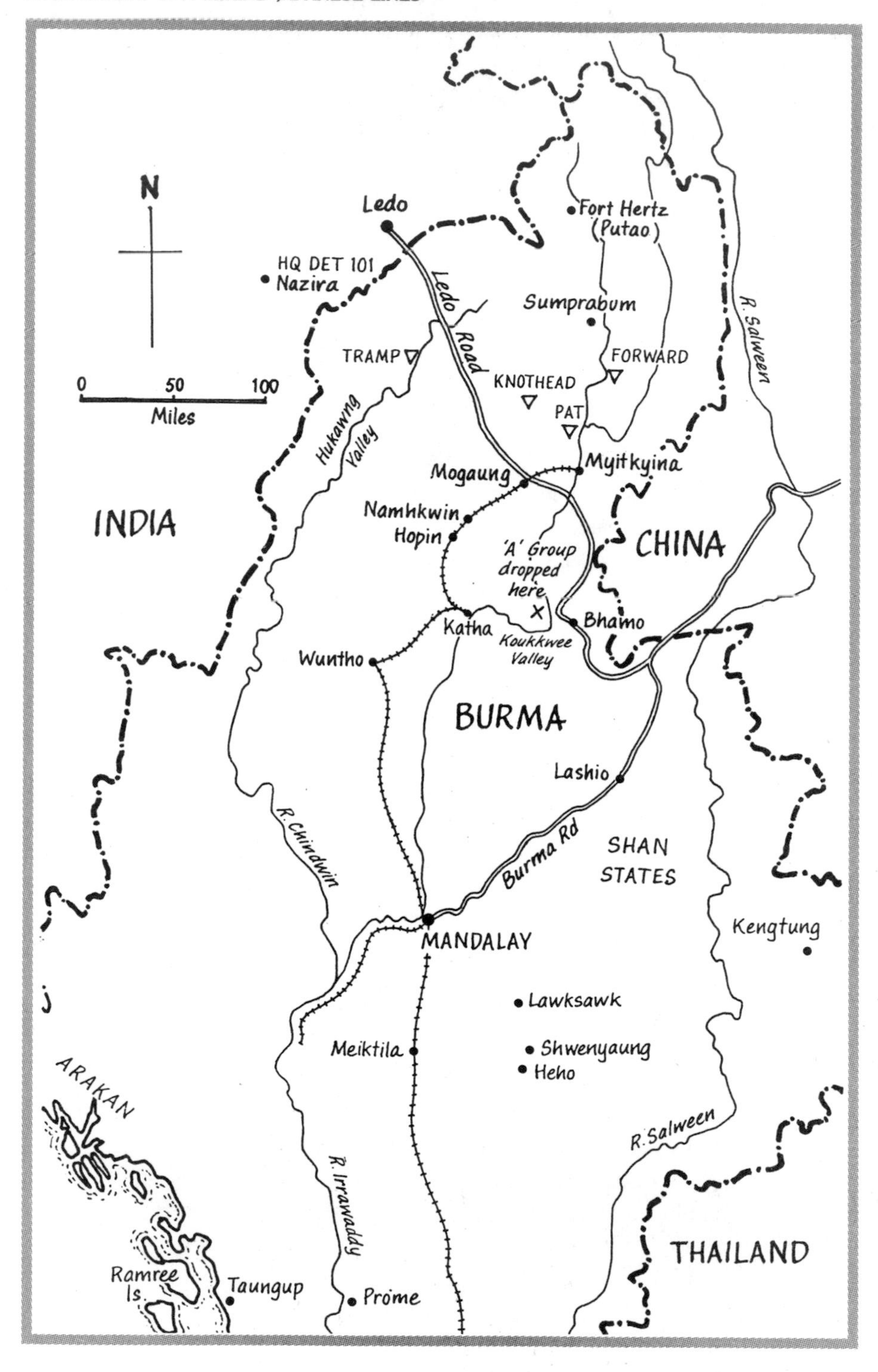
N
0 50 100
Miles
Ledo
HQ DET 101
Nazira
Ledo Road
Fort Hertz
(Putao)
Sumprabum
TRAMP
KNOTHEAD
FORWARD
PAT
R. Salween
Hukawng Valley
Mogaung
Myitkyina
INDIA
Namhkwin
Hopin
'A' Group dropped here
CHINA
Bhamo
Katha
Koukkwee Valley
Wuntho
BURMA
Lashio
R. Chindwin
Burma Rd
SHAN STATES
MANDALAY
Kengtung
Lawksawk
Meiktila
Shwenyaung
Heho
ARAKAN
R. Salween
R. Irrawaddy
THAILAND
Ramree Is.
Taungup
Prome

9
Detachment 101: Behind Japanese Lines

In January 1942 the US Army Chief of Staff, General George Marshall, appointed Major-General Joseph Stilwell Commander of all American forces in the China–Burma–India (CBI) theatre and, under Chiang Kai-shek, Chief of Staff of Allied forces in China. The same month Stilwell received a paper from Colonel Preston Goodfellow, the head of SA/G (Special Operations) at Donovan's Office of the Coordinator of Information, the predecessor of OSS. In it he proposed that a specially trained detachment be sent to the CBI to mount intelligence and sabotage operations behind Japanese lines in Burma or China.

Stilwell initially refused to approve the project, but when asked to nominate an officer of his own choosing to lead the unit he changed his mind and proposed Carl F. Eifler, a reserve officer who had once served under him. In peacetime, Eifler had been the Deputy Collector of Customs in Honolulu and was now serving as an infantry captain in Hawaii. In mid-February Eifler was given his assignment and he immediately recruited four others from his regiment: Captain John Coughlin, who became his second-in-command; Sergeant Vincent Curl; Captain Archie Chun Ming, a medical officer; and Captain Robert Aitken, a member of the Hawaiian Department's Intelligence section. It was on this nucleus that the new unit, officially called the Co-ordinator of Information Service Unit Detachment 101, was activated on 22 April 1942, the first ever in American military history to be established for clandestine warfare.

Although it had no predecessors, it was decided that the unit's title must not give the impression that it was entirely new, hence the name Detachment 101 and not simply '1'. Its brief was wide-ranging and reflected the breadth of clandestine operations in which OSS was involved during the war: subversion by MO (Morale Operations), propaganda, and intelligence as well as sabotage and guerrilla warfare. It also mounted escape and evasion operations for downed USAAF personnel, deployed a Maritime Unit (MU) and Operational Groups (see Chapter 9) in the Arakan, and its advanced intelligence bases even served as weather stations and air-raid warning networks for the USAAF flying supplies into China. Eventually, other OSS branches – including R & A, and R & D – were represented in the Detachment (see Chapter 14).

While the first American recruits were being trained the Japanese were over-running Burma. By May Stilwell, who had been commanding two Chinese divisions in Burma, had been driven back into India. The Japanese conquest of Burma closed the Burma Road along which Chiang Kai-shek's Nationalist forces fighting the Japanese in China had been kept supplied. A substitute supply route was therefore urgently required and in July 1942 the Americans started an air supply route, nicknamed 'The Hump', over the Himalayas to fly supplies to China from India. They also planned a new road (called the Ledo Road and then the Stilwell Road) which was to start from Ledo in northern India, pass through the Hukawng Valley, southwards to Myitkyina, and then through Bhamo to join the Burma Road near the Burma–China border.

Stilwell announced that the Allies had taken 'a hell of a beating' in Burma, but that he was determined to return as soon as possible. As an initial mission he aimed to clear northern Burma of Japanese so that the Ledo Road could be completed. While this was being done he wanted, by guerrilla action, to deny the Japanese the use of Myitkyina airstrip to prevent Japanese fighters harassing US aircraft flying over 'The Hump'. So when an advance party of twenty officers and men from Detachment 101 arrived in India in June 1942, Stilwell informed Eifler that he wanted the Detachment to operate in Burma not China and that he wanted 'to hear a lot of booms' coming out from that country.

The unit's first instructions from Stilwell, dated 15 September 1942, stated that 'the following initial specific mission is given you for immediate execution: To make plans for denying the use of MYITKYINA AERODROME to the Japanese as an operating field. This is your primary mission. In the accomplishment of this mission, without any desire to restrict you, it is desired to indicate that destruction on the railroad, the firing of railroad cars and the sinking of vessels carrying fuel will all contribute to the general success of your operations. Effective destruction of important bridges, such as the R. R. bridge near MEZA would reduce rail shipments of gasoline to a negligible amount. You should make a careful estimate of the situation and plan on your action, then inform this headquarters of your general plan. Subsequent missions will be given you from time to time, but for these you will submit your plans for approval before executing them... Liaison with British authorities should be initiated to the end that no possible cause for mutual interference may arise.'

Liaison with the British was in fact carried out through SOE's India Mission with which an agreement was signed maintaining full co-operation between the two organisations. This included collaboration in training, selection of personnel, exchange of intelligence information, and use of supplies.

In October 1942 Eifler established his base headquarters on a tea estate near Nazira in the Northern Indian province of Assam and it took until the end of the year for him to recruit and train the necessary number of Burmese nationals.

Eventually, there were as many as 26 schools to teach Detachment members espionage and sabotage techniques. By 25 November the detachment contained 85 personnel but it then ran short of funds. So acute was the financial situation that, before it was solved, the officers 'were called upon to put up their personal funds to buy food and pay agents who were on the verge of quitting'.

On 26 December 1942 Eifler led the first Detachment 101 group – two American officers, seven British officers, and five Burmese – into Burma to establish a supply and communications base at Sumprabum, 50 miles into the jungle south of Fort Hertz. Sumprabum was the nominal capital of the Kachin hills, the home of the Kachin tribesmen who were to give such staunch support to the unit. Sumprabum means 'jungle grass mountain' in the Kachin language and Eifler described it as containing 'three or four houses, a small church, a school building, and one other building. There was also a broken-down Chevrolet car with the remains of a dead Chinese soldier in the front seat.'

Shortly afterwards Stilwell issued another order to Eifler which was to have a far-reaching effect on the Detachment's activities. After detailing how contact with the British and their V-Force patrols (intelligence patrols) was to be maintained, Stilwell ordered Eifler to make contact with the Kachins and to establish friendly relations. 'Get them to make reports on Jap movements, dispositions, strength, etc.,' he wrote. 'Set up locations for future supply and chain of communication. Tell them Chinese are with us. Reassure them about treatment by Chinese [the Kachins feared the Chinese who often raided into their territory]. Tell the right ones we will give them some weapons.'

Contact with the Kachins was really the making of Detachment 101 for these fierce hill tribesmen made ideal guerrilla material. They are of Mongolian stock, a short sturdy people with friendly, cheerful dispositions. 'Extraordinarily loyal and brave,' wrote one Detachment member, 'they are at the same time fierce to their enemies.' When Stilwell, impressed by the numbers of Japanese killed by the Kachins under their Detachment 101 leaders, asked a village headman how he, Stilwell, could know if the toll on the Japanese had not been exaggerated, the headman took a bamboo tube off his shoulder and shook out its contents on the table. 'Count them', he replied, 'and then divide by two.' The objects were the shrivelled ears of Japanese corpses.

The Detachment's communications base, which was set up in a one-time American Baptist Mission building half-a-mile outside Sumprabum, would handle all the messages from agents who would subsequently be sent behind Japanese lines. The first of these sub-stations was established 250 miles inside Japanese-occupied territory on 7 February 1943. Other intelligence networks then began to be formed near potential targets by Burmese agents parachuted into Japanese-held territory and these played a key role in supporting the sabotage and guerrilla operations which were to follow. During the course of 1943 several airstrips for light aircraft were also built by the Detachment behind enemy lines and were so cleverly camouflaged that the Japanese never discovered them. The first of the light aircraft under the Detachment's control landed behind enemy lines with Eifler aboard on 1 October 1943 and from then on the air component of the Detachment increased considerably.

In accordance with Stilwell's directive, the unit's first sabotage operation was to attack road and rail communications into Myitkyina from the south. It was undertaken by an eight-man team, which included a British officer, a Karen tribesman, a Greek and several Anglo-Burmans. Initially, it attempted to penetrate the Japanese lines overland from Fort Hertz. But after probing the Japanese defences with the help of British-led Kachin Levies, half-trained guerrillas who defended their hills with an assortment of weapons including flintlocks and shotguns, it was decided that the only practical method of reaching the areas where they wanted to mount sabotage operations was to parachute in.

Impressed by the fighting quality of the Kachins, Eifler added four of these tough hill tribesmen to his team, designated A Group, but the Detachment's biggest difficulty lay in obtaining the necessary aircraft to parachute the team in and to keep them supplied from the air. Eifler partly overcame this problem by striking a deal with Air Transport Command Headquarters: in return for air transport and parachute training for the Group the Detachment would help rescue the crews of aircraft that had crashed or been shot down in the Kachin territory of northern Burma.

Air reconnaissance photographs showed that the Koukkwee Valley about 100 miles south of Myitkyina was an ideal drop zone for A Group. It would establish a base camp there and then attack the railway line which lay about 40 miles to the west. The twelve men were dropped in two groups during the first week of February with orders to cut the railway running through Mogaung to Myitkyina. Then the group was to recruit a force of guerrillas from the Kachins who lived in the Kachin hills south-west of Myitkyina, in order to harass road and river traffic from Myitkyina to Bhamo.

A base camp was established deep in the jungle where two of the Detachment and the four Kachins remained while the others, divided into parties of two, attacked three wooden bridges across the railway line and laid charges on the line itself between Hopin and Namhkwin. A dress rehearsal was held at the camp on 14 February for which the demolition party donned local native dress, described in the group's after-action report as being 'old colored shirts, longyis or shan pants, dirty canvas shoes, and mufflers used as head gear'.

On the night of 22 February the party laid the first batch of charges on the line using a three-day time delay fuze. The next night two lieutenants in the Burma Rifles, Dennis Francis and Red Maddox, the red-haired son of an Englishman and a Burmese girl, attacked a large bridge over a *chaung* near Namhkwin; the target for Jack Barnard and John Beamish was a similar one further south just outside Hopin; and Pat Quinn and his partner, a young Greek named Aganoor, were given the task of destroying a small bridge half-way between Namhkwin and Hopin. The three parties agreed to rendezvous under a big tree near the bridge supporting the road across the Tangwin stream.

'We set to work immediately, making as little noise as possible,' wrote Pat Quinn in his report, 'as the bridge was less than 100 yards from Yagyigon village, but found considerably difficulty in placing the charges as the plastic explosive, which had been kneaded during the day with grease, had hardened and we spent some 20 minutes or so kneading it again. Thereafter better progress was made and the job had almost been completed when there was a dull heavy explosion from the direction of Red's bridge.'

This explosion aroused the local police and lights began to appear in the village. As the bridge Quinn was working on was in full view of the village he said in his report that he decided to abandon any attempt to destroy it and that he and Aganoor removed the explosive and threw it in some nearby bushes. However, another report says that the charge did detonate but prematurely because of a faulty time delay. Certainly, there seem to have been two explosions that night.

'Our haste to get away from the place was to no avail,' Quinn wrote in his report, 'for we had already been spotted and were called upon by the local police patrol to stop. These men were armed with rifles, shotguns or pistols but they did not open fire on us because they thought we were unarmed, seeing as we were dressed like Kachins...' As the police closed with the two men they turned and emptied their pistols at their pursuers, dropping four. There are different accounts of what happened next, but Quinn says he ran one way and Aganoor another, and that he did not see Aganoor again, but it appears that Aganoor attempted to cover Quinn and was killed by the police patrol. He was the Detachment's first casualty.

In his after-action report Maddox wrote that he and Francis laid charges on the Namhkwin bridge – a steel structure 250 feet long and 100 feet high – and on the railway line, and that these demolished the bridge and destroyed a length of the line, but Barnard and Beamish on hearing the two explosions returned to base without laying charges on their target. When no one turned up at the rendezvous they returned to where they had hidden their supplies and Tommy guns before starting the attack. They waited there for 48 hours but when the others did not arrive they returned to the base camp only to find it deserted, Barnard and Beamish having already moved it to a safer location. On 27 February Quinn joined Maddox and Francis, and the three men eventually made their way back to Fort Hertz, arriving there on 16 May. Barnard and the rest of the group withdrew by another route and remained in the field for some weeks, not returning to Fort Hertz until 11 June.

Besides their sabotage work A Group had, the official OSS history recorded, 'supplied a great deal of information on economic, social and political matters in northern Burma upon their return. Included in the intelligence secured were lists of trustworthy villages and village headmen... Natives holding key positions under the Japanese were also listed, including former employees of the British government who had transferred their allegiance.'

The success of A Group prompted Goodfellow to write to Eifler: 'we have been very pleased and proud of the way you handled things under conditions which would have discouraged most officers. You men and the officers in your command are doing outstanding work and are the envy of the OSS.'

While A Group were still behind Japanese lines, B Group, composed of six Anglo-Burmans, were flown from Kunming in China and dropped by parachute into Japanese territory near Lashio. Nothing further was heard from them and on 4 March Radio Tokyo announced that 'six British spies' had been attacked by 'patriotic' Burmese and that three had been killed and three captured. 'This recent incident', the announcer trumpeted, 'shows that any and all attempts by Britain to win and cajole the Burmese will end in failure and disaster. All the Burmese people, from the humble villager to the patriotic leader, realise the danger of John Bull.'

Another disaster occurred when at the request of the British a sabotage group (W) comprising six Anglo-Burmans were sent to cut the Prome–Taungup highway in the Arakan by which the Japanese, fighting off a British advance down Burma's west coast, were being supplied from the south. The Group was landed from the sea by British submarine on the night of 7/8 March on Ramree Island near Sandoway. The landing was very rough and the men and their supplies had to be hauled by a line with which Eifler had swum ashore. Eifler, who received a severe blow on the head when landing, later wrote that he then 'shook hands with the lads, told them to get the stuff under cover before daylight was almost in the sky, and if they were discovered, not to be taken alive'. Unfortunately for them, as another OSS party learned when it went ashore in the same place some months later, the group was unable to follow Eifler's advice. Instead they were captured, tortured, and killed.

These disasters prompted Eifler to press for his own transportation so that his agents could be infiltrated with less risk of being detected. In particular, Eifler stated in a report to Donovan, the unit needed a motor boat like the ones used for 'rum running during the days of prohibition', because the Detachment needed to use the methods of a smuggler. This it received as well as several light single-engined aircraft.

Intelligence-gathering groups (J, L and M) from the Detachment were also infiltrated during the first half of the year and were controlled by two advance bases code-named 'Knothead' and 'Forward'. Besides recruiting native personnel these provided useful information for those who had begun to build the Ledo Road between northern India and China. By the end of the year there were eleven wireless sets behind Japanese lines feeding back regular intelligence including bombing targets for Tenth USAAF.

By October 1943 the Detachment numbered 35 men – American, British, Anglo-Burmans, and others – twenty of whom had had experience of being parachuted behind Japanese lines. Non-American personnel amounted to 225 instructors, agents and students, 50 cooks and bearers, 50 Gurkha guards, and 30 miscellaneous employees. During the next months the Detachment's operations in Burma were expanded by establishing a new base camp, code-named 'Pat', in the Pidaung forest. This was commanded by the two Anglo-Burmese lieutenants from A Group, Patrick Quinn and Dennis Francis, whose orders were to raise a force of about 400 guerrillas to harass the Japanese along the road and railway from Myitkyina to Mogaung. A new group ('Tramp'), led by another A Group veteran, Captain Red Maddox, was to be moved into the Chindwin River valley and recruit about 300 guerrillas. Finally, the two existing bases, 'Knothead' and 'Forward', were to expand their guerrilla forces to 1,000 and 1,500 guerrillas respectively, the former to harass the Japanese along the watershed of the Irrawaddy and extend guerrilla operations southwards, the latter to operate behind Japanese lines in the Hukawng Valley.

Up to this time the function of Detachment 101 had been mainly to act as an advance screen which provided intelligence on Japanese dispositions and to make contact with the Kachins with a view to recruiting them as guerrillas. But at the end of 1943, when Eifler – because of injuries he had received when landing on Ramree Island earlier in the year – was replaced by Colonel William R. Peers, Stilwell launched his offensive to clear northern Burma of Japanese and capture Myitkyina, and in this campaign Stilwell foresaw that there would be an important part for guerrilla warfare. He therefore directed, in February 1944, that the Detachment expand its guerrilla forces, which it called Kachin Rangers, to about 3,000 men so as to assist the advance of his troops down the Hukawng Valley, and by April he had ordered a further increase, to about 10,000.

Spearheading Stilwell's Chinese forces in the Mogaung Valley was a long-range penetration group of specially trained American troops which operated just ahead of Stilwell's forces and some fifteen or twenty miles behind enemy lines. Officially designated 5307th Composite Unit (Provisional), it was widely known as Merrill's Marauders after its commander Brigadier-General Frank D. Merrill. During the Marauders' advance southwards Detachment 101 provided it with guides and fed back intelligence to it on Japanese dispositions. On one occasion, when one of the Marauders' battalions was almost surrounded, a group of 200 Kachins led by a Detachment officer harassed the enemy's rear. On another, the eight Americans and 331 Kachins which composed the advance base 'Knothead' worked with two Marauder battalions to deceive the Japanese into thinking that Stilwell's forces were much larger than they actually were.

During April, after the Marauders had been seriously weakened by high casualties, they were reinforced by groups of Kachins from the Detachment. One of these groups, designated K Force, led by Detachment officers from 'Pat', helped make a surprise attack on Myitkyina air strip while those from 'Forward', now comprising a thousand Kachin Rangers, undertook diversionary operations north-east and east of Myitkyina. Soon after a 101 Kachin agent, N'Naw Yang Nau, had guided the Marauders to the airstrip, it fell on 17 May, but the town held out until 3 August, and in the siege which followed the Detachment helped contain the Japanese along the left flank from the Irrawaddy east to the Chinese border.

Because of their age-old clashes with the Chinese, the Kachins were accustomed to the type of guerrilla warfare the Detachment waged, but at first the Americans were less adept, for they thought it unmanly to cut and run after a successful ambush. Instead, they were inclined to stay and fight it out and it was not until they had been left behind by the Kachins a couple of times that they learned that the art of guerrilla warfare is to inflict the maximum number of casualties on the enemy while suffering as few as possible themselves. This was proved by the ratio of Kachins killed to the fatal casualties the Japanese suffered: it worked out at one to twenty-five.

During the Detachment's support of Merrill's Marauders the Kachins used their favourite form of ambush. The first requirement, Peers later recorded, was a well-laid ambush position along a well-used Japanese trail. If possible the site should be overgrown with heavy jungle foliage. 'The Kachins would take particular pains to ensure that it appeared natural,' Peers wrote, 'no footprints, no broken branches, no disturbances of any kind. There were numerous plants along the jungle trails which could forecast the ambush: if touched, they wilted immediately. The guerrillas knew everything there was to know about rocks, plants, trees, weather. Their efficiency was based on their knowledge of all things. They undertook an ambush with the same preoccupation one finds in an architect planning a building.

'When the site was selected the Kachins took strips of bamboo about two feet in length and cut them into knife-like spears about three-fourths of an inch wide. These they hardened over a fire until they were as strong as steel, sharp as daggers. They called them *pungyis*. The *pungyis* were then set in the ground in the undergrowth alongside the trail with the heads pointing in towards the trail. In effect, this was an ingenious kind of natural trap, deadly as a land mine. Then automatic weapons – British Bren guns approached the ideal automatic weapon for jungle warfare – were sited to fire up and down along the long axis of the ambush area. This done, the ambush was complete and ready to go.

'Through their own intelligence nets our guerrillas learned when a Japanese column was moving and about when to expect it. When the Japanese column came into the ambush area, the scouts and advance guards were allowed to pass through. As the main enemy body reached the ambush area, the guerrillas with automatic weapons opened fire on the column. This, in itself, generally took quite a heavy toll, but the principal reaction it caused was for the enemy to run and dive for cover into the underbrush. Rather than cover, they found the planted *pungyis*: men flinging themselves down were impaled before they hit the ground. No clothing was protection. The *pungyis* passed through leather easily. The low *pungyis* tripped a man over, so the longer ones caught him full in the chest. Rarely could a human being survive the physical and psychological shock. The bamboo caused a ragged wound that festered readily, was painful and slow in healing. It was a cruel death, and would have been more so if some of the guerrillas could have had their way. They proposed treating the *pungyis* with poison. This was in violation of the rules of land warfare and, remembering General Stilwell's strong views, I said no.'

In the next phase of Stilwell's drive south, the capture of Bhamo and Lashio – to re-open that part of the Burma Road to China to which the Ledo Road would be connected – the Detachment's various bases were integrated into a system for directing the numerous agents now behind enemy lines as well as the ten American-led Kachin battalions, each a thousand strong. These helped the British 36th Division by protecting both its flanks during the battle for Katha, and during the last six months of 1944 the Detachment's forces were the only Allied troops between Katha and the Chindwin River which guarded the Ledo Road from the possibility of any Japanese counter-offensive against it.

'The guerrilla tactics employed during the Lashio campaign were a very fluid type of warfare,' the OSS official history observed. 'The enemy's superiority in numbers and armament forced the Detachment's battalions to rely upon surprise, speed and freedom of movement. Ambushes, weapons blocks and hit-and-run attacks killed enemy personnel and destroyed communications and equipment without involving the guerrillas in pitched battles against overwhelming odds.'

The capture of Lashio on 7 March 1945 completed Stilwell's campaign to clear the Burma Road in the area. During it the unit killed an estimated 4,350 Japanese and had taken another 53 prisoner. Its own casualties were one American and 75 Kachins killed, and 125 Kachins wounded. By then the Detachment's total strength amounted to 566 Americans and 9,200 Kachins.

In its final campaign, between 8 May 1945 and 15 June 1945, the Detachment was ordered to clear all Japanese pockets of resistance from the Shan States down the Heho–Kengtung Road, which would ensure that the Japanese could not mount any counter-offensive against the Burma Road. Again, against an enemy with superior weaponry, the Detachment avoided pitched battles and relied on hit-and-run tactics and ambushes. One of these actions the OSS official history picks out as being outstanding of its kind. It took place on 17 May along the Lawksawk–Shwenyaung road. 'Hand-grenades connected by primer cord [Cordtex] were hidden every three yards along a hundred-yard section of the road, while the ambush party took up positions at both ends. Two hundred Japanese came down the road with advance and rear guards of 25 men each. When the main body was inside the trap, the grenades were electrically detonated and the guerrillas opened fire. The Detachment suffered no casualties but the Japanese lost half their men.'

For its outstanding work during this last campaign the Detachment was awarded a Presidential Distinguished Unit Citation which stated that 'under the most hazardous jungle conditions, Americans of DETACHMENT NO. 101 displayed extraordinary heroism in leading their co-ordinated battalions of 3,200 natives to complete victory against an overwhelmingly superior force. They met and routed 10,000 Japanese throughout an area of 10,000 square miles, killed 1,247 while sustaining losses of 37, demolished or captured 4 large dumps, destroyed the enemy motor transport, and inflicted extensive damage on communications and installations.'

In his chapter on the unit in *The Secrets War*, James R. Ward sums up its activities by saying that its greatest effectiveness was in the field of guerrilla warfare and its pioneering use of air and radio communications to support and co-ordinate guerrilla warfare activities. Fortunately, its members had time to learn through trial and error, and to build an intelligence base before having to undertake guerrilla warfare. They also built up a very efficient supply organisation so that by early 1944 they could support by air the large guerrilla force they then created.

But perhaps the greatest praise was rightly reserved for the men whom the Americans led. 'As always,' Peers wrote after the war, 'the Kachins were the vital force of 101 in guerrilla operations. They were the fighters who raised the flag of freedom in the jungles of Burma. As guerrillas, they never lost a battle. It was the Kachins who wrote the splendid accomplishments of 101.'

10
SOE and the Atomic Bomb

By far the most important Allied sabotage operations of the Second World War were the attacks SOE mounted at Vemork (Rjukan) in Norway where the Norsk-Hydro plant was producing heavy water for Germany's atomic bomb research. The crucial importance of this operation is highlighted by the biographer of the German physicist, Werner Heisenberg: 'Hitler's whirlwind military victories in 1940 gave the research group [German scientists working at the Kaiser Wilhelm Institute for Physics in Berlin] sudden access to the materials necessary for a serious [atomic] bomb program – heavy water from the Norsk-Hydro plant in Norway, captured in May; thousands of tons of uranium ore from the Union Minière in Belgium, seized a few weeks later; and use of the only cyclotron – albeit still unfinished – on the continent of Europe, part of the spoils from the fall of Paris in June.'

The route Heisenberg and his colleagues had taken in their research for an atomic weapon meant that heavy water (deuterium oxide) was essential for the construction of an atomic pile in which plutonium was produced. At that time the Norsk-Hydro plant was only manufacturing small quantities of heavy water for experimental purposes – about 10kg a month – but this was nowhere near enough for Heisenberg's requirement which was measured in tons. As early as April 1940 the British knew that the German firm, I. G. Farben, had been trying to purchase whatever heavy water the plant could produce and the following year the scientific adviser to Britain's Secret Intelligence Service (MI6), R. V. Jones, was alerted to the fact that Germany had demanded a huge increase in heavy water production at the plant.

'As soon as I had joined Intelligence,' Jones wrote, 'I had briefed agents and other sources to look for traces that might indicate German developments, including the production of heavy water at the Rjukan plant in Norway, where surplus hydro-electric power was used on a routine basis to electrolyse natural water and so leave a concentration of heavy water in the residue. I therefore jumped one afternoon of 1941 when I received a telegram from Norway saying that the Germans were stepping up the production of heavy water at Rjukan.'

When Jones told the head of MI6's Norwegian section about this alarming development, his immediate reaction was that the telegram was 'bloody silly.

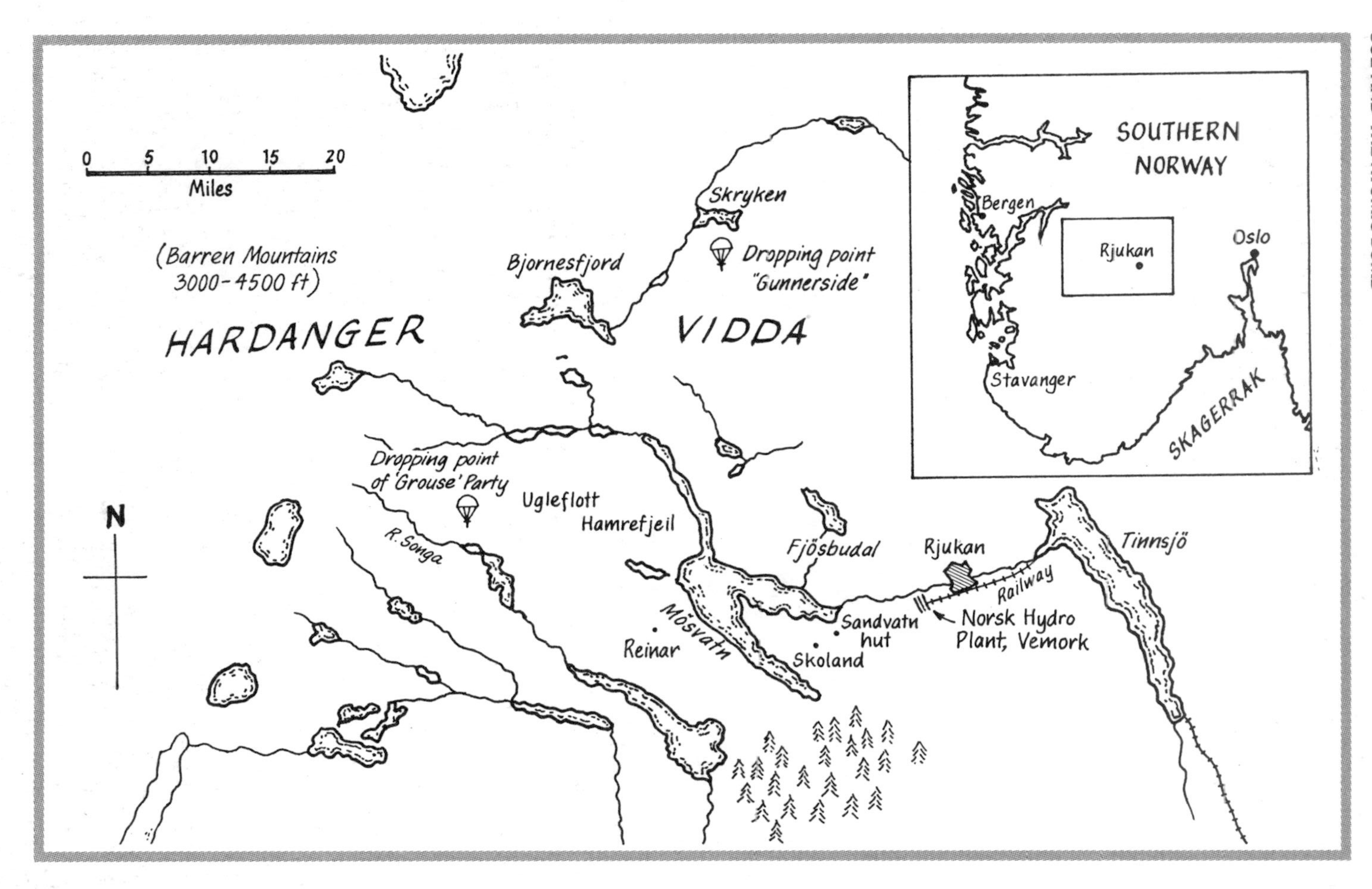
0 5 10 15 20
Miles
(Barren Mountains 3000–4500 ft)
HARDANGER
Skryken
Bjornesfjord
Dropping point "Gunnerside"
VIDDA
SOUTHERN NORWAY
Bergen
Rjukan
Oslo
Stavanger
SKAGERRAK
Dropping point of 'Grouse' Party
Ugleflott
Hamrefjeil
N
R. Songa
Fjösbudal
Rjukan
Tinnsjö
Railway
Mösvatn
Reinar
Sandvatn hut
Skoland
Norsk Hydro Plant, Vemork

Whoever heard of heavy water?' Jones quickly persuaded him that the telegram was anything but bloody silly and that more information was needed. Consequently, the source of this intelligence, the Norwegian scientist Professor Leif Tronstad, was brought to England and arrived with the disturbing news that heavy water production had been increased to 4kg a day. This convinced the highest authorities that Germany was working on an atomic bomb and that denying her scientists the heavy water they needed was the best, indeed the only, way of creating an irremovable bottleneck in its production.

The urgency of the situation obviously overcame – or perhaps the overwhelming authority of the War Cabinet did so – the usual rivalry between MI6 and SOE, for the matter was now referred to SOE and the two organisations worked closely to mount an effective operation. SOE arranged for one of Tronstad's contacts, a foreman at the Norsk-Hydro plant, to take part in a daring operation to capture a Norwegian coastal steamer, and bring it to Aberdeen. When he arrived in Aberdeen this contact, Einar Skinnarland, immediately volunteered to return to Vemork to gather the necessary intelligence. He was given a hurried parachute training course and just eleven days after arriving in Britain he was dropped back into Norway on the night of 28 March 1942. Because he had undertaken his voyage during his annual leave he returned before it had expired, and so his absence was not even noticed.

Under such rushed and dramatic circumstances it is not surprising that Skinnarland had problems. His dispatcher reported that the Norwegian had been reluctant to jump, and that the pilot had been forced to fly backwards and forwards for about 20 minutes before Skinnarland could be induced to leave the aircraft. But jump he did eventually and in due course earned the praise and admiration of all who worked with him. What's more he fed back the required intelligence which included detailed plans of the plant and how it was defended. 'Skinnarland's information was precise,' wrote Major-General Colin Gubbins, who was SOE's director of operations and training at the time, 'but it had to be transmitted in a roundabout way through Oslo, and frequently from more distant places.'

Having received the necessary intelligence, SOE parachuted into Norway a party of four Norwegians on the night of 18 October 1942. Code-named 'Grouse', its mission was to prepare the way for an attack on the plant the following month by a Combined Operations party of 34 engineer Commandos code-named 'Freshman'. Once this had been achieved they were to stay in Norway to organise and train local guerrilla detachments. 'Grouse' was led by Jens Poulsson and his three companions were, as he described them, the W/T operator, Second Lieutenant Knut Haugland (keen and clever); Sergeant Klaus Helberg (a worker, and as hard as nails); and Sergeant Arne Kjelstrup (clever and careful).

The agreed dropping zone for the party, on the mountainside west of Ugleflott in the Songadal, proved very rocky, and Helberg was injured, and took a week to recover. Also, their supplies were scattered far and wide, and the party had to work for two days to collect it all and put it in order. They made a depot and placed in it half their food and what equipment they did not need immediately. Haugland tried to make contact with England but without success, and on 22 October they began their march towards Vemork. They had to take with them their food for 30 days and about 250kg of equipment which included their wireless, two accumulators, a Eureka aircraft homing device (see Chapter 3), a hand generator, and a Sten gun. Initially, this was broken down into eight 30kg loads. Each man took one load, then returned for the second, which meant they had to travel triple the distance they covered every day. Luckily, after a couple of days, they acquired a ski toboggan on which they put the heavy equipment, and were able to pack what remained into four rucksacks.

They found huts to stay in at night, but the ground was rugged, and the snow heavy and deep, and if they left the ski tracks they sank up to their knees. To make matters worse the weather was mild and the snow stuck to the bottom of their skis which slowed them down. But they did not want to use the little bit of ski wax they had in case they needed it for a hurried withdrawal.

The mild weather meant that the ice on the lakes, rivers and marshes was unreliable and could only be walked on in places and the surface water covering it soaked their feet. Poulsson twice fell through ice while crossing rivers. These conditions sapped their strength and they had little to eat: a day's ration was just a quarter of a slab of pemmican, a handful of groats and one of flour, four biscuits, a little butter, cheese, sugar and chocolate.

On 30 October they reached Reinar by which time, Poulsson wrote in his after-action report, 'we were fairly done in, and I had a throbbing boil on my left hand'. Eventually, on 6 November, they reached their chosen base, the Sandvatn hut at Grasfjell, some five kilometres from Skoland where 'Freshman' was due to be dropped during the November moon period.

On 9 November Haugland contacted England and said the party was in position to receive 'Freshman', and on the night of 19 November it received the code-word 'Girl' which meant that 'Freshman' would arrive that night. The Commandos were dispatched from Wick in Scotland, but the gliders crashed and those in them were either killed or were shot by the Germans. Poulsson reported that they heard one of the aircraft and that it seemed to have detected their Eureka, but it then turned away from the DZ and nothing more was heard until a message the next day told the Norwegians of the disaster. They were warned that another attempt would be made the following month, this time by a party of six Norwegian parachutists code-named 'Gunnerside'.

The members of 'Gunnerside' were given intensive ski training in Scotland and practised laying their demolition charges on an exact mock-up of the high-concentration plant, the part of the Norsk-Hydro complex which produced the heavy water. But Tronstad knew how difficult the task was going to be now that the Germans had been alerted by 'Freshman', and he told the team honestly that they only had a fifty-fifty chance of carrying out the operation, and even less than that of getting out alive.

While the 'Gunnerside' party were undergoing their training Poulsson and his men moved farther north to the Grasdals hut, which belonged to the Norwegian resistance leader at Rjukan, and the party's code-name was changed to 'Swallow'. These additional security moves were necessary because the 'Freshman' disaster had made the situation very dangerous for the four men.

When the Germans discovered that the Norsk-Hydro plant had been the Commandos' objective, they mounted large cordon and search operations in the neighbourhood, and began a round-up of all those who might have been involved in aiding the attack. By January they had increased their forces in the area to nearly 300 men, brought in anti-aircraft guns and searchlights, and had erected two direction-finding stations to try and pinpoint Haugland's radio.

Each member of 'Swallow' had narrow escapes from the Germans. And although it had been agreed, for the sake of security, that there would be no contact with Einar Skinnarland before the attack on the plant, the team had trouble with charging Haugland's wireless batteries. This forced them to contact Einar Skinnarland's brother, Torstein, who worked at the nearby Mösvatn dam, and then the shortage of food drove the party to seek Einar's help. He kept them supplied as best he could and gave them a rifle and cartridges for hunting reindeer. He also helped with the troublesome accumulators, and relayed intelligence to them about the German defences in and around the Norsk-Hydro plant. Torstein was arrested during the German round-up following 'Freshman' but Einar found a safe hiding place on a farm. After Christmas he joined 'Swallow' for a while but left before the 'Gunnerside' party arrived.

The weather continued to be bad – too bad to hunt reindeer – and on 18 December 'Swallow' had run out of dry wood. The next day they moved to another hut and on 23 December Poulsson at last managed to shoot a reindeer and 'we celebrated a happy Christmas'. Soon there were plenty of reindeer. Haugland quickly learned how to stalk them, and took over most of the hunting. Poulsson recorded that they shot and ate thirteen reindeer, but early on they often had to mix Iceland moss with their food to make it go round.

The party certainly had enough time on their hands to prepare their meals because 'Gunnerside' did not appear during the moon period in December because of bad weather, and in January when the weather was perfect, the aircraft could not make contact with 'Swallow's Eureka, and returned to base. At the start of the next stand-by period, on the morning of 17 February, the signal came through that the parachutists would make a third attempt. The party laid out their signal lights and activated their Eureka, but nothing happened. Next day, however, Poulsson received a signal that 'Gunnerside' had already been dropped by parachute near the Bjornesfjord, a frozen lake on the barren Hardanger Vidda plateau some 30 miles north of the group's position. This, Poulsson wrote, 'surprised us not a little'. A storm then blew up and it was not until 23 February that Poulsson was able to dispatch two of his team to meet the parachutists.

'Gunnerside' was led by Lieutenant Joachim Ronneberg, and the five other Norwegians were Knut Haukelid, Fredrik Kayser, Kasper Idland, Hans Storhaug, and Birger Stromsheim. In contrast to 'Swallow' the jump took place in perfect moonlight, with the wind blowing at about 25mph. The team jumped from about 1,200 feet, higher than was normal, and so were in the air longer than they were used to. Their dispatchers had done an excellent job for they found when they landed that the distance between the first and last 'chute was no more than 800 yards. The supply containers were the last stick to arrive and landed close together near a place suitable for establishing a depot. There was only one minor mishap: the wind whipped one of the rucksack parcels across the ground at such a speed that no one could catch it. But they kept it in sight and after 2½ kilometres it became jammed in the only open ice-crack they encountered on the Vidda, and they were able to salvage it.

When the storm arrived the party sheltered in a fishing hut. After several days it abated but as they were preparing to move out a trapper appeared, having followed their trail in the snow from their depot where they had landed to the fishing hut. They interrogated him closely and did not form a good impression of him. Ronneberg ordered him to accompany them and he was given a toboggan to haul.

'If necessary', Ronneberg wrote tersely, 'we could liquidate him in the mountains', but later, after he had guided them to their destination, by night and day by an excellent route they thought better of him and let him go with a warning to keep his mouth shut. Then the party saw two bearded skiers in the distance and Haukelid donned his camouflage ski-smock, a civilian ski-cap, and skied to meet them while the rest of the party took cover. If the bearded skiers were strangers to the area Haukelid was to say he was a reindeer keeper. However, such subterfuge proved unnecessary as 'a wild yell of pleasure from the three told us that we were in touch with "Swallow"'.

The 'Gunnerside' party was taken to the hut which the 'Swallow' team were using as their base. While Ronneberg and his men rested, Helberg went to Rjukan to meet one of Einar Skinnarland's contacts who gave him the latest intelligence on the strength and positions of the German and Norwegian guards around the Norsk-Hydro plant. The next day, 25 February, both parties started the two-day journey to another hut from which the operation was to be launched. This lay at an altitude of about 800 metres in a remote valley leading to the Mösvatn road.

The saboteurs left the hut at 2000 on 27 February. The demolition party of Ronneberg, Stromsheim, Kayser, Idland and Storhaug were to break in and lay the charges while the covering party of Haukelid, Haugland, Poulsson, Kjelstrup, and Helberg would make sure they were not disturbed while in the building, and would cover their escape.

The plant was on the far side of a 600-feet-deep gorge at the bottom of which was an ice-jammed river. Normal access from the Möstvatn road was via a small suspension bridge. But as this was guarded by two German soldiers this approach was ruled out; killing the soldiers would bring instant reprisals on the local inhabitants. Instead, the saboteurs skied and then walked along the Mösvatn road before making the steep and slippery descent to the river. They managed to cross this via a snow bridge which lay three inches deep in icy water. Then they climbed up the other side of the valley until they came to a narrow-gauge railway line which connected the plant with Lake Tinnsjö to the east. They walked along the line until they came to the gates through which the railway passed into the plant. They cut the chains on the gates and slipped through them. Some 10 metres below the railway gates was another gate which led to a store shed. This was level with the basement where the heavy water was manufactured, so the gate was opened from the inside to provide the demolition party with a quick means of escape.

'Everything was still quiet,' Ronneberg wrote in his after-action report. 'The black-out of the factory was poor, and there was a good light from the moon. The sign was given to the covering party, who advanced towards the German guard hut, and at the same moment the demolition party moved along the path behind the drying plant towards the door of the cellar.'

But the door to the high-concentration plant in the basement was locked and they could not force it. While searching for the alternative entry they had been told about – a cable tunnel – the demolition team became separated. Eventually Ronneberg found the tunnel and entered it with Sergeant Kayser. They went down a ladder into the outer room, found that the door leading to the high-concentration plant was unlocked, went through it, and caught the night-watchman totally by surprise. Kayser kept watch over the man while Ronneberg began laying the charges. This proved simple because the machinery was identical with the mock-up they had practised on in Scotland.

Ronneberg was about halfway through his task when suddenly someone broke the window which opened on to the backyard. But it was only the two other men in the demolition party who had not been able to find the cable tunnel and had decided to break in. Stromsheim clambered through the window and helped Ronneberg place the rest of the charges. When all was ready, Stromsheim checked everything twice while Ronneberg coupled up the fuzes.

Ronneberg wrote that he had originally intended to use a two-minute delay fuze, 'but as everything had gone so well up to now, we did not wish to run the risk of anyone coming in and spoiling our work', and he attached two extra fuzes, each of 30 seconds which must have given them – and the watchman – only just enough time to run from the building and take shelter.

When the sound of the explosion was heard – it was an undramatic dull thud – Haukelid reported that a German guard came to the door of the barracks. 'He showed no sign of alarm, flashed a torch in the direction of the Norwegian guardhouse, and disappeared back into the hut.' In a book he wrote about the operation Haukelid conjectured that the German had thought the snow had caused one of the mines protecting the plant to explode.

Probably the explosion was muffled by the basement's heavy concrete walls, but the charges certainly did their work as a report from an unknown witness in SOE's files records: 'I arrived at the scene about five to ten minutes after the action had been carried out. It was at once evident that the object of the action had been achieved. Each one of the 18 cells had been blown to pieces and their contents of lye and heavy water had long since run off in the drains together with the cooling water.'

Apart from the perfunctory inspection by the German guard the explosion caused no immediate reaction and both teams were able to make good their escape without a shot being fired. The Germans guarding the plant were slow to react, but once it was known what had happened *Reichskommissar* Josef Terboven, Norway's Nazi political chief, appeared and ordered hostages to be taken. The Commander of the German occupation forces in Norway, General Falkenhorst, also turned up to look at the damage, declared that it had been a military operation, and let the hostages go. It was, he said, the 'best job he had ever seen', and a huge sweep of the mountains by 12,000 troops was made in an attempt to catch the saboteurs.

But by the time the search operation got under way both teams were out of the area. Ronneberg and four other members of 'Gunnerside' set off, as had been planned in London, to seek sanctuary in Sweden. On their way Ronneberg left a message for onward dispatch to London. The most important part of it read: 'Attacked 0045 on 28.2.43. High-concentration plant totally destroyed. All present. No fighting.' The party endured some incredible hardships during its 400km trek on skis, but all five men eventually crossed the Swedish border on 18 March, and were back in England before the end of the month.

All the 'Swallow' team, except Haugland – who stayed behind until August to train Einar Skinnarland as a wireless operator – eventually reached England as well. But originally one of them, Klaus Helberg, decided to remain behind to help the local resistance, and his first act was to gather together in one place all the equipment and stores that the two parties had left behind.

On 25 March he went to the hut at Skryken in which the 'Gunnerside' party had sheltered when they had first arrived in Norway. The area had now become a restricted zone and Helberg soon realised there would be Germans everywhere. This was confirmed when he went into the hut for the Germans had ransacked it. He ran out to look around and immediately saw three Germans skiing towards him. He dashed back into the hut to get his pack, put on his skis 'and started off for all I was worth'.

The Germans, who were now about a hundred metres behind him, shouted to him to stop, and when he didn't, they began firing, rather wildly, at him. He increased his pace, which forced them to stop shooting, 'and then a first class long-distance ski race began. I had half a year's training to my credit, and was in splendid form.' But to his dismay he soon saw that although two of the men were already lagging, one, 'a big weather-beaten fellow' was not only keeping up with him, but was slowly gaining ground. For nearly two hours the two men skiied into the mountains, the sun getting lower all the time. Helberg made sure he skiied straight into it so that if the German paused to fire he would be dazzled by it. Still the German closed, until he was within 50 metres of Helberg, and when the Norwegian came to a downhill slope he knew that unless he did something the German would catch him.

'I therefore turned round, drew my pistol, and fired one shot. I saw to my joy that the German only had a Luger, and I realised that the man who emptied his magazine first would lose, because at that long range nobody would have a chance of hitting. So I did not fire any more shots, but stood there as a target.' The German, flummoxed by this unusual tactic, promptly emptied his pistol at Helberg and then started back the way he had come. Helberg pursued him at top speed to ensure that the German had no chance to reload, but then, knowing the other two Germans might appear at any moment, he stopped, took careful aim, and fired a second shot. The man staggered, slowed down, and finally stopped, his head hanging over his ski-sticks. Helberg did not trouble to fire again but turned and made his escape.

Knowing that next day the Germans would be able to follow his ski tracks, Helberg pressed on through the night, but in the dark he went over a high cliff and hurt his shoulder badly. All the following day he had to avoid the patrols and check points which had been set up to catch 'the Englishman'. That night he took shelter in a Norwegian's house where some German medical orderlies were billeted. They were sympathetic about Helberg's shoulder and one took him to see a local German doctor. The doctor said he should be X-rayed in Oslo and sent him to the nearest railway station in a German Red Cross ambulance which was, as Helberg remarked in his after-action report, a fine method of escaping from the restricted zone.

Helberg's troubles were not yet over. He went to a tourist hotel for the night where Terboven also happened to be staying. This hated figure was not politely received by some of the hotel guests and so everyone staying there was herded in a bus and dispatched to an internment camp, an action which Terboven quite frequently ordered if he was displeased with his reception. Knowing that his papers would not stand up to close scrutiny Helberg escaped from the bus, hurting his shoulder even more in the process. He then spent eighteen days in hospital, went into hiding, and was finally smuggled out of Norway and returned to England.

The sixth member of 'Gunnerside', Knut Haukelid, also remained behind to help form resistance groups in the area, and it was he who put the final touches to an operation which deprived the Germans of any chance of building an atomic weapon. For despite Ronneberg's message to London, and the eye-witness report in SOE's files, the high-concentration plant had not been permanently destroyed. It also soon became clear that the Germans were determined not only to pursue the saboteurs, but to get the plant working again as soon as possible. They had no luck in catching any of the saboteurs, but by April heavy water was again being distilled, the Germans having been able to divert to Rjukan the partially completed cells for another heavy water plant at Saaheim. And to avoid having to start the long laborious process from scratch they had shipped back from Germany nearly pure heavy water with which to 'prime' the high-concentration plant.

The resumption of heavy water production was soon known to London and on 3 August Tronstad stated that 'we must make the necessary preparations to attack it again' because 'export to Germany is taking place.' Another memo dated 10 August stated that the estimated daily output from 1 August 'is 4.5kg daily' and that only 1,200–1,500kg of heavy water had been lost, less than half what had originally been estimated. Further evidence of new activity at the plant was produced on 19 August when SOE Stockholm forwarded to London translations of two meetings at Norsk-Hydro which had recently taken place on the future production of heavy water at the plant.

It looked as if emergency action was needed immediately. But a memo in SOE files dated 16 October stated baldly that 'we have made a careful investigation of the possibilities of further sabotage of the High Concentration Plant at Vemork, and I regret to state that we have come to the conclusion that such an operation would not be practical politics at present... It would not be possible to attack the plant with any hope of success unless one could produce a body of at least 40 well-trained and heavily armed men, who would have virtually no hope of escape afterwards. An operation of this character could not in present conditions in Norway be carried out on a clandestine basis and could really only be done on the basis of a small Commando raid such as that which ended so disastrously on a previous occasion.'

This seemed to end the matter so far as SOE was concerned, but the problem was still unsolved and in November it was decided to mount a bombing raid. To minimise casualties it was turned over to the USAAF which specialised in daylight precision bombing and was timed to take place when the workers at the plant had left to have their lunch. Even so the 145 B-17s which released 400 tons of high-explosive on the plant killed 22 Norwegians in Rjukan and only twelve bombs of the thousand or so dropped actually hit the plant. But that was enough to put the hydrogen factory out of action, and because heavy water production depended on the factory this, too, ceased production. None of the high-concentration apparatus or its contents was damaged, but the raid convinced the Germans that there was no point in continuing to try and produce heavy water at the plant. Arrangements therefore began to be made to ship the equipment and all the heavy water in its various stages of concentration back to Germany.

When London heard that this might happen Haukelid was sent an urgent signal via Skinnarland's wireless set. Was it true that the heavy water was to be moved and, if it were, could he prevent its transportation? Haukelid, who had spent much of 1943 on the Hardanger Vidda reporting back on events at Rjukan, received confirmation from Rolf Sörlie, one of his informants at the plant, that the heavy water was to be removed. He radioed Sörlie's intelligence to London and on 12 February he received orders to destroy the heavy water.

'Gunnerside' and 'Swallow' had targeted only the high concentrations of heavy water, but this time the entire stock – which amounted to 17,450 litres in different degrees of concentration varying from 3.5 to 99.5 per cent – had to be destroyed. But the Germans had brought in two companies of SS troops to guard the area while the heavy water was being moved and this discounted any possibility of destroying it *in situ*.

Haukelid decided that he could either try to destroy the heavy water while it was being transported by rail to Lake Tinnsjö, or sink the ferry which was to take it to Tinnoset at the other end of the lake for onward transportation to Germany. Because civilian casualties would be inevitable Haukelid asked for, and received, permission to sink the ferry. But he had still not made up his mind which was the best method of attack when on the night of 14 February he left his base at Hamrefjell for Rjukan.

The news at Rjukan was not good; the locals said the Germans were expecting an attack. Security was tight and troops were everywhere, and the next day two light aircraft for patrolling over the mountains arrived at a nearby airstrip. Destroying the heavy water as it was being transported on the railway was no longer feasible, so sinking the ferry was now Haukelid's only option. But his equipment was quite inadequate for such a sophisticated act of sabotage; he had neither detonators nor time pencils. He managed to obtain detonators. but he needed a time delay mechanism (following good sabotage practice he in fact made up two independent ones) so he made an ingenious one with an alarm clock. 'The clockwork itself made one of the contacts while the alarm bell hammer striking against a metal plate completed the second contact. The metal strip was insulated from the clock mechanism with a bakelite plate.'

Haukelid was now informed that the heavy water would be shipped aboard the ferry on two railway wagons on Sunday 20 February. On the 18th he took a trip on the ferry and reconnoitred it to find the best place for the charge. As there were four watertight compartments he decided to place it in the forepeak thinking, quite correctly, that if it filled with water the railway trucks containing the heavy water would roll forward off the ferry and plunge into the deep lake.

In the early hours of 20 February Haukelid, Sörlie and two helpers drove to the ferry from Rjukan in a hired car. Haukelid, Sörlie and one of the helpers went aboard and found that there was a poker party in full swing. They went below, but the night-watchman must have heard them for he left the poker game and found them in the passenger cabin. 'We told him that we were on the run and he let us stay,' Haukelid recorded in his after-action report which he wrote when he reached Sweden at the beginning of March. While the helper engaged the man in conversation the other two 'wriggled through a hole in the floor and crept along the keel. I placed my charge just alongside the keel. It was a very confined space and difficult to get at. There was about one foot of water then about 50cm clearance up to the cabin floor. I put my charge down in the water. I had previously made a sausage of 8.4kg of 808 [plastic explosive] which would cut a hole about .6 metres square. I reckoned that this would sink the vessel in about 4 to 5 minutes. The clocks and the 9 volt batteries were in a box which I fixed to the stringers. I set the alarm for 1045 hours which was the time I had discovered on my own trip would bring the vessel to the best place. I had only about 2mm clearance on the contact so it was ticklish work. By 0400 hours all was finished so we left.'

Haukelid's device did its work to perfection. It exploded at 1100 while the ferry was halfway down the lake and the ferry, then 300 metres from the shore, sank immediately. It took with it fourteen Norwegians and four Germans, but the remaining passengers, who included the violinist, Arvid Fladmoe, were saved, though Fladmoe's Italian Tesore violin, worth 12,000 Kroner, received a soaking.

The ferry sank in more than 300 metres of water, far too deep for any of its cargo to be salvaged. But some of it was saved because four partly filled barrels of low-concentration heavy water floated to the surface and were salvaged. But the rest was consigned to the bottom of the lake and with it went any hope the Germans had of manufacturing a war-winning atomic weapon.

11

Abduction, Forgery, Pornography and other Black Subversive Operations

Black radio apart (see Chapter 7), Black operations designed to subvert the enemy came in many disguises. In January 1943 OSS formed its Morale Operations Branch (MO) to conduct all types of subversive activity. 'It is the function of the Morale Operations Branch', its initial orders stated, 'to attack the morale and the political unity of the enemy through any primarily psychological means operating within or purporting to operate within the enemy or occupied territories. The principal means to be employed are field agents, native residents of the enemy and occupied countries, rumours, printed matter and radio.'

In-fighting with the Office of War Information, lack of clear objectives, and lack of trained manpower, delayed the introduction of operations by the MO Branch and it was not until 1944 that it began to produce any written Black propaganda. One example of this was a weekly news letter, *Handel und Wandel*, which purported to be issued by German interests in Sweden for businessmen in Germany. Its intention was to subvert an élite group of German industrialists by impressing upon them the damage the Nazi party was inflicting on their commercial interests. One issue, for example, reported that Himmler was organising saboteurs in all industrial plants to ensure that the 'scorched earth' policy of destroying anything of use before the advancing Allies arrived was carried out ruthlessly. All factory owners were urged by *Handel und Wandel* to form groups to counter these saboteurs.

In central Italy where it was not possible to use Black radio to any extent OSS concentrated on printed Black propaganda material. Its most ambitious project was an underground newspaper *Das Neue Deutschland*. This purported to be the mouthpiece of the German peace party which aimed at ending the war, liquidating the Nazi Party, and forming a democratic state. Its tone was semi-religious and it was sufficiently effective for a special warning to be issued about it and for Himmler's SS publication, *Das Schwarze Korps*, to print a front-page denunciation of it.

Another inventive piece of OSS printed Black propaganda was a circular letter from a 'League for Lonely Women' disseminated by members of the French and Italian resistance in August 1944 for German soldiers to pick up. These soldiers, when on leave, had only to pin an entwined heart symbol (provided with the letter) on their lapel to find a female companion. 'Don't be shy,' the letter ended. 'Your wife, sister and girl friend is one of us. We think of you, but we think also of Germany.'

As an example of disruptive propaganda this is hard to beat, but the official history of the OSS does not record its effect if any on German morale. It certainly had repercussions on the Americans for copies were found on German prisoners of war, and US Army Intelligence, thinking they were genuine, fed the story to the American press which published their contents believing them to be true.

Sometimes the OSS were able to exploit a tactical situation with great success by employing printed Black propaganda. A field message, dated 10 March 1945, records that OSS operatives reported that when an Italian Fascist division, the Monte Rosa, arrived at the Brenner Pass, *en route* to join the Germans fighting in northern Italy, several hundreds of its members had deserted as soon as the train had entered Italy. 'It was made up of Italians interned by the Germans in the Balkans and given the alternative of slave labour or the Army. Their morale obviously was soft, yet the Germans needed them badly and intended to use them on the lines... SI and SO followed the Monte Rosa, and later the San Marco, Littorio, and Italia divisions until they settled near La Spezia.'

A partisan band in the area was now brought into the action to issue to the Italian troops 'passes' from a self-styled 'Patriots' Committee' which invited the troops to join the partisans. 'Actually,' the operative writing the report added, 'we didn't know whether the Partisans would honour that pass, but we didn't give a damn; the idea was to make the Italians completely useless to the Germans. The effects were cumulative. The appearance of the MO leaflets aroused German suspicions. Kesselring was forced to interlard the Italians with German units he badly needed elsewhere. When the Italians reached the front lines they deserted in whole platoons armed with surrender passes dropped to them by PWB [Psychological Warfare Board]. They were withdrawn in 15 days.' There were claims that an estimated 10,000 deserters were affected by this operation, and others like it.

Another successful MO operation in Italy was 'Sauerkraut'. Italian prisoners of war, carefully screened to ensure they were firmly pro-Allied, were infiltrated in German uniforms behind the German lines after the failure to assassinate Hitler in July 1944. Their objective was to post a fake military announcement by Field Marshal Kesselring that he was resigning his command because 'the war is lost to Germany' and that senseless slaughter would be the only result of Hitler's order to fight to the last. This ruse must have had its effect because on 13 September Kesselring was officially forced to deny authorship of the announcement, and other, similar 'Sauerkraut' operations were mounted as a consequence.

In May 1943 the Chief of MO issued a catalogue of operations that he considered fell within the description of Black operations for subverting the enemy:

'bribery and subsidies, blackmail, counterfeiting of currency, ration cards, passports, personal papers of enemy prisoners or dead, rumour, abduction, chain letters, poisoning, distribution of and instructions on how to use toy gadgets and tricks, assassination by suggestion or agents, illness and epidemics by suggestion or agents, and divers manipulations such as black market in neutral countries, etc.'. The numbers of Allied operations which fell within these Black categories were legion. The earliest British one was disseminated by Section D, the predecessor to SO2, the sabotage branch of SOE. Friendly letters were sent by a Section D operative from the USA to senior Nazi Party officials in which the writer said that he was sorry to hear that there was a severe food shortage in Germany and that he would be sending the recipients of the letters a food parcel. These were sent by sea and included printed propaganda as well as food. At the same time the Gestapo were alerted in the hope that the officials would be harassed. According to the head of Section D this did occur.

Another was an SOE plan to bribe the Vichy French naval commander in Madagascar prior to the Allied invasion of the island in May 1942, while a third, code-named 'Blackmail', attempted in 1942–3 to bribe the crew of the Italian ship *Gerusalemme* to sail it from the neutral port of Lourenço Marques. Tangier and Algiers were OSS centres for spreading rumour – or 'sibs' as the British called them, from the Latin *sibilare*, to hiss or whistle – and for buying foreign currency at advantageous rates.

Both organisations used black market operations for trading currencies (see Chapter 13 for SOE's largest and most successful). OSS operatives bought ten million French francs from intermediaries acting on behalf of Arab speculators. Lisbon was also a centre for purchasing currencies at advantageous rates. The OSS bought more than a million dollars-worth of various currencies (other than the Portuguese escudo) on the open market there and in early 1944 discovered that much of the French currency it had purchased had been smuggled from France by German legation and consular officials in Portugal!

The counterfeiting of currency was another area of co-operation between OSS and SOE. Under the code-name 'Grenville' SOE printed in London large amounts of counterfeit Japanese military currency for the use of agents in the field in the Far East, and for the intended purchase of rubber and other essential commodities. The OSS also worked on counterfeiting the same currencies; a memo in SOE files, dated 6 December 1943, records: 'OSS, working with agreement of US Treasury, have achieved perfect imitations of Japanese Burman 1-rupee notes and expected to achieve similar results for Malaya. Considerable quantities of the Burmese notes were stated to be already in circulation and being utilised by BB400 [the code-name for a member of the Indian Mission]. Further, OSS were working on other issues, such as Siam.' SOE's products were not so perfect – the Japanese detected that the Malayan currency was counterfeit. The notes were a tenth of an inch too long and the smoke from the steamer on the back of the ten-rupee note was omitted.

Instructions for ageing the notes were as follows: 1. soak very briefly in very weak tea. 2. fold into four or crinkle. 3. place under blotting paper and flatten with hot iron. 4. fold again into four and lightly sandpaper edges where folded. 5. rub floor dirt into note with rag cloth. The OSS history records that garden soil could not be used as it left a residue which could easily be detected; and that genuine new French notes had to be specially prepared for agents going into the field by being pinholed and aged. This was because only banks and accredited government agencies were ever issued with new notes and the banks always pinned bundles of notes together after they had been counted.

Bribery, blackmail, and abduction were all employed by SOE when, towards the end of the war in the Far East, it worked to prevent the Japanese implementing a 'scorched earth' policy in Malaya. 'Military personnel, officials and employees have been bribed to give information,' one SOE report of 10 July 1945 revealed. It went on: 'Blackmailing responsible personnel connected with targets and threats of a "dim" future that awaits them on our arrival should they not co-operate with us, have all achieved results. The kidnapping and conditional restoration of wives and mistresses have also been successful.'

Forgery is not named in the MO Chief's list, but it was extensively used by both OSS and SOE for a wide variety of purposes. In his book, *The Fourth Arm*, Professor Cruickshank adjudges that one of the most successful ploys used by British forgers was to produce counterfeit German food ration coupons. These were dropped over Germany with the object of disrupting the German system of rationing scarce food and of causing the maximum problems to those who, wittingly or unwittingly, used them. The Germans reacted strongly, tightened up the rationing system, and issued warnings that anyone caught using the forgeries would be heavily punished, perhaps even executed. If anyone, the warning said, drew rations to which he was not entitled, 'he is playing a game which may proved very dangerous for him'. Plenty of people did play it, however, and Cruickshank gives a number of examples where German citizens were given heavy prison sentences, and at least one was sentenced to death.

Forgeries and Black printed matter – many of them produced by a Black propaganda unit run by Ellic Howe – were also disseminated by SOE agents in occupied Europe to reinforce the rumours and innuendos of Black radio broadcasts. These ranged from fake stamps to 'malingering' booklets, manuals disguised as innocuous books which explained to members of the armed forces how they could fake illness or injury so as to avoid active duty.

In April 1944 the news issued by the Black radio station, *Soldatensender Calais*, became the basis for a newspaper which was run jointly by OSS and SOE. Called *Nachtrichten für die Truppe*, it was dropped by air for German troops in north-west

Europe. Though it purported to be written by Germans, it did not attempt to pretend it was German. Sefton Delmer, who ran *Soldatensender Calais*, described it as being 'off-white' as the origins of its news prevented it from being pure white propaganda.

'Of all the enterprises I launched during the war,' Delmer wrote, 'this "news for the troops" is the one of which I am proudest. For this was a joint British-American venture and the readiness with which my American friends at OSS and SHAEF's American Psychological Warfare boss General Bob McClure placed a team of first class editors and news writers under my orders, I still consider it to have been the greatest compliment paid me at any time in my war-time career... Every night, for 345 consecutive nights, they put the paper together from the news and talks of the *Soldatensender*, which they sub-edited and rewrote for print.'

Ellic Howe believed that such success as *Nachtrichten* could claim was more due to the inadequacy and inefficiency of the German news service than to the newspaper's intrinsic merits. He records that German prisoners, when interrogated about their reaction to *Nachtrichten*, said that they were almost without news from home and that *Nachtrichten* arrived promptly 'like the morning mail'. In reacting to its contents a Magdeburg newspaper described it as printing 'facts on its front page which more or less tally with our own OKW reports. In this way it gains the confidence of the reader and appeals to his sense of impartiality. It even mentions decorations awarded to members of the Armed Forces and the special performances of German divisions. When it has thus lulled the reader's suspicions to sleep with its exemplary objectivity it serves up fat lies and filthy calumnies... According to one issue an accurately described BdM [Nazi organisation for teenage girls] leader had arrived recently at one of the health resorts in our Gau [region] for prolonged treatment for a nervous breakdown. The fact that any ordinary citizen can get such treatment, in spite of the bomb terror, is of course omitted. Investigation revealed that the whole story is quite untrue.'

Pornography was another Black subversive operation not listed by the Chief of MO. But Sefton Delmer records that SOE 'were constantly clamouring for printed pornography' and a discreetly censored SOE file in the Public Record Office has details of Japanese pornographic leaflets prepared by SOE in London at the request of SOE's India Mission. 'We have had a lot of difficulty in getting hold of anyone to play the more stirring scenes,' an SOE officer wrote in reply from London, and lamented that the path of the pornographer was a thorny one. There was, he wrote, tongue firmly in cheek, 'a certain amount of red tape to be unwound before we got our subjects stripped for action.'

However, with the help of a film director, Scotland Yard, MI5 – which mysteriously possessed a photograph with the necessary content – and the Home Office – whose libraries, it was suggested, might be able to provide a model for the more risqué scenes! – five leaflets showing a profiteer eating, smoking, drinking, bathing, and fornicating with a number of pretty girls were produced on highly glazed paper. London apologised to India that the background of the finished leaflets looked 'a bit austere' but that with the Japanese 'the play is apparently the thing, and the scenery is kept simple'. The leaflets were produced in a suitable format for distribution by shell or mortar. There is no record that they ever reached their targets or that there was any attempt to disseminate them.

Delmer's unit produced only three pieces of pornography 'not because I was squeamish, but simply because I did not think the effort involved on our part would be justified by the subversive effect on the Germans'. One of the pieces was designed to plant in the minds of German soldiers abroad what the millions of male foreign workers in Germany were doing with the soldiers' women at home. It was a two-page folding leaflet containing, under the heading *Lieb Vaterland magst ruhig sein* (Dear Fatherland you may rest assured), a very gloomy picture of a snow-covered soldier's grave somewhere on the Eastern Front. The heading was the first line of a very famous German patriotic song from the days of the Kaiser 'The Watch on the Rhine'. Overleaf was another caption and picture, but instead of the caption being the second line of the song, *Fest steht und treu die Wacht am Rhein* (Firm stands and true the watch on the Rhine), it read *Fest steckt's und treu der Fremdarbeiter 'rein* (Firmly sticks it and true, the foreign worker in), and underneath it was a coloured picture of a naked girl, painted in the photographic style so favoured by Hitler, who is about to lower herself on to the erect penis of some dark-haired, dark-skinned non-German.

'My SOE friends ordered these leaflets by the thousands,' Delmer wrote, though Ellic Howe records that only 5,000 were printed. 'But, ironically, not because they found them to be subversive of German morale, but because they found them excellent for the morale of their men distributing them!'

12
SOE's F Section

Six different SOE sections worked in France: F, RF, DF, EU/P, AMF, and the Jedburghs (see Chapter 15). F Section – formed at the same time as SOE itself, in July 1940 – though not the largest was arguably the most important of these sections, and the acts of sabotage its agents performed contributed substantially, perhaps critically, to the success of the Normandy landings on 6 June 1944 (D-Day).

RF was set up in the spring of 1941 to co-operate with de Gaulle's Free French forces; DF, part of F Section until the spring of 1942, ran escape lines; EU/P was a liaison section between the Polish government-in-exile and SOE, and dealt with the numerous Poles living outside Poland, half a million of them around Lille and St-Etienne; and AMF, based in Algiers, worked into southern areas of France for twenty months during 1943–4. Initially, AMF worked mainly with the supporters of Giraud but after October 1943 it switched to the Gaullists.

Within France there were several different, and distinct, groups of resisters. The main ones were the *Armée Secrète*, who were Gaullists; the communist-controlled *Francs-tireurs et Partisans* (FTP); the *Armée de l'armistice*, the disbanded French Army in Vichy which supported de Gaulle's rival, General Giraud; and the Maquis, a general term covering all forms of outlaws from the Vichy regime, particularly those attempting to avoid the *Service du Travail Obligatoire*, or forced labour in Germany.

Such a profusion of secret services and resisters inevitably caused friction and confusion. On one occasion F Section personnel who turned up at a drop zone to collect supplies found RF personnel already in possession of it; on another, an SOE-controlled group reconnoitring the Bordeaux docks prior to attacking German shipping there saw their targets destroyed under their noses by a group of Royal Marine canoeists using limpet mines – which, ironically, had been supplied by SOE. And even when all the other groups of resisters agreed to collaborate in the lead up to the Normandy landings in June 1944 some FTP groups refused to do so.

This friction and confusion was often compounded by rivalry and open dissension in the field which sometimes involved the Allied personnel who had been sent in to help the resistance of every political shade. For instance, one SO officer, who had been dispatched as an instructor to an SOE circuit in the Toulouse area in July 1944, later reported a particularly unpleasant fracas in which he found himself. The officer needed more petrol for his car than the local resistance leader had given him. When this was pointed out by the member of another group who was with the American an argument broke out.

'There were some heated words and I was puzzled because I did not know at the time there had been a previous incident involving Robert and Rammon. I asked Rammon to let me eat in peace and discuss his affairs with Robert at some other place. He turned to me in anger and began to abuse me as a "meddling" Allied officer, etc. He ordered Robert placed under arrest. Robert attempted to draw a pistol and was set upon by several officers under Rammon, one of whom waved a pistol in my general direction. Why, I don't know because I made no attempt to interfere. Rammon beat Robert about the head and face while others held him. The man was hustled off to jail. Rammon invited me to a duel at 50 paces with pistols. I did not accept because the Articles of War forbade it, and too, the range was too great. I proposed fists at two paces. This did not come off.'

At a higher level the French capitulation in the summer of 1940 had led to bitter political divisions both inside and outside France which could not be overcome by the common cause of defeating the Nazis. As a consequence F Section was not allowed any contact with the Free French authorities and the section was known, on the insistence of the Foreign Office, as the 'independent French' section. All knowledge of it was kept from the Free French and when they found out about it their fury was unbounded. De Gaulle, who had his own resistance organisation in France, adamantly refused to admit that F Section had any right to operate in his country without his approval – though in the field, as will be seen with Harry Rée, the two organisations did co-operate on occasions.

De Gaulle continued to the end to show little gratitude for those who played a part in liberating his country. In September 1944, when he was visiting Toulouse, he denounced as mercenaries the organiser and members of the local SOE circuit (*réseau*) called 'Wheelwright'. The circuit's organiser, George Starr, replied that many of his circuit held French commissions and that the circuit, in any case, was under the direct command of one of de Gaulle's own generals. This impressed de Gaulle not at all and Starr was ordered to leave immediately and was threatened with arrest when he refused. Eventually, de Gaulle relented, rose from his desk and shook Starr's hand, but this was in recognition of Starr's courage in defying him not because the General accepted Starr's presence in France.

The friction with de Gaulle meant that F and RF Sections in London worked independently of each other. RF Section recruits were nearly all French citizens but F Section relied largely upon British and Commonwealth citizens, many of them of Anglo-French parentage, though some anti-Gaullist Frenchmen were employed.

The aims of the two sections were also different. F Section, which from 1943 included SO personnel from the OSS, concentrated on industrial sabotage and arming resisters, and, once the Allies invaded, to foster, with the help of all internal resistance forces including the Maquis, the advance of Allied forces. RF, while involved in a number of sabotage operations – notably the activities of the 'Armada' *réseau* which disrupted vital military canal traffic throughout north-eastern France in 1943 – was mainly concerned with triggering 'an explosion of French opinion that would with Allied help dispose at once of the Germans and of Vichy'. Orders for RF were jointly drawn up by SOE and the Free French, the former having the power to veto them should it wish to do so.

As the war went on the political shift towards de Gaulle became more marked and by February 1944, when de Gaulle formed the French Forces of the Interior (FFI) to command all French resistance forces, it was practically complete. The FFI was commanded by Koenig, one of de Gaulle's most outstanding fighting generals, and on 1 July his staff became an amalgam of the F and RF Sections, and those of de Gaulle's resistance organisation, the *Bureau de Recherches et d'Action à Londres*. This gave the FFI operational authority over all SOE's French sections and all resistance groups in France which agreed to come under it.

The first head of F Section was Leslie Humphreys who had been Section D's representative in Paris. In December 1940 he was succeeded by H. R. Marriott. He held the post until September 1941 when Major Maurice Buckmaster, who had worked for the Ford Motor Company in France in the 1930s, assumed control of it. Buckmaster, who remained the section's head for the rest of the war, 'set about communicating his boundless enthusiasm to as many colleagues and agents as he could. He had useful and extensive contacts in France, and knew the country well. He was a colourful and in many ways a controversial figure; he had considerable gifts of leadership, and some of his most successful agents long admired him. Others did not; he was by no means universally popular, but no better head for the section was ever in sight.'

Buckmaster's second-in-command was Nicholas Bodington who was to organise the 'Pedlar' circuit in the Châlons-sur-Marne region after D-Day. He had worked for Reuters News Agency in Paris before the war and spoke French perfectly; 'he could pass for a Parisian without a tremor', M. R. D. Foot wrote in his outline history of SOE, 'and had a brilliant and versatile mind as well as high courage, offset by some character defects, including an apparently insatiable desire for money.'

By the spring of 1941 F Section was ready to infiltrate its first agents, but there was no transport available to deliver them. In early May three of them were killed and two others were wounded during an air raid while waiting to leave the

Section's holding flat. A sixth, a wireless operator named Georges Bégué, had been out on the night the flat was bombed, and on the night of 5/6 May 1941 he was parachuted into Vichy-controlled central France, the first known F Section recruit to land in the country (according to a cryptic entry in SOE's War Diary, an unnamed one, was landed in Brittany by boat in March 1941).

From then on most F Section agents who managed to escape the attentions of the Gestapo served for a time in France before being withdrawn to England, by light aircraft or boat, for rest, consultation, further training, or detailed interrogation before being returned to their *réseaux*. Some agents were infiltrated and exfiltrated several times; others, their cover blown, were not allowed to return to France.

Bégué made his way to the house of a friend of one of F Section's officers. He introduced Bégué to two local tradesmen who were willing to let their premises be used for clandestine purposes. Bégué reported back to London and within days three more agents were dropped into the area. One of them soon opted for the quiet life. Another, a director of a firm of French scent makers, attempted to start his own *réseau* in southern Brittany before joining the third agent, Baron Pierre de Vomécourt, as second in command of de Vomécourt's *réseau*, 'Autogiro', which Vomécourt began organising in and around Paris.

De Vomécourt, described as a 'vigorous, talkative, good-looking man in his middle thirties, a good shot, a fast thinker, full of energy and enthusiasm', was to play a central role in establishing F Section in France and was its first *chef de réseau*. The Free French had shown no interest in him, so he had joined F Section but soon found, as others did in those early days, that SOE knew frighteningly little about conditions in his country. 'It seems extraordinary', he informed the French historian, Marcel Ruby, many years later, 'that SOE, now hovering on the brink of its début, had no liaison at all with British Intelligence [MI6] which had been involved in French affairs for years. It was to prove a costly mistake. SOE knew literally nothing about life in France since the Occupation, not even the cost of living or the restrictions that had been imposed. This nearly led to my being arrested the very morning I arrived. I had, obviously, been parachuted "blind": in other words, there had been no indication lights for the aircraft, no reception committee for me. As the blackout was in force throughout France, it isn't surprising that I should have been dropped about eight kilometres from the intended spot. But I eventually found a road and signposts showing place names that I recognised, and at last I reached a little station on the line to Châteauroux.

'Noticing a few people entering a café opposite the station, I went in too, being absolutely frozen: it was 5.30 in the morning and I had had no sleep. I asked for a cup of coffee laced with cognac. "It's our day without", snarled the café owner. Seeing that I didn't understand, he said it again. I didn't want to cause a fuss, so I just mumbled: "Oh, I see..." But I'd been spotted already. As a precaution, I left the train one station before Châteauroux and went the rest of the way on foot. Just as well! I heard later that at Châteauroux station the police had been scrutinising everyone who arrived by train. The man at the café had telephoned them to say he had heard an aircraft circling that night – and that this clown, who didn't know what "day without" meant, had just caught the train. That's how much SOE knew about what was happening in France.'

The fact that Pierre de Vomécourt had not been told that French cafés were only allowed to sell alcohol on alternate days nearly cost him his life. It was on such tiny threads of information that the lives of many agents hung and was the reason why, in the early days, Buckmaster sought such intelligence above all else.

Pierre had two brothers, Jean – the eldest – and Philippe and Pierre promptly recruited both of them and divided France between them to recruit anti-Nazis who were prepared to form resistance groups to fight the occupiers. Jean, who lived at Pontarlier near the Swiss border, took charge of the eastern part of the country; Philippe that part which lay south of the Loire; while Pierre went to Paris and took charge of northern and north-western France. Although SOE normally financed all its circuits, in this instance the brothers put a good deal of their own money into the formation of these early *réseaux*.

Through Bégué's wireless Pierre arranged for Philippe to receive two containers of arms, ammunition, and plastic explosive. They were parachuted to him on 13 June 1941 and were the first of nearly 60,000 SOE dropped into France during the course of the war. However, Bégué's messages were detected almost immediately and the Vichy police began to hunt for their source. To cut down on his transmission time Bégué suggested using the BBC to broadcast messages which indicated whether an operation was about to take place and if so when. His suggestion, which had already been proposed elsewhere within SOE, was accepted and from October 1941 the BBC broadcast of personal messages to resisters became an important part of SOE's radio communications with those in the field.

During the course of 1941 other F Section agents were parachuted into the Vichy-controlled part of the country (known as the *zone libre*) to start the long-drawn-out process of starting *réseaux* and collecting and hoarding the supplies of *matériel* dropped to them. One of them, an SOE staff officer named Jacques de Guélis, recruited a number of exceptional agents, including one of F Section's most outstanding early helpers, an American journalist named Virginia Hall. She arrived in August 1941 as an accredited correspondent of the *New York Post*, registered with the police, and took up residence in Lyon. She proved a vital cog in the ever expanding network of F Section circuits and nearly all F Section agents dropped into the *zone libre* passed through her hands.

Two other outstanding agents arrived in September: Ben Cowburn, an oil technician from Lancashire, who immediately began a country-wide survey of likely oil targets for sabotage; and Michael Trotobas who during a second tour in 1942 set up an important sabotage circuit called 'Farmer' in and around Lille. Others dropped with them or followed shortly afterwards and by the end of the year 24 had been parachuted into the country. But a third were captured and many of the rest had to go into hiding. Among those arrested was Bégué – he later escaped, returned to England via Spain, and became F Section's signals officer – and his successor as Pierre de Vomécourt's wireless operator who was subsequently shot.

It was not an auspicious beginning but the Vomécourt brothers were still at liberty and active. The SOE War Diary records that in September Pierre's agents wrecked a couple of trains and some railway turntables at Le Mans, and that they also managed to hinder the production of a machine tool factory; Jean's influence reduced the output of a number of coal mines; and Philippe, having been appointed a railway inspector and started the 'Ventriloquist' *réseau*, dislocated German traffic whenever he was able. A wireless operator, N. F. R. Burdeyron, who had been dropped to help form a circuit in western Normandy in July 1941, was also still at liberty and he encouraged friends in Lisieux to commit minor sabotage in their factory which made breech-blocks for naval guns. He had no explosives but managed to derail a couple of German troop trains by removing a length of rail. It was not much but at least it was a start.

Throughout 1942, F Section continued to infiltrate agents and supplies into France. It concentrated on trying to build up new *réseaux* and supplying them with arms and explosives, and training the ever-increasing number of recruits. For example, during the autumn and winter of 1942/3 one of its agents, V. H. Hazan, trained more than 90 volunteers to act as instructors in elementary weapons and demolitions drill.

Little sabotage was achieved by F Section in 1942, partly because the Foreign Office was reluctant to allow overt sabotage operations in the *zone libre*, but also because the section's organisation in France was still in a formative stage. But Cowburn organised some unattributable sabotage in an aircraft engine factory when friends of his fed abrasives into machinery. Another F Section agent who arranged discreet sabotage operations was Sydney Jones, who arrived on the Riviera by boat in September. His mission was to establish a sabotage circuit in Marseille, and in due course he arranged the destruction of 50 German goods wagons as well as damage to some port installations before returning to England five months later.

These minor successes were overshadowed by a number of severe reversals, however, especially when Pierre de Vomécourt and several others, including Burdeyron, were arrested and 'Autogiro' was liquidated. Jean de Vomécourt was also caught, deported to a concentration camp, and eventually shot; and though Philippe remained at large until October 1942, he too ended up behind bars, though French Vichy ones not German. He eventually escaped and spent some time in England before returning to France.

Another reversal – for F Section spent much time trying to nourish it in 1942 – was a circuit called 'Carte' run by an artist, André Girard, who lived at Antibes. Girard, who was in touch with senior officers in the Vichy Army, promised much but delivered little. His lack of any sense of security, and the occupation of Vichy France in November 1942 by the Germans – who promptly dissolved the Vichy Army – resulted in the circuit's being wound up early in 1943. It also resulted, in April 1943, in the arrest of Peter Churchill (no relation of the prime minister) – who spent much of his time in 1942 acting as liaison officer between F Section and 'Carte' – and his courier Odette Sansom. The dissolution of 'Carte' left a vacuum which three new circuits eventually filled. One of them, 'Jockey', was organised by an outstanding F Section agent, Francis Cammaerts.

Cammaerts, alarmed by the careless behaviour of 'Carte' members, cut himself off entirely from them and started 'Jockey' from scratch. Before he recruited anyone he watched them for some weeks before approaching them; and then insisted that they did the same for any sub-agents they recruited. Eventually, he formed a security squad of seven or eight men, including two retired policemen, who spent their entire time not only shadowing likely recruits but those who had already joined – including Cammaerts himself.

'He insisted that the men should automatically work out for themselves a perfectly good reason for all their actions,' noted the January 1945 transcript of Cammaerts' interrogation by SOE, which is in the organisation's files, 'in case of snap controls or surprise arrests. He did not allow any material to be transported uncamouflaged... He advised his men not to spend more money than they had done previously, and to keep as unnoticed as possible... His groups were never more than 15 men, and should this number be exceeded he advised the group chiefs to divide into sub-groups.' He kept his identity, and even his nationality, a close secret and while he could contact the group leaders they did not know how to contact him. Such caution eventually paid dividends.

Among the other agents parachuted into France in 1942 were Francis Suttill who organised a large *réseau* called 'Prosper' in Paris and the surrounding area; a Mauritian, Claude de Baissac, who ran what was to become one of F Section's most successful circuits, the 'Scientist' *réseau* in the Bordeaux area; Roger Landes, code-named 'Aristide', who became 'Scientist's wireless operator; Tony Brooks who was to create a highly successful *réseau* called 'Pimento' among railway workers in southern France; and de Baissac's sister Lise, whose task was to form a *réseau* called 'Artist' near Poitiers. Two other F Section female agents also entered France that year to act as couriers for Suttill: Andrée Borrel and Yvonne Rudellat.

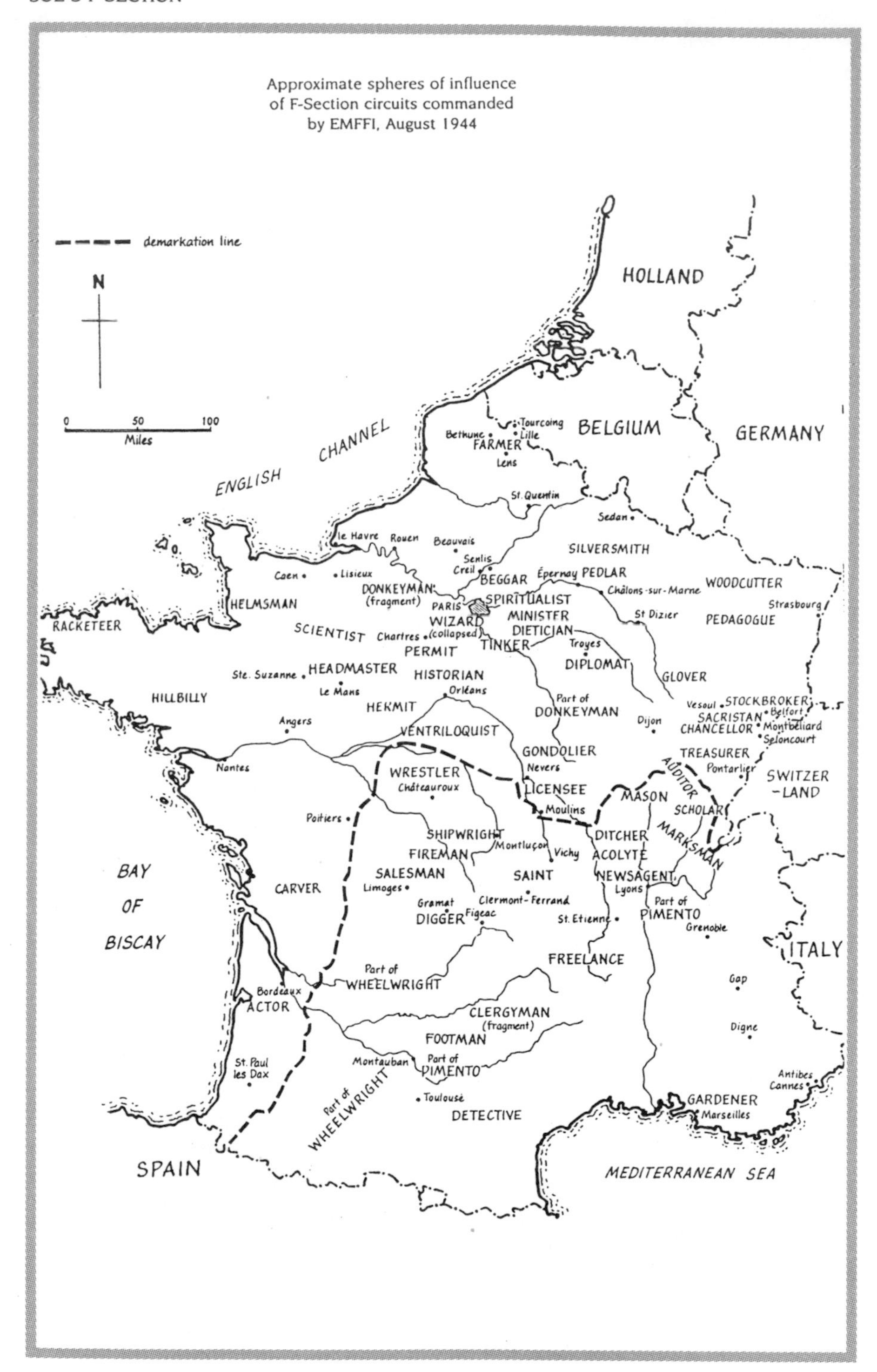
Approximate spheres of influence
of F-Section circuits commanded
by EMFFI, August 1944
demarkation line
N
0
50
100
Miles
HOLLAND
BELGIUM
GERMANY
ENGLISH
CHANNEL
Tourcoing
Lille
Bethune
FARMER
Lens
St. Quentin
Sedan
le Havre
Rouen
Beauvais
Senlis
Creil
SILVERSMITH
BEGGAR
Épernay
PEDLAR
Châlons-sur-Marne
WOODCUTTER
Caen
Lisieux
DONKEYMAN
(fragment)
PARIS
SPIRITUALIST
MINISTER
St Dizier
Strasbourg
PEDAGOGUE
HELMSMAN
RACKETEER
SCIENTIST
Chartres
WIZARD
(collapsed)
DIETICIAN
TINKER
Troyes
PERMIT
DIPLOMAT
Ste. Suzanne
HEADMASTER
HISTORIAN
GLOVER
Le Mans
Orléans
HILLBILLY
HERMIT
Part of
DONKEYMAN
Vesoul
STOCKBROKER
Belfort
SACRISTAN
Montbéliard
Seloncourt
Angers
VENTRILOQUIST
Dijon
CHANCELLOR
GONDOLIER
TREASURER
Nantes
WRESTLER
Châteauroux
Nevers
AUDITOR
Pontarlier
SWITZER
-LAND
LICENSEE
MASON
Moulins
SCHOLAR
Poitiers
SHIPWRIGHT
Montluçon
DITCHER
MARKSMAN
FIREMAN
Vichy
ACOLYTE
BAY
OF
BISCAY
CARVER
SALESMAN
Limoges
SAINT
NEWSAGENT
Lyons
Gramat
Clermont-Ferrand
Part of
PIMENTO
DIGGER
Figeac
St. Etienne
Grenoble
ITALY
FREELANCE
Part of
WHEELWRIGHT
Gap
Bordeaux
ACTOR
CLERGYMAN
(fragment)
Digne
FOOTMAN
St. Paul
les Dax
Montauban
Part of
PIMENTO
Antibes
Cannes
Part of
WHEELWRIGHT
Toulouse
DETECTIVE
GARDENER
Marseilles
SPAIN
MEDITERRANEAN SEA

The appearance of the Germans in the *zone libre* was a mixed blessing for SOE. Some imprisoned agents were released by their basically pro-Allied jailers and the Foreign Office restrictions on overt sabotage were lifted. But Virginia Hall had to flee Lyon. Despite being handicapped by an artificial leg – the result of a pre-war shooting accident – she crossed the Pyrenees and eventually reached England. It was as well she did so for the incoming chief of the Gestapo in Lyon was reported by another agent as saying that 'he would give anything to put his hands on that Canadian bitch'.

In the occupied zone Suttill's 'Prosper' network expanded rapidly in the early part of 1943 as he recruited agents who then started sub-circuits of their own. These soon stretched from Nantes, through the middle Loire and Paris up to the Belgian border around Sedan, and 'Prosper' replaced 'Carte' as F Section's leading *réseau*. It received substantial supplies of arms some of which Suttill passed on to local communist resistance groups.

'Germans are killed daily in the streets of Paris,' reported one of Suttill's friends in March 1943, and added that '90 per cent of these attacks are made with arms supplied by us.' In April Suttill used one of his sub-circuits to attack the power station at Chaingy near Orléans, temporarily severing the power supplies. 'Prosper' agents covered most of Normandy, but in April 1943 another circuit, 'Salesman', formed by a French journalist, Philippe Liewer, began operating between Rouen and Le Havre. Liewer worked on the principle that 'small is beautiful' and made no attempt to recruit in large numbers which he could easily have done. Instead, he picked about 350 men who were 'thoroughly trained, well armed, reliable and competent'. With them he performed several acts of useful sabotage in the autumn of 1943 which including putting an electricity sub-station near Rouen out of action for six months.

The most outstanding coup of 'Salesman' was sinking a 900-ton minesweeper which had been repaired and overhauled in a shipyard near Rouen. On the day its trials were satisfactorily completed, and after 12 million francs worth of ASDIC equipment, 20 tons of ammunition, and supplies for three months, had been loaded, three of Liewer's agents slipped aboard and placed a delay charge of 3lb of plastic explosive, which Liewer himself had made up, as near to the bottom of the hull as they could.

'At 11 p.m.', a report in the relevant SOE file records, 'the charge exploded, making a very satisfactory hole, later ascertained to be 5 feet by 3 feet, and the ship sank in six minutes. It could be seen next morning with just the tip of the funnel showing above the water.'

The Gestapo arrived promptly but ingenious questioning of the men they knew had had access to the ship, and then threats of a firing-squad, failed to elicit who had done the deed. The German Admiralty also decided to make its own investigation. This resulted in a confrontation which has all the classic ingredients of a West End farce and reveals to the modern reader the German armed forces' feelings for the Gestapo.

'Hating the Gestapo quite as much as the Army does,' the SOE report, which was quoting Liewer, continued, 'they [the German Admiralty] brought in their own experts, two of whom entered the water at 2 p.m. and pronounced that, by the size and characteristics of the hole, the charge could only have been an external one! Baffled, the Gestapo was forced to release the thirteen workmen who departed, honour vindicated, to their homes.'

This was not the end of the affair for the explosion had taken place on the side next to the quay, so the sentry guarding the quay was arrested. So were the crew who, on returning from their last night ashore, gave vent to their delight on finding they no longer had a ship. At a subsequent court-martial the sentry, and the member of the crew 'whose joy had been the most unbounded', were sentenced to be shot and the rest of the crew were rapidly recruited into the German Army and dispatched to the Eastern Front. 'Justice having been so satisfactorily assured,' the report concludes, 'the Gestapo and the Admiralty – and the workmen – returned to their respective businesses.'

In north-east France three *réseaux* were brought into being during 1943: 'Musician', 'Farmer' and 'Tinker', all of which did useful sabotage work. 'Musician', organised by a Canadian named Gustave Bieler, was formed in the area around St-Quentin. In February he derailed a troop train near Senlis and by the latter half of the year, when his wireless operator, Yolande Beekman, joined him, his teams were sabotaging the main line from St-Quentin to Lille about once every two weeks. He also kept his friends among the railwaymen – always the most militant resisters – well supplied with abrasive grease which wore out the parts it was applied to instead of lubricating them. No less than ten locomotives were immobilised with it that autumn.

The organiser of 'Farmer', Michael Trotobas, maintained excellent security because he often chose his men from the local underworld who were accustomed to keeping their mouths shut and acting discreetly. He also had invaluable help from local Poles who preferred to work with him than with the local EU/P circuit. The group's first successful sabotage operation against the local railway network took place in February 1943 when 40 railway trucks were destroyed and the Lens–Béthune line was blocked for two days. By the summer Trotobas and his men were perpetrating derailments at the rate of fifteen or twenty a week which caused considerable disruption to local railway traffic.

On the night of 27/28 June Trotobas carried off a spectacular coup. Dressed in civilian clothes and equipped with a Gestapo pass, he took twenty of his men, all wearing gendarmerie uniforms, to one of the country's largest locomotive works in the Lille suburb of Fives under the pretext of checking the works' security arrangements. They laid charges on the transformers and were just retiring when one charge exploded prematurely. It says much for the coolness with which Trotobas operated that he persuaded the night-watchman to do nothing until he, Trotobas, had returned with the local fire brigade and a team of investigators. He and his men then made good their escape. Their night's work damaged 22 transformers and destroyed four million litres of oil.

So renowned did Trotobas become, and so loyal were his followers, that even after he was shot and killed by the Gestapo in December 1943 his circuit survived. Within days of his death his men sabotaged the railway repair shop at Tourcoing and destroyed eleven locomotives.

'Tinker' was organised by Ben Cowburn – now on his third mission – and operated around Troyes until Gestapo pressure forced its suspension at the end of the year. On the night of 3/4 July 1943 he and five other men destroyed six engines in the town's locomotive depot and badly damaged six others. They laid the charges with a good deal of fumbling – 'the difficulty', Cowburn subsequently wrote in his report, which is in SOE's files, 'of struggling about underneath the mechanism of a big engine in absolute pitch darkness has to be experienced to be believed' – and then beat a hasty retreat.

About half an hour after they had left they heard the first charge explode. Cowburn conjectured that this must have been a premature explosion because he had set two-hour time pencils. They increased their pace to get out of the area as quickly as possible and the charges then began to detonate at the rate of one every ten or fifteen minutes. Cowburn counted thirteen of them.

As soon as the first had detonated all the local police and German garrisons were rushed to the depot and began to search it, not realising that more than one locomotive had been attacked. When the second charge exploded they quickly evacuated the depot and surrounded it from a distance.

'I understand', Cowburn wrote, with unconcealed glee at the Germans' discomfort, 'that in the early hours of the morning Oberst von Litroff, the German military commander at Troyes, came himself and rebuked his men for their nervousness and chattering teeth. He climbed on to one of the engines which was on the transfer line, as nobody realised that these engines had been doctored also. No sooner had he got on to the footplate than the engine next to him blew up. The colonel sprang off and scurried across the line to his waiting car.'

Cowburn's operation against the railway depot at Troyes showed that it was possible to destroy a valuable target without creating widespread destruction and killing civilians in the process – which would inevitably have occurred had the RAF decided to attack it. This fact was used by Harry Rée to create a new form of clandestine attack: sabotage blackmail. He used it with great effect against the Peugeot car factory at Sochaux, a suburb of Montbéliard. The factory, which had been converted to produce German tank turrets and aero-engine parts, had already been bombed by the RAF. The raid had caused casualties and damage in the town but had failed to put the factory out of action.

Rée, who was the organiser of the 'Stockbroker' *réseau* in the Belfort area, heard from friends that the Peugeot family might be pro-Allied. He was put in touch with one of them, Rodolphe Peugeot, and suggested to him that it was better for him to allow the factory to be sabotaged than for the RAF to mount another raid. Peugeot saw the logic of this and once Rée had established his bona fides, by getting the BBC to broadcast a short message suggested by Peugeot, this audacious piece of sabotage blackmail succeeded brilliantly and production at the factory was stopped for most of the rest of the war. The local French Gaullist resistance leader provided the men from the factory for the operation while Rée provided the explosives from the stores parachuted to him.

Many years later Rée described the extraordinarily cool-headed approach of the saboteurs who destroyed the factory's transformer building. 'They were playing a game of football together while a friend went to get the key [of the transformer building]. Some of the German uniformed guards started playing football with them, and they organised a little match – France v. Germany. The French team not only had these bakelite bombs in their overall pockets, they had revolvers too – they felt they wouldn't be doing things properly unless they acted like cowboys! And one of them took a kick at the ball and one of these magnetic bakelite bombs fell out of his pocket, and one of the Germans said, helpfully – "*Attention, vous avez laissé tomber quelque chose, monsieur*". And the player simply said, "*Merci*", picked it up, smiled at the helpful German, and went on playing. Mad – but somehow typical of the resistance people I worked with.'

When the Germans, after months of effort, managed to find an essential replacement machine it was promptly destroyed by 'Stockbroker' agents as it sat in the factory yard waiting to be unloaded. Rée later tried the same tactic on the Michelin family, whose tyre factory was based at Clermont-Ferrand; and when the Michelins refused to co-operate the RAF bombed the factory, damaging it badly.

The official history of the OSS records the trail of industrial wreckage which Rée and his men left behind them. They destroyed 'the Leroy foundries at Ste–Suzanne, and the Usines [works] Winmer at Seloncourt; disabled locomotive turntables and engines, and derailed trains loaded with German troops and equipment; and blew up the Usines Maillard in the Doubs, the Koechlin works at Belfort, and the telephone exchange at Dijon, as well as hangars containing German Army supplies at the airfield near Vesoul, loading cranes at Montbéliard and Nevers, and a steel railway bridge over the Haute Saône Canal.'

Three *réseaux* were also formed in eastern Brittany and the Vendée during 1943. One of them, 'Sacristan', was run by E. F. Floege, an OSS agent who was Chicago born. But he had lived in Angers, where he ran a bus company, for so many years that he spoke perfect French, and English with an accent. In August another OSS SO agent, André Bouchardon, was dropped to him as his wireless operator and by the late autumn the group had received enough supplies to start serious sabotage operations. But Floege's son, who was acting as his father's courier, was arrested and broke down under interrogation. As a result the Germans tracked down Bouchardon, cornered him in a local restaurant, and after a struggle shot him in the chest. Supposing him to be dead they threw his body into the back of their car without searching it; but during the journey Bouchardon recovered sufficiently to draw his revolver, shoot all three of its occupants, and escape from the wreck. He subsequently joined up with Floege and hid in Paris until one of the escape lines spirited them across the Pyrenees. The file on Bouchardon's debriefing by SOE in April 1944 records that he made the journey with the Gestapo bullet still lodged in his thorax.

Although 1943 produced several notable sabotage successes for F Section, disaster struck many of the *réseaux* that had carried them out. The 'Prosper' and 'Scientist' circuits were both betrayed. Suttill was captured and was later executed, but de Baissac escaped to England. 'Musician' and 'Salesman' were broken up, and even the highly successful Harry Rée, having been wounded in a fight with a German, was forced to flee to Switzerland. Many others were less lucky. They were captured, tortured, and eventually shot, though a few survived the horrors of the concentration camps and a few more escaped before they could be shipped to the camps. By the time that France was liberated in August 1944, 43 F Section circuits had ceased to function either through enemy action, because London had ordered the withdrawal of their personnel or, in one or two cases, because of internal stresses.

As early as August 1943 F Section's role in the invasion of north-west Europe was delineated by a special SOE/SO planning group and subsequently summarised in a history of Special Forces Headquarters in SOE's files: 'A preliminary increase in the tempo of sabotage, with particular attention to fighter aircraft and enemy morale; attacks on local headquarters, simple road and telephone wrecking, removal of German explosive from mined bridges likely to be useful to the Allies, and more and more sabotage as the air battle reached its climax; and then, simultaneously with the seaborne assault, an all-out attack on roads, railways and telephones, and the harassing of occupation troops wherever they could be found by any available means.'

To carry out these plans SOE quickly needed to replace the personnel who had been captured in the field and to increase the supply of arms, ammunition and explosive to the resistance groups who were to help SOE fulfil its mission. SOE replaced lost circuits or renewed them so successfully that there were more than 50 F Section *réseaux* in being when the areas in which they operated were either overrun by the advancing Allied armies or were abandoned by the Germans, and half of these were formed in 1944, seven of them after D-Day. During April and May 1944 alone, sixteen agents were received by the 'Stationer' circuit, which had been organised the previous year by Maurice Southgate in the area south of Châteauroux.

Among the most outstanding of these new or revived circuits was 'Actor', organised by Roger Landes on the remains of 'Scientist' in the Bordeaux area, which armed more than 2,000 men ready for D-Day. The havoc these men wreaked between April and September 1944 was so extensive that it took a ten-page appendix in Maurice Buckmaster's book, *They Fought Alone*, to detail all their acts of sabotage. One of their more spectacular operations was mounted in June when they laid an ambush on the RN 157 out of Bordeaux, destroying 24 trucks of a German motorised convoy, killing 162 Germans, and wounding 182. The rest of the convoy was unable to get through the ambush and was forced to return to Bordeaux. Landes lost fourteen killed and 42 wounded in this episode. Another took place in July when a group of Landes' saboteurs blew up 456,000 litres of petrol and 200,000 litres of oil at St-Paul-les-Dax.

De Baissac was dropped back into France in February 1944 and started a new 'Scientist' circuit around Chartres which did useful work at the time of D-Day. Liewer, having escaped to England after the betrayal of his *réseau*, was dropped back into France the night after D-Day to start 'Salesman' up again near Limoges. He took with him Violette Szabo, 'one of the best shots and the fiercest characters in SOE'. She proved this a few days later when, after severely twisting an ankle while trying to escape from a group of Germans, she held off her pursuers with a Sten gun which allowed one of Liewer's men who was with her to escape. When her ammunition ran out she was captured and eventually executed.

In April three OSS SO personnel working with F Section, Bassett, Beugnon, and Martin, were dropped to form a circuit, 'Beggar', north-west of Paris. By D-Day they had 91 men working for them and this number had risen to 305 by August. They repeatedly cut railway and telephone communications from Creil, Senlis, and Beauvais, and blew up several trains including one loaded with tanks. Two other SO personnel, Floege and Bouchardon, the 'Sacristan' team who had returned to England the previous year, were dropped in May to take control of 'Stockbroker', its SO chief, who had been dropped in April to replace Rée, having been killed the previous month. These two invented, just as had Rée before them, a new form of sabotage.

'They had at their disposal', the official history of the OSS records, 'almost no arms and very few explosives. Forced to improvise, they soon developed a cheap method of sabotage. Stopping a train about three kilometres from the tunnel near the Montbéliard station, they persuaded the mechanics and other personnel to leave, got up steam and started the train off on its own. The latter collided with a stationary train in Montbéliard station. This was the first "phantom train", an operation which was subsequently widely used throughout the region. In early June, for example, 'Stockbroker' derailed a train in the Baume-les-Dames tunnel, and a few hours later a second piled on top of the first. At the time of the arrival of the Allies, the Maquis in the region comprised 3,200 men, led by "Alfred" [Floege]. Of these 1,800 were well armed and had considerably damaged the forces of the Germans retreating eastwards.'

In June 1944 Virginia Hall, now a member of OSS, returned as a wireless operator. She was based in central France for about four months, arranging supply drops for the local Maquis, before moving to the Haute Loire in the Massif Central. She had had no training in sabotage, but the teams she recruited accounted for four bridges, the destruction of a key railway line, and several derailed freight trains. In Gascony George Starr, the organiser of 'Wheelwright' – one of the few surviving circuits from 1942 and now well stocked with arms and explosives, and with exceptionally strong local support – welded communists and non-communists into one fighting unit which in due course was the first Allied fighting unit to enter Toulouse. 'Marksman', another surviving circuit from 1942, took over most of three departments on the Swiss border on the heels of the occupying troops.

George Hiller, who was dropped into the Lot in January 1944 to form 'Footman', had an instant and important success. Almost as soon as he arrived he was approached by the foreman of a factory at Figeac which was turning out 300 variable-pitch propeller blades a week for the Luftwaffe. Hiller, who used the name of Georges Prudhon in the field, had only to construct explosive charges for half a dozen of the most important, and irreplaceable, machine tools in the factory and all work there ceased, making it 'as important a piece of industrial sabotage as F Section did anywhere'.

Hiller's principal mission was a political one: he had to find and recruit to the Allied side a powerful resistance leader known as Colonel Veni, and then to act as his liaison officer. In this he was eventually successful, but on 23 July his car was ambushed by the Germans outside Gramat. He was badly wounded, but managed to escape, dragged himself 1½ kilometres to get assistance, and spent the night covered in leaves in a ditch while the Germans searched for him. He recovered in a Maquis hospital from where he continued to direct the work of his *réseau*, though his radio operator now took control of it.

In April 1944 Southgate's 'Stationer' brought the Dunlop tyre factory at Montluçon to a halt with 2lb of well-placed plastic explosive. Shortly afterwards Southgate was captured and 'Stationer' was divided into two new circuits, 'Wrestler' and 'Shipwright', which were organised by his courier, Pearl Witherington, and his principal wireless operator, Amédée Maingard. Witherington, a British subject, subsequently controlled 2,000 armed resisters in the northern half of the Indre, who ensured that the main railway line from Paris to Bordeaux was almost permanently cut. The Germans were so enraged by her activities that posters with her photograph were widely distributed offering a reward of one million francs for her capture, but she remained at liberty and at the time of writing is still alive. She was recommended for the Military Cross, but as women were not eligible for this decoration she received a civil MBE instead. She returned this, saying she had done nothing civil, and the authorities had the good grace to replace it with a military MBE.

All these *réseaux* and others were alerted by the BBC on the night of 5 June to start their rail sabotage operations which would isolate the Normandy landing area from German reinforcements, and of the 1,050 planned 950 took place. The best known example of the delays the resistance caused the Germans was when the 2nd SS Panzer Division *Das Reich* was ordered to the beachhead on D+1 (7 June) from its base near Toulouse. Short of fuel because 'Wheelwright' had been busy blowing up its petrol dumps, the division turned to the railway. But this was soon denied it by 'Pimento' which cut all rail communications between Toulouse and Montauban, and by 'Wrestler' and 'Shipwright' which carried out 800 acts of railway sabotage in the Indre department during June. This left the division with no alternative but to march, but F Section circuits, including de Vomécourt's 'Ventriloquist' and de Baissac's revived 'Scientist', laid ambushes on all the roads, causing not only casualties but traffic jams which the Allied air forces were not slow to target. Normally the distance between Toulouse and Normandy could have been covered in three days: it took *Das Reich* no less than sixteen, and when it arrived the fighting quality of its soldiers 'was much below what it had been when they started'.

In eastern France the resistance delayed the 11th Panzer Division. This had taken a week to get from the Eastern Front to the Rhine; it took three more weeks to reach Caen. And when, on 15 August, the Allies landed in the south of France ('Dragoon'), F Section circuits were equally effective: Brooks' 'Pimento', Richard Heslop's 'Marksman', and Cammaerts' 'Jockey' all wrought considerable damage on German transport and lines of communication, the last keeping open the *route Napoléon* from Cannes to Grenoble via Digne and Gap which enabled 'Dragoon' forces to outflank the Germans in the lower Rhône Valley.

The activities after D-Day of the British and French members of F Section have been widely written about by them, and by others. What are not so well known are the activities of SO officers who were attached to F Section circuits after D-Day as additional radio operators or as instructors in tactics and weapons. Reports on, and by, these men in OSS files show that their contribution was considerable, but there is only room here to quote from two of them.

One of the first SO officers to be dropped into France after D-Day was Second Lieutenant Robert A. Cormier, an arms and demolitions expert. He and two

British wireless operators were parachuted in on 7 July to help create the new 'Pedlar' circuit in the region around Châlons-sur-Marne. The organiser of 'Pedlar' was Major Nicholas Bodington, Buckmaster's second in command. He did not arrive, by parachute, until two days later, having needed dental treatment in London. The circuit's second in command, Captain Harratt, rather unusually, travelled overland from Gibraltar, being for some unspecified reason unable to parachute.

SOE had no contacts in the Châlons-sur-Marne area so the parachutists were dropped into the Aube where Yvan Dupont had created a new circuit, 'Diplomat', to take over where 'Tinker' had been forced to leave off. There were strong groups of Maquis working with Dupont, which had managed very efficiently to isolate Troyes after D-Day, and they sent a twenty-strong reception committee to collect Cormier, the two operators, and the nine containers and fifteen packages that were dropped with the men. All landed safely, but soon after the men had been whisked to a safe house in a car it was found that 250 Germans had surrounded the woods in which the reception committee were sheltering with the containers and packages. The committee escaped but all the equipment and supplies were lost.

While Bodington went with one of the wireless operators into the Marne region, Cormier and the other operator waited in a safe house some ten kilometres from Troyes. During their wait, which lasted two weeks, Cormier kept himself busy by instructing groups of Maquis and taking part in several derailments. 'We blew up one petrol train which was unable to move from a small railway station because railway lines were continually cut. We also blew up two reservoirs which were used by the Germans for water supply for railway engines [and] 25 pylons which ran power from France directly to Alsace and Lorraine.'

When Bodington returned, Cormier and the operator were sent south-east of Châlons-sur-Marne while Bodington and the other operator made their way to Epernay to the west. Cormier established his headquarters in the house of a distiller and began making contact with small groups of Maquis so that he could arm them with weapons dropped to him by SOE. The distiller, who was so well in with the Germans that a colonel had set up his headquarters in his house, possessed trucks and a car. This was invaluable to Cormier because he was not only able to move around as he liked but could carry arms and explosives in hidden compartments under the vehicles. 'On trips', he noted casually in his after-action report, 'we usually had two or three Germans in the truck with us which avoided our being stopped or questioned by German patrols.'

Instruction took place mostly in the nearby woods. 'Each man was given a weapon which we taught him to strip, load and fire. Before any member of the group went into action he knew his weapon thoroughly. Each member had fired at least ten shots from his weapon. We held each group responsible for at least four sabotage acts a week, such as railroad lines, tearing down telephone wires, killing isolated Germans, laying tire bursters and making general nuisances of themselves.'

On 14 August Cormier, working with the St-Dizier group of Maquis, ambushed two lorries, destroying them both and killing ten of their occupants. On 20 August, with the Cirey group, he attacked three lorries, destroying two of them and killing about fifteen Germans. 'We attacked with 50 men. The duration of the attack was 30 seconds. We had no casualties.' The same day Cormier was called by Bodington to Epernay and on his instructions blew up the main Paris-Strasbourg line in six places and then returned. On 30 August with five men he attacked a tank. 'We blew off one track. The Germans then blew up the tank as they were in retreat and had no time to repair it.'

Once the Allied armies had passed through the area, the Maquis with whom Cormier and Bodington were working began clearing the area of isolated pockets of German resistance before Cormier returned to England on 24 September.

Another circuit which received SO help was 'Fireman' when First Lieutenant William J. Morgan was parachuted in on 13 August. 'Fireman' had been formed in March 1944 by two Mauritian brothers named Mayer to work with the Veni groups around Limoges.

Rather to Morgan's surprise none of the reception committee ran forward to greet him when he landed, though he knew he was in a friendly area because he could hear French being spoken all around him as the containers and packages that had also been dropped were collected. 'Taking my time, I rolled up my parachute. While doing so I heard one Frenchman say to another, "there's a container over there that is moving", pointing in my direction. The other Frenchman replied, "Well, that's your territory, go over and get it." The first Frenchman then came running in my direction and when almost upon me said, "How did you get here before I did?" I replied, "I am an American", whereupon his face froze into a horrified expression and he turned on his heels and ran to his comrade. The two of them returned slowly pointing Sten guns in my direction.'

After this dubious reception Morgan was soon involved in the work of the circuit, and on 23 August he was requested by the local resistance leader to organise the ambush of a German armoured column which was moving along Route Nationale 145 towards Montluçon, north-east of Limoges. Morgan decided the best place to do this was at a village on the route where there was a small bridge. He gathered 40 men who were armed with four Bren guns as well as the usual Sten guns, rifles, and hand- grenades.

Morgan had been ordered by London the previous day not to destroy any more bridges. To keep within these orders he decided to damage it just sufficiently so that the German column would have to halt to repair it, and his men were placed in various ambush positions including all the small roads, which had been blocked with felled trees, leading away from the main one. The villagers were told to leave and the men settled down to wait. Morgan's orders were specific: not to fire until the column had halted, to pick off drivers and officers first, and to use grenades against the lorries before opening fire on them. The ambushers were not to be in too great a hurry to withdraw. If necessary, they were to stay all night and were to fire at least two magazines of ammunition.

The German column, headed by a tank, arrived at 2300 and stopped at the bridge. 'I was afraid', Morgan wrote in his after-action report, 'that the Maquis soldiers might lose courage and not open fire because the German were following their usual tactics and firing everywhere about them. Suddenly, I heard our Bren guns open up. At the same time at my ambush behind a tree about 40 metres from the road, I saw in the very dim light of one of the lorries a German soldier talking heatedly to another German soldier while pointing and gesturing in my direction. I opened fire and saw both men drop, and believe it or not, the damn Sten jammed. But I had the most tingling sensation of pride as I heard the Maquis give tit for tat. From time to time the grenadiers would let a gammon [grenade] fly; the noise of a gammon is the most delightful noise from an ambush.'

After half-an-hour the firing died down. The Germans sent out patrols but at dawn the next day some of Morgan's men were still in position and began firing on the column again at 0730 when it moved off leaving behind it three wrecked lorries. Morgan's Maquis leader estimated 120 Germans had been killed, but Morgan thought twenty was a more likely total. The Maquis had no casualties.

There is no absolute agreement among historians as to the number of agents F Section infiltrated into France or the number of circuits that were formed, though the most likely figure for the latter is nearly 100. In 1981 Buckmaster told the French historian Marcel Ruby that 'from June 1944 onwards there were 53 groups in communication with us, from all over France... I had 480 officers working for me, 440 men and 40 women. The casualty rate was exactly 25 per cent: we lost 120 agents.'

13
Walter Fletcher's Activities in Rubber Smuggling and Black Market Currency

To judge the value of most subversive operations was impossible. But the exact monetary worth of the subversive activities of one SOE operative, Walter Fletcher, was calculated by the China representative of SOE's Financial Controller to be exactly £77,741,758. Fletcher's dealings are a good example of how far SOE, while holding its nose, was prepared to go in employing any illicit means to achieve a desired end.

In trying to smuggle raw materials out of Japanese-occupied territory, which was his first venture (code-named 'Mickleham'), Fletcher was certainly attempting to subvert the Japanese war effort. His second – dealing in black market currency in China – might not appear so clear cut. But Fletcher's set-up was adjudged by the representative of SOE's financial controller in China, who was in a position to know, as being 'a true Fifth Column organisation'.

The representative, who in February 1946 co-authored a history of Fletcher's activities, then went on to say that this second operation (code-named 'Remorse') 'could have harnessed the trading proclivities of all Chinese and, as was proved through operations such as 'Waldorf' and 'Embryo', this form of activity was capable of very remunerative development', which sounds as if the writers did not believe 'Remorse' was properly exploited, and, indeed, there is evidence in SOE files that it was not.

Lest this should appear a curious attitude to have towards an allied power – even as ambivalent a one as China – it must be remembered that the Nationalist government which ruled those parts of the country not occupied by the Japanese was, in the words of an India Mission officer, 'utterly corrupt, nationalistic, ambitious but intrinsically unpatriotic, anti-foreign, autocratic/dictatorial'; that the provincial governments and the Chinese Army were tarred with the same brush; and that there were 'many people who are ready to sell their soul and country to the highest bidder for money or goods or power, and even ready to risk their lives for that'.

So subversion did not necessarily have to be confined to a declared enemy, or a recalcitrant neutral, if it suited SOE's purposes. The economic undermining of a morally dubious ally – even one supported by so powerful a nation as the United States – was all grist to the mill so far as SOE was concerned, and an internal SOE paper, dated 27 December 1944, sums up Fletcher's operation without pulling any punches. 'It is inevitable that in carrying out its work it pays considerable sums in bribes – or allows people to earn large amounts as "rake-off" – and thus enables HMG [His Majesty's Government] through SOE to influence many people; not only financiers who get their commission but also various generals and war lords; other beneficiaries are those groups of people called guerrillas, but who are in truth better described as trading companies, who exact tolls in some form or another on all goods which pass through the area under their control.'

Fletcher, the chairman of the London rubber broking firm of Hecht, Levis & Kahn, was the son of a naturalised Austrian subject and was, by all accounts, an ebullient character. He was also very large, so large that in those days when aircraft could easily be overloaded he was counted as two people whenever he flew. Hugh Dalton, SOE's first political head, remarked that Fletcher was a 'thug with good commercial contacts' who was well suited to SOE; and an SOE officer summed him up as being 'not exactly the person to be trusted with the private means of a widow or orphan', an assessment which apparently confirmed the suitability of his appointment.

If a doggerel he wrote about himself is accurate, Fletcher was a humorous *bon viveur* rather gone to seed:

'Garrulous, old, impulsive, vague, obese,
Only by luck not "known to the police",
Wedded to Wine and Food, and oft-told tales,
Stuffed over-full, as *foie gras* is in quails.
A mind once keen, now almost in eclipse,
A figure, too, that looks like an ellipse;
This, and no more, be Walter's epitaph:
"In war's worst hour he sometimes made us laugh".'

Although he saw himself as 'over the hill', Fletcher's mind, as will be seen, was still fertile enough to conjure up some of the most bizarre schemes of the war. His recruitment into SOE in August 1942 followed a discussion between Mr A. C. Baker, a former British adviser to Kedah and Kelantan in Malaya, and British officials in London which took place on 10 April 1942. During it Baker raised the possibility of smuggling rubber – which the Allies were desperately short of – out of south-east Asia. He suggested that Sumatra was a more likely source than Malaya because the Sumatrans would be more likely to help in 'dangerous smuggling enterprises'. He said the rubber could be transported in dhows to Ceylon or southern India and that the pilgrim traffic to and from Jeddah, which would probably continue, would be a useful conduit for infiltrating agents into

Malaya or the Netherlands East Indies. He thought the best method might be to open a receiving point in Ceylon for the rubber, letting the news get around, 'and Chinese and Arab enterprise would do the rest'.

The idea appealed, the Americans expressed interest, and it was agreed that SOE would handle the British end of the operation as it was 'a covert project of the buccaneering type'. On 6 July Oliver Lyttelton, the British Minister of Production, under whose aegis SOE mounted 'Mickleham', cabled Sir Clive Baillieu, the head of the British Raw Materials Commission in Washington, that he was sending Fletcher over to the United States to discuss the scheme with him and with a Major L. W. Elliott. Elliott was an American rubber expert who had been appointed, under the American Board of Economic Warfare, to run the American operation from Australia.

During the meetings Elliott suggested an island in the Tenimber group some 300 miles north of Darwin, as a suitable collecting point; from there it would be relatively easy to ship it to Australia. He also suggested that the British could best contribute by 'driving' the rubber into his area by dispatching agents to disseminate the news that high prices for rubber were obtainable at collecting points in the eastern islands of the Netherlands East Indies. Fletcher agreed but added that 'a higher price than that mentioned at the meeting would have to be paid to start the flow... A black market to be effective must offer very considerable profits when the risks involved are not a fine or imprisonment, but certain death for the operator and probably wholesale massacre for his family and friends.'

The British government was realistic about the prospects for 'Mickleham' but decided it should go ahead, not only because of the shortage of rubber, but also to boost British prestige in the Far East, which badly needed boosting. Official approval was given in August 1942 and Walter Fletcher was appointed the British representative. Being a businessman through-and-through Fletcher played for high stakes, and he requested £500,000 to start 'Mickleham'. The Treasury demurred and gave him £100,000. The US Board of Economic Warfare was even less generous to Elliott, allotting him only $100,000.

In early October Fletcher flew to India to become an independent part of SOE's India Mission. From the start he must have realised the difficulties involved in extracting rubber in any quantity from Japanese-occupied territories and that for 'Mickleham' to be a realistic proposition he would have to obtain rubber from other sources as well. He soon proposed that rubber be smuggled into China from French Indo-China which, although occupied by the Japanese, was still under Vichy French administration and had a large stockpile of rubber. But how to pay for it and how to obtain Chinese approval and acquiescence in the scheme?

In a memo dated 27 October 1942 Fletcher ruled out trading rubber for Lend-Lease goods because the Americans would view this as a breach of the Lend-Lease Act. But it was all too clear, he wrote, that the Chinese war lords were not only purchasing war materials 'at almost any price' but they were snapping up any goods that might retain their value after the war, local jewellery being particularly popular. 'This has given me an idea which may give us the chance – diamonds.' They were easy to transport and were a stable international currency. What's more they were produced within the British Empire and were therefore available without the strings that were attached to Lend-Lease.

From family connections with De Beers, Fletcher added – he seemed to be something of a name-dropper – he had no doubt that there were high quality diamonds available from both the diamond-producing companies and from the South African government. Such an idea, he was sure, would appeal to Smuts, the South African prime minister, who was imaginative enough to 'be fired by the plan to mobilise usefully, for the war effort, packets of stones lying hidden in safes and vaults'. He then went on: 'at first blush it might seem easier to try and mobilise local stones, such as rubies, emeralds, saphires [sic], etc., but... the Rajahs here, who have always acquired the best ones and have vast stores of them, would create difficulties.'

At the top of this memo, scribbled in pencil, was the comment by an astonished official in Baker Street: 'Do you understand that B/B300 [Fletcher's codename] hopes to pay for rubber with rubies?' The Treasury was agog. Presumably Fletcher required finished gems not industrial diamonds? Was he also intending to use them to 'influence personally' members of the Chinese government? (As the official historian of SOE in the Far East remarks, the Treasury's vocabulary did not extend to the word 'bribe'.)

The importance of how the rubber should be paid for rather dwindled in importance as the means of collecting it loomed larger and larger, and eventually proved unsolvable. On 4 December Fletcher wrote to Baker Street that he no longer believed that 'Mickleham', as originally conceived, was practicable. In the longer term, say one year, the scheme could yield good results, but all the viable collecting points for the rubber were in Japanese hands. He therefore thought it better in the immediate future to build up a sound organisation in preparation for the next military advance which would secure them. He had, he admitted, also found it impossible to recruit suitable agents and even if he could acquire them there was no way of transporting them because there were too few submarines or aircraft available for clandestine missions.

Elliott, too, had got nowhere in finding suitable collection points, though a memo sent to Fletcher shows that he had not drawn a complete blank. 'Our people in Australia [presumably Special Operations Australia, see Chapter 8],' the memo said, 'had been successful in assisting Elliott to secure 3½ tons; this is better than a poke in the eye with a blunt stick.'

In the normal run of events this admission of failure would probably have meant the end of 'Mickleham'. But Fletcher being Fletcher immediately turned loss to profit. Smuggling rubber out of Japanese-occupied territory and transporting it by sea might not be immediately possible or economically sound, but why not use existing Chinese smuggling organisations to bring in not only rubber but other much needed raw materials such as quinine?

'Existing smuggling organisations, chiefly Chinese, for other commodities, must be roped in,' Fletcher argued ingeniously in his memo of 4 December to Baker Street. To narrow the objective to rubber alone was missing the opportunity to employ existing smuggling chains. There was, he said, quite a big traffic in tungsten between Thailand and Japanese receivers in southern China, which was 'largely under the benevolent wink of the Yunnan government', and he was in the process of working out a way to offer better financial inducements to the smugglers to reverse this process, not just to get his hands on the tungsten, a valuable commodity, but to acquire a working interest in an organisation which then could be turned to smuggling rubber. Equally, he added, any organisation smuggling quinine from Sumatra could be used just as well for smuggling rubber. It was getting in on the act that was the problem. He concluded his message by asking if the money voted to him could be used for obtaining other materials and it ends on a tactful note which may have been received somewhat sceptically in Baker Street. 'Please tell D/FIN [SOE's financial controller] I am using money with as great an economy as possible.'

To back up his claims that he should cast his net wider, at the beginning of 1943 Fletcher set up an economic intelligence unit at Meerut, India, under Major John Newhouse and a Dutch civil servant, Mr B. S. Van Deinse. This reported that several strategic materials – agar-agar, cutch, benzoin, silk, quinine, and mercury – could be obtained and smuggled out of Thailand, French Indo-China, southern Yunnan, and Japanese-occupied territory.

Fletcher's mention of quinine in his memo to London coincides with a memo to Baker Street of 18 December 1942 from an unnamed agent working in the United States. He said that a Mr Mitchell of the American Red Cross asserted that he knew someone who had told him that 'The American government will go as far as to deal with the enemy provided they can get quinine smuggled from Japanese-occupied territory into China for export to the USA.'

In fact, so keen were the Americans to get their hands on quinine, essential for the suppression of malaria which was decimating their troops in the New Guinea campaign, that the OSS investigated the possibility of smuggling it from Bandoeng in Java where a manufacturing plant was still operating.

It is therefore not wholly surprising that when Baker Street replied to Fletcher's memo on 5 January 1943 SOE agreed that he should try and muscle in on existing smuggling chains and concurred that 'it would probably be a mistake to narrow the objective to rubber alone'. Soon afterwards, the Ministry of Production approved the use of Fletcher's money for purchasing other materials and expressed particular interest in quinine and kapok. The Treasury also gave its formal approval. What SOE's long-suffering financial controller thought about it all is not known.

For Fletcher, who must have guessed that his days with SOE were numbered unless he came up with another scheme, this was just the lifeline he needed. But the cautiousness of London exasperated him and on 7 January a memo showed his frustration, particularly over SOE's tardiness in grasping the essentials of certain financial transactions. 'What a sorry tale,' he wrote. 'I have been educated to believe Britannia rules the waves and SOE waives the rules – but not so.' Hardly a fair comment in view of what was to transpire. Despite the difficulties he was encountering he ended the memo in ebullient mood. 'Like Houdini, who is now my patron saint, the more we are shackled the quicker we shall emerge triumphant.'

And emerge he did; on 25 February 1943 Lyttelton confirmed that he wanted 'Mickleham' in its new guise to continue and that he appointed Fletcher his representative in China to extract rubber stocks known to be in northern French Indo-China and elsewhere.

On 21 May 1943 the British Ambassador, Sir Horace Seymour, received a letter from the Chinese Foreign Affairs Ministry giving the Chinese National Government's approval for this plan. By then Fletcher had set up a company in China, with Chinese participation, and had opened a headquarters in Kunming and a branch in Kweilin to handle the materials that were to be smuggled in from Japanese-occupied territory. These were then to be flown out by the US Army Air Forces – for the whole operation was, from the beginning, a joint Anglo-American undertaking, though the Americans were not always kept informed about Fletcher's dealings. (When 'Mickleham' became the cover for 'Remorse', the Americans were not told until SOE was more or less forced to provide some sort of explanation when General Wedemeyer assumed command of US forces in China at the end of 1944. The explanation was, to say the least, disingenuous, and showed, as the official historian of SOE in the Far East points out, 'the lack of trust between the Allies in the field of special operations in the Far East'.)

On 20 April, having been given permission to operate in China, Fletcher wrote a memo from Chungking, enthusing about his prospects. He had already had many talks and meals with the 'big boys in the racket' and that there were 'plenty of fish ready to play, but I shall have to follow a narrow way between having too many at it, and not being in the hands of one man'. He was sure his new contacts would produce results. As the official historian comments, his means of expressing himself must have raised the chaste eyebrows of Whitehall.

The next day an SOE staff officer visiting Chungking wrote to London: 'B/B300 is with us, large as life and twice as agile', and went on to explain that Fletcher's biggest problem was the exchange rate. 'If he uses the official rate his prices will be futile. If he uses the black rate he can do a great deal but will run foul of Kung and the Stabilisation Board.'

This soon proved to be true, for however lavish the meals 'the big boys' – presumably the bigtime smugglers – produced nothing, for inflation and the poor rate of exchange imposed on Fletcher made any profit for them impossible. The only way to make 'Mickleham' Mk II financially viable was for Fletcher to obtain currency at black market rates while ensuring that the cover he provided for the commercial activity of his agents trading with and in enemy-occupied territory was effective. Also, Fletcher and Colin Mackenzie, the head of the India Mission, soon realised that there was little hope of obtaining anything from the Japanese-occupied territories without a much more high-powered organisation. Wirelesses for their agents in the field and an efficient sea transportation service were just two of the requisites.

In June the Ministry of Production had started to backtrack by requesting Fletcher to restrict his purchases to rubber, and to obtain small quantities of agar-agar to test its quality. When Fletcher said he could obtain quinine the Ministry replied that the price he was quoting was seven times the price in London – though in fact he eventually did purchase over a period of time, and with the Ministry's approval, five tons of the drug.

The same month SOE's London Controller of Missions, who was visiting Meerut, re-assessed 'Mickleham' with Mackenzie and Fletcher, and decided that a new approach was again required. On 3 July the London Controller cabled the CD, Charles Hambro, that 'as a result of his visit to China B/B300 has rightly or wrongly absolutely convinced himself only effective method of getting substantial quantities rubber from occupied territories into free China in present peculiar situation existing latter country is to go into smuggling racket himself through syndicate which he has formed with certain Chinese associates. Proposed methods not only constitute very different idea of how he should work from anything entertained when he left London but raise important issues such as other commodities which would have to be smuggled at the same time, character of financial transactions necessary to run such an organisation, and repercussions on relations with Chinese and Americans.'

The London Controller suggested that it was not reasonable to expect Fletcher to put his case by telegram and that he should be allowed to return to London to explain it, something which Fletcher had been agitating to do since May. Permission was at last granted and on 5 August Hambro cabled the London Controller and Mackenzie that 'we are now in discussion with B/B 300 and he is making strong point of great advantage 'Mickleham' is and will be to SOE [India] Mission.' Was this correct, Hambro wanted to know, and he ended the cable by saying that at least one staff officer in Baker Street 'feels personally that on balance he [Fletcher] is more trouble than he is worth'.

Mackenzie's reply was cautious, but he did say there were intelligence advantages to be had from 'Mickleham' and the following month the head of MI6, Major-General Menzies, wrote to Lyttelton saying much the same thing, and requesting that 'Mickleham' be retained. However, neither Lyttelton nor Baker Street felt that they could any longer support 'Mickleham' and SOE's political head, Lord Selborne, Minister of Economic Warfare, wrote to Menzies suggesting that if he wanted the operation as an intelligence conduit MI6 should take it over. There is no reply in the files.

After a series of discussions, and special pleadings by Fletcher, Lyttelton put his foot down: 'Mickleham', as it stood, was to be discontinued and on 6 October Selborne wrote to Fletcher confirming this. On the bottom of the copy of Selborne's letter to Fletcher someone scribbled in pencil: 'This isn't the end. Of that I'm quite certain.' He was right.

On the same day Fletcher wrote to Van Deinse that 'the real trouble is that the scheme is a hybrid and all those ministries to whom it might be of use – War Production, Supply, MI, MEW, SIS, SOE, each in turn take the line – "yes, this is grand, but why should we pay the bill for what, after all, is going to be quite largely to the advantage of others?"'

But Fletcher, who must have been, figuratively speaking at least, very quick on his feet, was still not finished. He came up with a new idea, probably one he had had up his sleeve for some months: he turned 'Mickleham' on its head. Smuggling would no longer be the objective, it would merely become the cover to (a) acquire Chinese National Dollars via the black market and (b) obtain intelligence from Japanese-occupied territories via the 'Mickleham' agents there. He even boldly proposed that the organisation be 'greatly expanded', explaining that 'those with whom we wish to deal in the Black Market in a large way are themselves big men and will not deal with what they know to be a small organisation... it must be an undertaking which is known to be large, well financed, and fair in its dealings.'

The Chinese had three official rates: 120 Chinese National Dollars (CND) to the pound for diplomatic missions, 80 to the pound for military missions and businessmen, and 160 to the pound for European salaries. As the open market rate for notes was 400 to the pound, and the potential rate against rupee or sterling credits was in the range of 320–350 CND to the pound, it was not difficult to see that profits could be made and that by being forced to use the official rates the British Military Mission, the British Embassy, and British businessmen, among others, were losing heavily. The Chinese, Fletcher argued, would be quite happy with what he proposed so long as they saw a profit in it.

As for the intelligence part of the new operation the Americans, who would not be interested in the black market aspect of it, did want intelligence 'and want it "hot".' No doubt encouraged by the interest shown by the India Mission and by MI6, Fletcher proposed that the new intelligence network be entirely separate from any other, though it would be under a central co-ordinating authority, and that it would need radio links with India and in China, together with the necessary codes. And, oh yes, he wanted to appoint a local accountant as 'a fairly large sum – between £300,000 and £500,000 – appears necessary for this work'.

All this must have all been greeted with astonishment by Baker Street. But the Treasury, always the most cautious and conservative of ministries, saw the advantages that might accrue from Fletcher dealing in black market currency. It therefore readily agreed with his new plans and soon made sure that all British organisations in China dealt directly with him. A note for a meeting between Fletcher, Menzies, SOE and the Treasury on 12 October summed up the situation succinctly: 'MK (MICKLEHAM) is dead. REMORSE arises from its ashes.'

Three days later Fletcher wrote to Mackenzie: 'Naturally I was sorry that MK has ceased to exist. It was always difficult and its demise is due to insufficient means to carry it through, apparent great improvement in the rubber situation, about which I am a little doubtful, but in the final issue, officials in the Ministry of Supply and Ministry of Production not really liking our methods.'

The financial dealings of 'Remorse', now a Treasury undertaking, were put under SOE's Financial Controller, with Mackenzie only being responsible for the intelligence and operational side of the operation. Even after the decision had been made to make MK just the cover for 'Remorse', talks dragged on. Then the decision makers were struck by flu and there were still more delays, so it was not until January 1944 that 'Remorse' was officially sanctioned.

On 18 January Desmond Morton, Churchill's link with the intelligence community, wrote to SOE's Colonel Harry Sporborg from Downing Street that Fletcher had just visited him to ask his advice about an anti-scorch scheme which Fletcher was also working on.

'I have to admit that even regarding him with a super wary eye, I am not unimpressed,' Morton commented. But his discussion with Fletcher left him with the impression that Fletcher's 'undoubted enthusiasms and method of work might easily betray him into playing one alleged master off against his real one' which was SOE.

'It seems to me that SOE is the operator,' Morton wrote. 'If things go wrong it will be SOE which will be held to blame. I do hope, therefore, that someone in your party feels really responsible for Fletcher, and is able on the one hand to control his exuberance, but on the other, to get the best value out of him and whatever it is he has created. It is hot stuff, but so is curry and some people live on that.'

Soon after his visit to Morton, Fletcher returned to China to take up his duties 'as Head of an SOE operational organisation in China', as a memo to CD's deputy noted on 12 January 1944. It also noted that 'At the request of 'C' [Menzies], HM Ambassador Chungking, the DMI, and other official departments in China,' SOE had undertaken to obtain Chinese dollars at a better rate of exchange than the existing official rate which was 120 dollars to the pound. The demand for these dollars 'is acute', the memo pointed out, for British government departments in China were at the mercy of China's high inflation rate. As a result salaries bore no relation to the cost of living, and made it impossible to grade allowances fairly or accurately. Fletcher, the memo continued, would obtain the dollars in 'straight black market operations whereby those Chinese who wish to buy Rupees will be encouraged to do so' and by importing into China articles of small bulk but high value, such as diamonds, which could be sold on the open market.

Fletcher, the memo went on, would not take part in any transactions personally and that a Chinese company had been set up for this purpose which would also obtain the necessary dollars by ordinary commercial methods. 'Firstly the company will attempt direct and legitimate trading in those goods which are at present being hoarded in China as a hedge against inflation. Even if economically unsound, this trading will provide good cover to the company's other activities. Less legitimately the company will use the existing smugglers' routes to and from Japanese-occupied territory to purchase other commodities easily resaleable at a profit in China.'

The connection between Fletcher and the company would be quite open because Fletcher, for cover purposes, had been given the title of 'Ministry of Production Representative' and he would be purchasing various commodities in which the Ministry was interested. Ostensibly, the company was to be financed with Chinese capital though in fact the Treasury had sanctioned up to £300,000 to finance it. This sum would be initially required to cover the inevitable delays in obtaining repayment from black market transactions.

This was all very well, but, as the SOE history of Fletcher's activities pointed out, London had dragged its feet so much and there had been so many delays that good opportunities had already been missed. 'A large amount of the quinine available during the first tour had gone into the hands of the Japanese and our best Chinese contacts had gone stale and had been attracted by other interests.'

Nevertheless, once 'Remorse' got going 'an extremely active three months followed'. The valuables smuggled into China were sold at a good profit. On 10 July London dispatched 71 Omega pocket watches, 29 Longines pocket watches, and 40 wrist watches, valued at £700, all obtained from Lisbon, and a further 200 wrist watches were dispatched soon afterwards for sale in China. The first batch of watches was followed on 13 July by a pearl necklace costing £1,000, and a cable of 12 August referred to an eight carat stone and that there was difficulty in disposing of the present stock of diamonds 'but will gradually reduce to a few stones required for bribery and similar purposes'. In March 1945 an assignment of diamonds was sold at a currency exchange rate of 1,340 CND to the pound, more than twenty times the official exchange rate. Altogether watches worth four million CND, diamonds and pearls worth ten million CND, medical drugs worth twenty-four million CND, and cigarette paper worth sixty million CND were sold on the black market.

But these sales were dwarfed by the currency transactions which made huge profits and by the end of the war the customers of 'Remorse' included seven military organisations, eleven diplomatic missions, the Red Cross, the Friends' Ambulance Unit, ICI, Reuters news agency, and seven other commercial organisations.

The intelligence part of 'Remorse' appears not to have contributed much, if anything, but its financial transactions were a staggering success and it had its finger in a number of financial pies. In 1943 the manipulation of blocked rupee accounts brought a net return to the Treasury of £259,540 and the purchase at black market rates of French Indo-Chinese piastres for operational purposes saved more than 800,000 rupees. After the war 'Remorse' supplied released internees in the Shanghai and Tientsin areas with funds, and a financial plan was evolved to strengthen the Hong Kong dollar. This last succeeded brilliantly, for financial manipulation and a strong press campaign improved the exchange rate from 25 to 300 CND to the Hong Kong dollar which lowered the cost of living for the one million-odd inhabitants in the colony.

From the files it would appear that 'Remorse' was so successful that it became – or certainly tried to be – autonomous, extending its operations in all sorts of ways. When the Indian and Chinese governments became embroiled in a trade squabble 'Remorse' obtained silkworm eggs on the black market to sustain the Kashmir silk industry which produced parachutes. 'Embryo', a 'Remorse' operation designed to employ 500 guerrillas behind Japanese lines for some nefarious but unnamed activity (almost certainly smuggling), had to be abandoned when it was thought there would be political repercussions from Chungking, though the guerrillas did work behind Japanese lines for some months. 'Nonchalant', an operation to lure skilled dock labour from Hong Kong, was financed by 'Remorse', as was an operation code-named 'Waldorf' which assisted some 5,000 French troops who had escaped into Yunnan after the Japanese takeover of French Indo-China in March 1945. Neither the Chinese, nor the Americans, nor UNRRA, would help the French, so 'Remorse' stepped in, erected camps for them and supplied them with more than three million CND and 123 tons of supplies.

It is difficult not to draw the conclusion from the relevant files that the backing accorded Fletcher was at times less than whole-hearted. Given the wildness of some of his schemes this is not surprising; perhaps the surprising thing is that

Baker Street stayed the course with him. It was wise to do so for it meant that the Treasury profited by more than £77 million. This alone made SOE's contribution to the war effort a substantial one.

How warmly Fletcher was congratulated on his success is not known. But in November 1945, when 'Remorse' was finally closed down – and after Fletcher had become the Conservative MP for Bury – SOE's director of finance cabled Calcutta that 'owing to his many public and business activities [Fletcher] is I regret no longer a member of SOE but I am glad to think that this has coincided with the termination of REMORSE's magnificent career.'

14
OSS Operational Groups

The OGs were uniformed OSS units formed from volunteers who were trained parachutists and were skilled in sabotage. They were as the report on their operations in southern France notes 'the first real use of the American Army of Organised Guerillas, of highly trained bi-lingual officers and soldiers who operated in small hard hitting guerilla bands, behind enemy lines', though it could be argued that Detachment 101 (see Chapter 9) had the distinction of first fighting with guerrillas.

One of the forerunners of the American Special Forces, or Green Berets, the purpose of the OGs was to work in small groups with guerrillas to harass the enemy in enemy-occupied territory. From August 1944 they were known officially as 2671st Special Reconnaissance Battalion, Separate (Prov.). Company A consisted of groups formed for operations in Italy; Company B comprised those that would operate in France, and Company C those that would operate in the Balkans. A group that would operate in Germany was formed in the spring of 1944, and was attached to Company A. By August 1944, when OGs in the UK were controlled by Special Forces HQ in London and those based in Algiers by the Special Project Operations Center, the total number of men serving in the OGs was about 1,100.

Volunteers were given intensive training courses designed to make them, as the official OSS history noted, 'proficient in demolitions; small arms (both of American and foreign make); scouting, patrolling and reconnaissance; first-aid; unit security measures; living off the land; knife and hand-to-hand fighting; camouflage, map reading and compass; and equipment and methods of operation of airborne and seaborne raids. A large percentage of the tactical exercises were conducted at night. Operational training included mountain operations, parachutage, amphibious operations, skiing and mountain climbing, light artillery, radio operation, and advance espionage techniques. Aggressiveness of spirit and willingness to close with the enemy were stressed.'

The OSS's Operational Groups Branch was established in May 1943 and its first members were recruited from infantry and engineer units of the US Army. The composition of a group was originally four officers and 30 men, which was divided into two sections of sixteen men, each section being sub-divided into two squads. In the field, however, group size varied from larger than standard to one officer and two men.

Volunteers from an all-Norwegian US Army unit (99th Infantry Battalion) were formed into the Norwegian Special Operations Group (NORSO) for operations in Norway. This was activated in April 1943 in liaison with the Norwegian military attaché in London. It was given preliminary training in the United States before being sent to Scotland in December 1943 for further training at SO and SOE training schools.

But OGs first saw action in the Balkans when fifteen officers and 110 men were sent to Yugoslavia's Dalmatian Islands in October 1943, and others followed in January 1944. These worked mainly with British Commandos on operations which would give them experience prior to seeing action elsewhere in Europe, and in the Far East. Besides working with SO personnel to supply Tito's partisans, OGs defended Vis from German attack and subsequently harassed German garrisons on some of the Dalmatian Islands, and were involved in attacks on Solta, Brac, Hvar, and Korcula, and made reconnaissance patrols on two others to ascertain the German order of battle.

The eight-man OG which raided Korcula Island in April 1944 did not have a medic with it, a lack which its commander, Lieutenant Dobriski, was to rue. After a two-hour trip in an open boat from the nearby island of Lastovo, the OG was met by partisans who took them to a cave where the Americans slept the night. Next morning it was decided to ambush the daily German foot patrol which operated between the towns of Blato and Smokvica. 'In its essence', the after-action report recorded, 'the final plan seemed clear-cut: the eight Americans, combined with twelve more partisans, would lie in wait at a selected point along the road; the enemy would be offered a possibility of surrendering; those that refused that gracious offer would be used for target practice. The Kommandant [of the partisans], a very rugged character who had battled for three years in the mountains on the mainland, was a little amazed that the Americans should feel it incumbent to be so generous; he was not disposed, however, to offer any arguments. Whatever the Americans wanted to do was – within reasonable limits – satisfactory to him.'

The party left the cave in the early evening and marched for two hours to the spot where the ambush was to take place. 'Two automatic rifle teams were picked up *en route*; one was to aid in the ambush and the other was to cover our getaway. Only incongruity during the march: the lone partisana in the party held up the march for five minutes while she picked violets for her lapel.'

The plan went awry from the start for the group was still organising itself on the hillside when the spearhead of the foot patrol, five Germans on two motor cycles, one riding in a side-car, suddenly appeared. Surprise was mutual but as the ambushers had been seen, the Kommandant, closely followed by everyone else, opened fire. One partisan nearest the road even threw rocks. The Germans abandoned their motor cycles and fled for cover, but three were killed immediately. In the following fire-fight with the other two, Dobriski was wounded in the thigh and the remaining two motor cyclists were killed. The group then withdrew before the foot patrol arrived and made their way back to their base. It was a nightmare journey; the wounded man was in great pain and though he was evacuated successfully the after-action report pointed out how essential it was to have a medic in the OG team because 'It was only by pooling the knowledge of the entire party that enough [medical information] could be gathered to treat the wounded man. Even then, there were several tenuous moments, when no one was certain that what had been done should have been done.'

OG teams also saw action in Greece, a number having been formed at the request of the Greek government-in-exile. When in the summer of 1943 OSS recruiting officers visited Camp Carson, Colorado, in search of Greek-speaking personnel, so many of the 122nd Infantry Battalion volunteered that the whole unit was offered to OSS, and from it a total of seventeen officers and 205 men were chosen. In early 1944 these Greek OGs were sent to Cairo, and between 23 April and 7 September fifteen officers and 159 men in seven separate parties, numbering between three and fifteen, were infiltrated into Greece by sea or air to mount sabotage operations against the Germans (see Appendix for summary of damage inflicted). These seven groups participated in a joint SOE-OSS operation, code-named 'Smashem', launched on 8 September to harass the withdrawal of German troops from Greece.

The first section (Group I) was infiltrated at Parga by landing craft on 23 April and reached its base at Romanon in the Epirus two days later. It subsequently took part in three ambushes against German convoys which destroyed nineteen trucks and killed and wounded a number of Germans. It also blocked off any German interference with the Parga landing beach and the route inland from it which was the main lifeline feeding resistance forces in the area. The section had to be withdrawn on 5 September because of ill health.

The second section (Group VII) was parachuted into the Peloponnese on 16 May to attack the Patras-Corinth-Athens railway line. It remained for 38 days before being forced to withdraw because of intense German activity caused by the success of its mission. It re-entered Greece on 16 July, this time at Parga where it joined forces with Group I and took part in several ambushes with it. In August it moved up to Macedonia to attack railway lines near the Yugoslav border as part of 'Smashem' before being withdrawn on 20 November.

The third section (Group V) was also infiltrated by sea at Parga on 21 May 1944, and remained in Greece for 163 days. It had to move right across the country to reach its base north-west of Salonika some 30 miles from the Yugoslav border where its principal target was the Salonika–Athens railway line.

Unlike the first two sections it suffered battle casualties – five lightly wounded – but killed, captured, or wounded nearly 700 Germans and caused extensive damage to the railway system and other industrial targets. Its original commander, Lieutenant George Papazegleu, was injured in a fall in July and was replaced by Lieutenant Len Peyten who 'led the group with distinction in a great number of operations'. These included attacks on three troop trains which caused large loss of life among their occupants; attacks on the German garrison at Yannitsa and on a German railway blockhouse which killed all its occupants; and the destruction of a chrome mine. It was exfiltrated on 1 November.

The fourth section (Group II) to enter Greece, on 18 June, also caused extensive damage and heavy German casualties. It was led originally by Lieutenant John Giannaris but he was wounded in action on 8 September and was evacuated ten days later. On 25 September leadership of the group was taken over by Lieutenant Nicholas Pappas who had been second in command of Group III which had entered Greece in July. The target of Giannaris and his men was also the Salonika–Athens railway line – which they attacked on numerous occasions from their base in the village of Papas, some 30 miles north-west of Lamia – but they also mined a nearby road. Their favourite area of attack was a five-mile stretch of railway line that ran between high hills in the mountains south-east of Papas. During one operation to sever the line one of the group was killed and Giannaris was wounded while going to his aid. Altogether, the group took part in fourteen separate operations, five of them with a British unit, the Raiding Support Regiment, and on most of them they were helped by the local Greek resistance movement which provided guides and muleteers. Several members of the group suffered from malaria and it was eventually exfiltrated on 30 October.

The fifth and sixth sections (Groups III and VI) were both landed at Parga on the same day, 19 July. They too had to move right across Greece to reach their bases, a sixteen days' hike which they made together. Group III's base was at Dheskhati, about 35 miles north-west of the town of Larisa. Larisa lay astride the main road communications between Athens and Salonika and these were the group's main targets. Before being evacuated on 7 November the group had attacked several convoys, destroyed a road bridge and generally disrupted the Germans' road communications. It suffered no casualties but inflicted more than 200 on the enemy. When the two groups reached Dheskhati, Group VI moved north-east to the area of Mount Olympus where it lived in the open on the mountain's eastern slope. Its main target, like that of Groups II and V, was the main Athens-Salonika railway line, but it also attacked local roads. It helped cause severe disruption to German railway schedules by persistently cutting the line and destroying two bridges before being exfiltrated on 11 November having suffered only one, non-fatal, casualty.

The last section (Group IV) to enter Greece was parachuted into the Drama area north-east of Salonika on 7 September. The area was occupied by Bulgarian troops and the Group had time to destroy only one railway bridge before Bulgaria sued for peace, bringing all operations to a halt.

The OGs were also very active in Italy and on the Island of Corsica. When Italy surrendered on the night of 8 September 1943, French Maquis groups on Corsica, which had been mainly garrisoned by Italian troops, seized control of key points. These groups then appealed for Allied help to fight German troops who were moving from Sardinia to Corsica. The Allies sent French troops to bolster the Maquis and an OG of two officers and 30 men accompanied them and helped to harass the Germans who were only using the island as a stepping stone to reach the Italian mainland. Once Corsica was liberated the following month it became an important forward base for the OG which, within an OSS HQ, operated from Bastia on the north-east coast (later the OG HQ was moved to Siena). In the following months OG personnel set up observation posts on German-held and unoccupied islands between Corsica and the Italian mainland, and reconnaissance and sabotage raids and pinprick attacks on coastal installations were made on the nearby mainland. In March 1944 a 15-man OG section, code-named 'Ginny', was landed on the mainland from Corsica as part of operation 'Strangle' which was designed to prevent, by ground and air attacks, supplies reaching the German front line. It landed successfully but was subsequently captured. Its members were interrogated and though in uniform were then shot. The German officer, General Dostler, who was directly responsible for this atrocity, was tried after the war and executed.

After southern Italy was cleared in September 1943 the OG set up their HQ at Caserta and a total of nine missions were dispatched through enemy lines to work with Italian partisan groups fighting the Germans in northern Italy. During the last month of the war OG teams, operating to the south of Piacenza and Parma, organised several successful road blocks and harassed German forces there. Others severed several important escape routes for the Germans retreating northwards towards Switzerland and Austria. One OG unit, which was controlling 15,000 partisans in the Genoa area, prevented the Germans from destroying the city's roads, and took 3,000 German prisoners. Another secured a guarantee from the Germans garrisoning Venice that installations would remain unharmed provided the Germans were not attacked by partisans.

Because of SHAEF restrictions the OGs, with two exceptions (the Algiers-based 'Emily' and 'Justine'), were not allowed into France until 15 July 1944. Their principal mission was to work with the Maquis to halt or delay the movement of German forces and to protect the flanks of Allied forces driving inland from the beaches in Normandy and in the South of France, where they had landed on 6 June and 15 August respectively.

Altogether thirteen OG sections (fifteen officers and men including a radio operator and a paramedic) were dropped into France from Algiers. The first, 'Emily', was parachuted to a Maquis reception committee at Gramat in the Lot on the night of 8 June 1944 with a mission to disrupt rail and road communications in the *département*. On the night of 11 June the section, working with local Maquis groups, badly damaged a steel railway bridge over the River Célé near Figeac which severed the rail connection between Paris and Toulouse. A few nights later several OG personnel from the section, again with the help of the Maquis, destroyed the Madeleine bridge which spanned the Lot south of Figeac; and in August 'Emily' personnel, protected by the Maquis, destroyed a 64-metre section of a railway viaduct at Souillac. 'Emily' personnel also arranged, through the Maquis, for the foreman of the Capdenac railway yard to disable 28 engines by removing irreplaceable parts from them.

'Justine', comprising two officers and thirteen men, was the next Algiers-based OG to enter France. It was parachuted into the Vercors on 29 June 1944 to help the resistance there who had, too early as it soon proved, risen against the Germans in the area. In his after-action report, the leader of 'Justine', Lieutenant Vernon G. Hoppers, wrote that he found that 'the Vercors region no longer was a Maquis headquarters but the headquarters of a Republic with an organised army, of about 5,000 men'.

The 'Justine' OG broke up into teams of two men each to instruct the Maquis in the use of British and American weapons which had been parachuted in to them. When they found that the men who were equipped with Springfield rifles were aiming the weapon with its anti-aircraft sight instead of its normal one they quickly realised the importance of their task. On 1 July two members of the Group went to reconnoitre Chabeuil airport east of Valence with a view to sabotaging it, and next day, with the aid of eight Maquis, they laid an ambush there, attacking three armoured cars with grenades and Sten guns. Two of the cars were destroyed and eighteen Germans were killed. The party then returned to the Vercors and on 7 July another ambush was laid at Lus-La-Croix-Haute by the entire group and twenty Maquis.

Hoppers' after-action report gives a vivid picture of the techniques the OG employed in ambushes as well as the atrociousness of guerrilla warfare. The ambush party moved into position about 0700 hours. The ambush spot, or Death Trap, as it was later named, was a strip of horseshoe-shaped road about 300 yards in length. A bazooka supported by a Browning Automatic Rifle (B.A.R.), the standard US infantryman's light machine-gun, was placed at each end of the horseshoe, and the 30-foot cliff overlooking the road was lined with Maquis armed with American Marlin submachine-guns and Gammon grenades; men were also positioned to prevent anyone approaching the ambush from behind. The ambush party had just got into position when a single truck was seen approaching from the direction of Aspres-sur-Buëch. It was stopped and the French driver reported that a German troop convoy of six trucks with 120 men was behind him. One hour and twenty minutes later the look-out spotted the convoy. The ambushers allowed the first truck to pass through the ambush spot, thinking that when it was picked off by the bazooka at the far end, it would block the road. But the second truck increased its speed and swerved around the first.

'The B.A.R. located to the left and rear of the bazooka for just such an emergency opened up and stopped the second truck. The third truck was hit by the

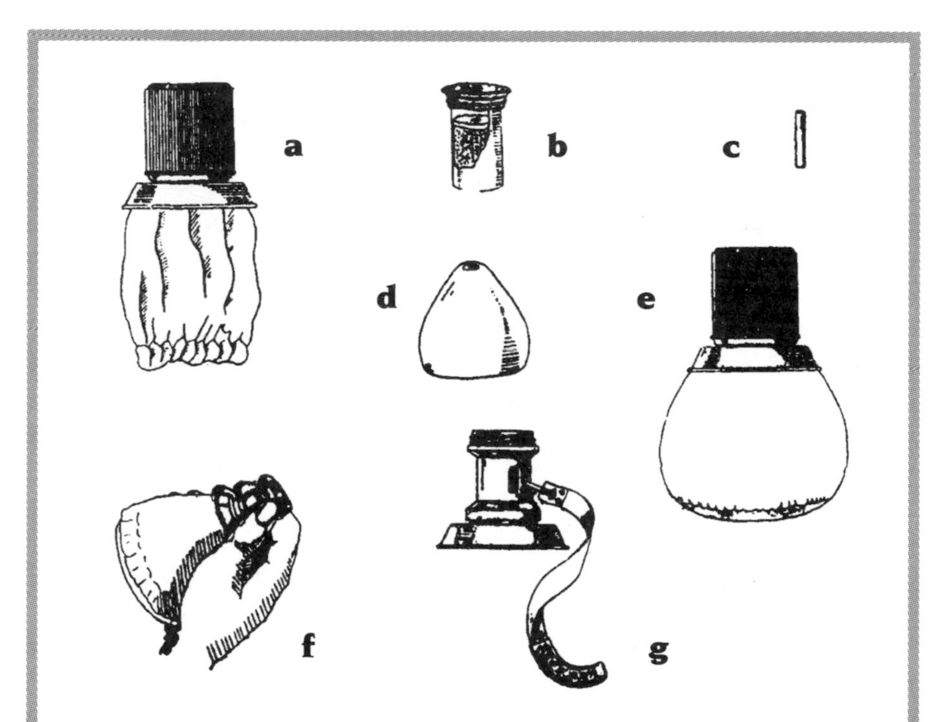

The Gammon grenade, named after its inventor, a Major Gammon, could be made up by the user as and when he required it. For use against armoured vehicles and trucks, it had to be filled with plastic explosive, but it could be filled with any suitable explosive as an anti-personnel weapon. It was made up of three parts: the percussion fuze and cloth bag (a), the primer cup (b), and the special short No. 8 detonator (c). One kilogramme of plastic explosive was moulded into shape (d) leaving a hole in its top for the primer cup. The detonator was inserted into the hole in the centre of the primer cup; this was then screwed on to the percussion fuze before the primer cup was fixed into the hole in the explosive, and the cloth bagdrawn over the explosive (e). To prepare the grenade for throwing the black bakelite cap of the percussion fuze was unscrewed and discarded. The white tape wound arund the top of the grenade was then held in place by thumb and forefinger (f). When the grenade was thrown the tape unwound in flight (g) which pulled out the safety in so that the grenade exploded on impact.

bazooka at the far end of the trap and the B.A.R. supporting him went to work on the fourth vehicle which was a bus. In the meantime when the first bazooka round was fired every man started to work with grenades, Marlins and rifles [to] liquidate the men in the rear of the trucks. We used Gammon grenades, filled with one pound plastic and one pound scrap iron. These grenades did a thorough job on the men closely packed into the rear of the trucks. On the second shot with his bazooka Sgt. Harp, who was firing at the cab of the third truck, caught the driver in the chest as he tried to get out of the door. The upper part of his body disappeared and his legs fell forward upon the road.'

When the surviving Germans piled out of the trucks and set up a mortar and a light machine-gun the ambush party withdrew, split up, and then re-assembled twelve hours later at a pre-arranged rendezvous. They knew one of the Maquis was dead but when a second did not turn up two men were sent in a car to search for him. They discovered him in a small village where he had been tortured to death before all the villagers. The Germans had broken his fingers and arms, gouged out his eyes, and bayoneted him in the stomach and chest. Villagers who had to bury the dead later confirmed that 60 Germans had been killed in the ambush and 25 wounded.

Twelve days later, on 19 July, the Germans launched a large-scale ground attack on the Vercors. This was supported by aircraft and by SS troops who were dropped by glider on to the plateau at Vassieux-en-Vercors. The 'Justine' OG, supported by 75 raw Maquis recruits, attacked these troops at dawn next day, but were driven off by automatic fire and by aircraft which continued to harass them all day. Nevertheless, the Americans kept the Germans confined to the village and this gave some of the population the opportunity to escape. The OG attacked again after dark and got within 200 yards of the Germans' position. The fire-fight lasted until dawn when the OG and the Maquis had planned their assault. But when the time came the OG found that only six Maquis remained with it and so, once more, it had to withdraw. Again, the Americans kept the Germans pinned down for the whole day but on 22 July they withdrew, first to St. Martin-Le-Colonel and then to the plateau above St-Marcellin. There they met one of the Maquis commandants who told them that the entire Isère valley had guards posted at 50-metre intervals, the Germans being determined no one would escape down it from the Vercors. That evening German troops flooded into the area and the OG was forced to go to ground.

'For 11 days the section laid in one spot,' Hoppers wrote in his after-action report, 'while German patrols scoured the woods and fired into the underbrush trying to scare the Maquis into the Isère valley, where many were shot trying to escape. For 11 days we ate nothing but raw potatoes and occasionally a little cheese. Not more than one man moved at a time; and then never more than fifty feet away from where we lay. The men were never allowed to speak above a whisper. The food which we did get was stolen at night from a farmer who lived close to the woods in which we were hiding. On the night of 6 August we received word from a Maquis that the bridge just outside Saint-Marcellin was no longer guarded. We immediately moved down from the plateau and force marched 40kms. into the region across the Isère.'

Eventually the OG made its way to safety and took refuge with the resistance in the mountains above Grenoble. Though the pressure of large German forces had resulted in the disintegration of 'Justine', the final paragraph of the after-action report recorded, with justifiable pride, that the Germans had thought there had been a battalion of American troops in the Vercors not just fifteen lightly armed men.

The other eleven Algiers-based OG ('Louise', 'Betsy', 'Ruth', 'Alice', 'Nancy', 'Lehigh', 'Helen', 'Lafayette', 'Williams', 'Peg', and 'Pat'), were dropped between mid-July and 2 September 1944 to work with the local Maquis and help the advance of 'Dragoon's forces by wreaking as much havoc as they could among the defending German divisions. Both 'Louise', which was first in, on 18 July, and 'Betsy', on 26 July, were dropped into the Ardèche, and were followed there, between 24 August and 1 September, by 'Lehigh', 'Helen', 'Lafayette' and 'Williams'. 'Nancy' (ultimately bound for the Italian border) and 'Pat' were dropped into the Vaucluse on 2 and 6 August respectively; 'Ruth' into the Basses Alpes, between Grasse and Castellane, on 4 August; 'Alice' into the Drôme on 7 August with orders to 'organise and strengthen the resistance forces' and to 'reconnoiter National Highway No. 7 [along the Rhône and] to destroy enemy communication lines'; and 'Peg' into the Ariège on 10 August.

The fifteen-man team 'Louise' was commanded by Lieutenants W. H. McKensie and Roy K. Rickerson. The team landed at Devesset, south of Lyon, and established their base in a stone-built schoolhouse near Aizac. Prior to the 'Dragoon' landings on 15 August the planners required the destruction of a bridge across the Rhône so as to block all river traffic; a railway suspension bridge some 50 miles north of Avignon was chosen by the local FFI under whose control 'Louise' was operating. The operation took place on the night of 23 July.

'Four charges of plastic were prepared for railroad overpass,' the after-action report records. 'The section was briefed at 1430 and started on the operation at 1930. At Antraigue we were joined by 25 Maquis to act as security. Lt. McKenzie [sic] and S/Sgt. Pelletier's squad with Maquis as security moved out in one truck... About twenty minutes time was consumed in placing three charges. A ten-minute time fuse was used and supplicated with a twenty-minute time pencil. Security was called in and personnel mounted on trucks before fuse was lit. Lt. Rickerson and men drove to the bridge. Maquis were let off both trucks to form a road block north of Viviers. Sgt. Boucher and a bazooka with Captain Montague [a British member of Jedburgh 'Willys'] and two R.A.F. men crossed the bridge to act as security on the east end. Lt. Rickerson and the remainder of the men set the charge...' Two days later the team learned that 'the suspension bridge had dropped flat across the river making it impossible for the barges and breaking all communication lines and power lines... Germans sent 500,000 litres of gasoline from Avignon en route to Valence by barge. Reaching Viviers, the barge could not pass and it turned back to Pont-Saint-Esprit.'

The day after that 'Betsy' arrived and the 15-man team set up a base camp at Vanosc, nearly Annonay, situated between Valence and Lyon. On 9 August it destroyed a railway bridge south-west of St-Etienne in the Loire, but it then suffered a number of casualties. First Vanosc was attacked from the air on 10 August and one of the team's sergeants was killed, and three of the men were wounded. Then a few days later, while trying to block the main road near Couiza in the *département* of Aude, five 'Betsy' personnel and eighteen Maquisards were engaged in a fire-fight with a force of 250 Germans in which one of the OGs' officers was killed and a sergeant was wounded while covering the retreat of the rest of the party.

In the meantime 'Louise' ambushed a column of 400 Germans, killing about 100 of them, and destroying one tank and six trucks with their bazookas and Gammon grenades. Then on 1 August the team derailed a train transporting sixteen tanks and supplies. Two weeks later four 37mm guns were parachuted to the OGs. The guns were all damaged but two were eventually made usable and were mounted by the OG on a hill overlooking Vallon which the Germans were evacuating. The official OSS history relates that with the help of about 40 members of the local Maquis, the OG killed some 200 Germans, but fails to add that 'The enemy countered the fire, flanked the position, and after a day-long fight forced McKenzie [sic], Rickerson, and their men, together with those FFI who stuck with them, to withdraw. The Germans captured the two 37-mm guns.' At the end of August 'Louise', now working with 'Lafayette', bluffed a retreating German column, sheltering in a valley near Chomérac, into surrendering and rounded up, with the help of the Maquis, 3,284 prisoners.

Between 1 August and 9 September OG teams were also dropped into northern and central France from England. The eighteen-strong 'Percy Red' was the first to be dispatched. The team and its supplies left Harrington airfield on the night of 31 July/1 August in four aircraft, to be parachuted into the Haute Vienne to co-operate with a strongly armed Maquis group there. Only one aircraft found the DZ that night, and the others had to return the following night and on the night of 5/6 August. When all the men and supplies had arrived the team set up its HQ at Sussac, the centre of local Maquis activities.

Specific missions for 'Percy Red' included the dislocation of local railways and roads, and the destruction of a wolfram mine near St-Léonard-de-Noblat, and to provide the Maquis with radio communications and demolitions support.

The team's first operation, on 11 August, was to attack an armoured train the Germans were going to use to open the railway south of Limoges which the Maquis had so far managed to keep closed. About 40 men took part in the attempt, which took place between Salon-la-Tour and Uzerche, but the train was guarded by 50 Germans who spotted the charges which had been laid on the line and in the fight which followed the OG's section leader, Captain William F. Larsen, was killed. Although the train was not wrecked it was forced to return to Limoges. The next day the team was joined by a Jedburgh team (see Chapter 15), code-named 'Lee', and the two groups, supported by the Maquis, then demolished a bridge across the Vienne in St-Léonard which delayed the Germans' withdrawal from Limoges. To prevent any Germans who were withdrawing from the south entering the city the OGs then 'blasted the national highway about 35kms south of Limoges. The local population assisted them in making a tank ditch across the highway. They still had a supply of mines so the surrounding terrain was mined and trees were cut down and booby trapped. All the side roads were booby trapped too. A railroad bridge was blown to block another road... Three days were spent in fortifying the city in this manner.'

The same night as 'Percy Red' destroyed the road bridge across the Vienne, and during the next night, four officers and 21 men of another OG ('Patrick') were dropped into the same area. They were commanded by a remarkable Russian *émigré*, Lieutenant-Colonel Serge Obolensky, then aged 54, whose mission was to 'conduct continuous attacks on rail, road and communications targets' but, more importantly, to protect from destruction, a hydro-electric plant at Eguzon in the Indre *département*.

'There was one company of Germans under a captain at the power-station in Eguzon, and there was a French force of the Pétain government to defend the balloon barrage and the electric transformers,' Obolensky wrote later. 'I arranged a meeting with the French officer, and told him I had orders to take and hold the power-station. I had, of course, placed my men in echelons in the countryside to give the impression that I had a big force with me. The French captain was stunned when I told him I had direct orders from General Koenig of the French army to take and hold Eguzon for France. Then I said that in no circumstances must the Germans be permitted to destroy the station.'

He told the French officer that he guaranteed safe passage to Argenton for the German force provided that they were out before dawn. If they were not he would attack. If the Germans double-crossed them and laid delayed charges before they left Obolensky would make sure they would not escape, and he sent some Maquis to block off the road. His bluff worked and the Germans left without attempting to damage the power-station. 'I think one factor that saved the station,' Obolensky commented, 'was that it supplied so much of Paris and they [the Germans] did not want it destroyed until they pulled out.'

The following week, on the night of 30 August, Obolensky and his OGs, with Maquis help, ambushed a stronger than expected force of Germans. The Maquis wavered but the OGs steadied them by holding their ground, and the Germans withdrew. On 7 September 'Percy Red' – which had clashed with a German bicycle patrol, attacked a German-held château near Le Blanc, killing two and capturing six, and had been involved in another skirmish with the Germans – was now ordered to join 'Patrick' and both groups again clashed with the Germans who suffered casualties. By now the members of 'Percy Red' were exhausted and as they had, in any case, achieved their objectives, they were withdrawn to England on 10 September by an aircraft from Le Blanc airfield.

'Donald', eleven-strong, was the second OG to be dispatched from England when it was dropped into the Finistère *département* on the night of 5/6 August, east of Landivisiau in Brittany. It successfully carried out its mission to prevent destruction by the Germans of the area's road and rail infrastructure and to work with Jedburgh team 'Hilary' in assisting local resistance groups. 'Percy Pink' was the next to be sent from England. Eight men of this 13-strong group was parachuted into the Dordogne on the night of 11/12 August, but efforts to dispatch the other five failed. The mission of 'Percy Pink' was to assist the local Maquis.

The eighteen-strong 'Lindsey' OG was dropped from England on the nights of 16/17 and 17/18 August 1944 with a mission to capture a hydro-electric plant in the Cantal *département*. With Maquis help this was successfully accomplished without a fight, but thereafter the OG was involved in several skirmishes with the Germans. The next OG to leave England was 'Christopher' which was dropped near Poitiers in the Vienne *département* to harass German forces withdrawing from Bordeaux. Thirty-two of its 55 men were members of the 'Norso' group who were seeing action for the first time. 'Adrian', comprising 32 men who were dropped on the night of 9/10 September, had a similar mission to harass the Germans withdrawing through the Dijon area and to delay – or, if possible, prevent – any moving northwards. Soon after landing they were joined by a Special Air Service team and together they laid an ambush and caused heavy casualties to German troops withdrawing from Dijon.

The operations carried out by OGs in France included the destruction of 32 bridges in the Rhône valley. They also killed 461 Germans, wounded 467, and, by greatly exaggerating their own strength, obtained the surrender of more than 10,000 others. OG casualties in France amounted to five killed, 23 wounded, and one missing in action.

In March 1945 the 'Norso' group at last had the opportunity of working together when some of them mounted an operation code-named 'Rype' (Norwegian for a ptarmigan). Thirty-six members of the unit, under the command of a future Director of the Central Intelligence Agency, Major William E. Colby, were dispatched to cut the Nordland railway line at two points in the North Trondelaag area to hinder the deployment of 150,000 German troops in northern Norway. Only four of the eight Liberator bombers dropped their loads on target, three returned to England and one got lost forcing the six men aboard to parachute into Sweden where they were temporarily interned. Only fourteen members landed at the reception area, a frozen snow-covered lake at Jaevsjo on the Norwegian–Swedish border, though eventually an arrangement was to be made with the Swedish police to release those who had dropped into Sweden and these were eventually able to rejoin the main party. Later, two aircraft carrying supplies and ten members of the party crashed, killing all aboard.

Colby landed safely on the lake and walked towards one of the signal fires where a figure was waiting. To be on the safe side Colby drew his pistol before approaching and uttered, in his elementary Norwegian, the pre-arranged password: 'Is the fishing good on the lake?' The answer should have been: 'Yes, particularly in winter.' Instead, the man said: 'To tell you the truth, it's no good at all.' This fazed Colby somewhat, but a Norwegian resistance officer who had dropped with the team was immediately able to identify the man as genuine.

After a tough six-day cross-country ski trek the sabotage party reached the Nordland railway, but their original target, the Grana bridge, was too heavily defended for their much reduced party to attack. Instead Colby chose to destroy a smaller railway bridge at Tangen. This was successfully accomplished on 14 April and eight days later 2½ kilometres of track was destroyed with plastic explosives. 'We split into teams,' Colby wrote later, 'silently crept to the line, placed our charges, and at midnight sharp the first went off. My team hadn't quite finished, but we quickly did so when a German flare went off fifty yards from us. A bullet kicked a pebble against my forehead, but I told Sivert Windh not to fire his Browning automatic rifle; I didn't want the Germans to know that a regular unit with automatic weapons was near them. We jumped the fence, retrieved our skis, and made fast tracks on the hard snow crust up the trail back into the mountains. Applying the lesson of my drop in France, I made the group keep going all the way back to base, taking a roundabout route to point the German patrols in the wrong direction until a friendly snowstorm covered our tracks.'

These two operations slowed the deployment of German troops from one battalion a day to one a month.

OGs were also sent to China in March 1945 where their mission was to form, train, and equip twenty Chinese Commando units – each about 200 strong – for operations against the Japanese in Japanese-occupied China; 390 OG personnel were involved in this task. Five of the Commandos saw action before the war ended.

15
The Jedburgh Teams in France

These three-man teams were sent into France on and after D-Day to help local resistance networks co-ordinate their efforts with the operations of the Allied armies, to give them a wireless link, to arrange arms and supplies for them, and to train resistance members in the use of the weapons and explosives dropped to them. They worked with SOE agents on the ground and with all the other different types of groups – such as the SAS, the American Operational Groups (see Chapter 14), and the Inter-Allied Missions – which were also dropped into France after D-Day.

The Jedburgh teams, or 'Jeds' as they were called, trained at Milton Hall, near Peterborough. It was not their purpose to take command of resistance groups, the French having their own leaders. In fact, when some were briefed they were encouraged not to go into action, though from the teams' after-action reports it is obvious that they could not, or did not, follow this part of their briefing. The head of one team ('Veganin') later wrote that to discourage participation in the fighting 'was a great mistake. After leading a successful military action and demonstrating one's own military prowess, the maquis were far more inclined to obey orders and held the team in greater respect.'

What the Jeds actually did is described by the official OSS historian: 'They suggested, helped to plan, and took part in sabotage of communications, destruction of fuel and ammunition dumps, attacks on enemy pockets cut off by the advance of the Allied armies and the procurement of intelligence. They subsequently provided liaison between American and British task forces and the Maquis, as various areas were overrun.'

Some teams, such as 'Andrew', accompanied an Inter-Allied Mission while others, such as 'Hugh', worked with SAS teams. At least one, 'Isaac', became an Inter-Allied Mission once it reached the field. They were all parachuted into their destinations except 'Julian II' which, on 18 November 1944, went in by road into the Alsace–Strasbourg–Mulhouse area where it remained until 20 February 1945. Its function was primarily for communications and intelligence purposes.

What was known as counter-scorching was also an important part of some Jeds' duties. This meant protecting important installations – bridges, power plants, and so on – to prevent the Germans, as they retreated, implementing a

THE JEDBURGH TEAMS IN FRANCE

'scorched earth' policy as they, and the Russians, had done with such horrific efficiency on the Eastern Front.

Nearly all the Jeds were dropped to receptions arranged by SOE agents and most, but not all, were dropped in uniform. Six were dropped into Brittany in June 1944 and seven to other parts of France. Another 79 were dropped during the next ten weeks, the majority during August after the Allies had broken out of their Normandy beach-head. Twenty-five teams were dropped by Special Project Operations Center (SPOC) from Algiers into southern France, the rest by Special Forces Headquarters (SFHQ).

Six teams were also dropped into the Netherlands in September 1944 in connection with 'Market Garden', the operation which attempted to capture the bridge at Arnhem. Later, Jed personnel who had worked in France volunteered to work behind enemy lines in Italy and the Far East. For example, several were involved in Operation 'Character' in Burma (see Chapter 16), though they were only known there as Jed teams when one or more of the team had been an original Jed. After the war the Jeds were regarded as one of the predecessors of the American Green Berets.

Jed teams comprised an officer of the country into which the team was being dropped; a British or American officer; and an American, British, or French radio operator. The role of the first officer was primarily liaison while the second officer dealt with supply and training of the resistance forces, and was responsible for supporting and protecting the third member of the team, the radio operator. Of the 93 teams dropped into France, only seven were tri-national. Of the remainder, seventeen had two Frenchmen, one had three Frenchmen, 29 had two Americans, and 39 had two Britons. Normally two of the team were officers, the third being a sergeant wireless operator. Their losses were 23 killed, nineteen wounded or injured, and four taken prisoner. Despite imaginative guesses for the name 'Jedburgh' by some writers, it was in fact simply the next on a staff list of code-names.

Special Forces personnel were attached to Army, Army Group, and Supreme Allied Headquarters to advise commanders in the field on the use of the teams and to maintain radio contact with them, via SOE's Jedburgh section, at Baker Street. SPOC and SFHQ had been formed in May 1944 as headquarters organisations to control all Allied clandestine operations into France. On 1 July there was a change in the command structure for SPOC and SFHQ when SHAEF delegated all resistance activities in France to General Koenig's Free French Forces of the Interior (FFI) whose staff comprised SOE, OSS, and Free French personnel.

These command changes caused disruption and a degree of bureaucratic muddle which were to be the cause of strong complaints from those in the field. The head of SOE's RF Section, Colonel Hutchison, who led an Inter-Allied Mission into France on 10 June, put in his report that 'the twelfth hour change of control in London... was almost disastrous. We in the field were left puzzled, angry, and despairing. We felt London's pulse beating more feebly...'

The effect on SPOC was even more marked, particularly as it occurred when many of the teams were about to be dispatched to France. The British head of Jedburgh team 'Veganin', Major Neil Marten, who later became head of SPOC's Jedburgh Section, wrote in his official report on the activities of the Jeds dropped from Algiers that the delays were 'the most criminal matter in the whole history of the Jeds... for some reason the majority of the teams were left waiting until the very last moment before they were sent in and it was impossible for them to do any good whatsoever.' In many cases, he said, the teams were 'utterly wasted' and Hutchison commented that though Jedburgh teams were more than justified 'the pity is that more were not sent sooner as requested. The Maquis wanted them and asked for them.'

Unlike other joint clandestine operations in Europe, where it was tacitly agreed that SOE was the senior partner, the Jeds were, from the beginning, a joint Anglo-American operation. Consequently, Major-General Gubbins, who was then head of SOE, paid close attention to them, 'devoting', as his biographers subsequently noted, 'what some of the older hands in Baker Street considered to be excessive attention to the recruitment and training of what was essentially a paramilitary force'. But Gubbins was an inspirational leader as well as a consummate administrator and his personal interest in the Jeds must have kept morale high. 'Whenever possible', his biographers continued, 'Gubbins made a point of seeing organisers, both before they set out for and on their return from their missions to the field. In handling these interviews, he was at his best. He briefed himself fully beforehand, showed an instinctive understanding of the problems facing the individuals concerned and took infinite trouble to remedy even the most trivial complaints.'

Equipment and arms probably varied, but the members of 'Alan', who were parachuted near Mâcon on 13 August, had an American 7.62mm carbine with a folding stock, a .45 Colt automatic pistol, and a Commando knife. 'We were, in fact, trained to use the latter for fighting by a diminutive Glaswegian PE instructor,' the English member of the team, Stanley Cannicott, later wrote. 'However, I am sure nobody ever used it as such – it would have been useful to cut our static lines if we got hung up in a tree and it served for preparing food.'

Food, of course, loomed large in the minds of all the teams and they were given lectures by a big game hunter on how to live off the land. Stanley Cannicott kept some of the lecture notes. 'It is important to reject all prejudice and every consideration except the bedrock necessity of getting food somehow in order to keep going. Rats and mice are both palatable meat. Rats, in fact, cooked in a stew might be mistaken for chicken. Dogs and cats provide excellent food and they are worth much trouble in capture by friendly advances. The liver, in particular, is excellent; it can be stewed with leaves and provides an excellent meal. The hedgehog would be a lucky find in a dry ditch. Turn it on its back, tickle the body lightly with a stick or the fingers. It will then poke out its head and neck which can be severed by a stroke, skin and cook as suggested for dogs and cats.'

However, Cannicott recorded that he knew of no Jed who ever had to go to such extremes in order to obtain a square meal. Even during training when, at the end of the day, they had to bivouac in a wood and were given a bag of flour and a dead sheep for supper, they ate well enough as 'we had not only the ex chef of the *Queen Mary* with us but also several French Foreign Legion types who were quite *au fait* with the killing and preparing of sheep.'

After some weeks of training the teams selected themselves. A French officer would team up with an American or British one and the two officers would then either be allotted a wireless operator or would approach one to join them 'as their child', and thereafter the team trained together as much as possible. The procedure was known as 'getting married' and though there were a few 'divorces' it seemed to work well enough.

When training was complete the teams waited at Milton Hall until one by one they were called to London for a final briefing. There were delays and as this was thought to have caused a drop in morale a distinguished American officer – 'the most decorated gentleman of the American forces' – came to give the Jeds a pep talk.

'We duly sat ourselves in the big hall,' Cannicott recorded, 'the British at the front sitting smartly, the French strewn around and the Americans lounging, as only Americans can do, at the back. After a short talk, this eminent gentleman looked us in the eyes and said "Men, don't worry, when you go out there we'll be behind you." Almost instantly a loud American voice from the back cried "Miles behind!" Some of us Brits blushed profoundly.'

An American Jed, William Dreux, a member of 'Gavin' which was dropped into Brittany, recalled how the trainees at Milton Hall had little time for the niceties. They liked to use a battle cry to show their derision for anyone uttering them, or for anything they did not understand or disapproved of. In the case of the Americans this included the pukka Indian Army colonel, named Spooner, who initially commanded Milton Hall with unbending discipline.

The battle cry – '48... 49... 50... some shit!' – derived from an American captain who, when under training in the USA to become a parachutist, was given the punishment of 50 press-ups by the sergeant instructor for turning up late. The captain counted each press-up out loud. Then he stood up, red-faced and breathless, and added with venom, 'Some shit!'

It was used with devastating effect when a distinguished civilian arrived at Milton Hall and said that he wanted to have a brief chat with the teams under training. He then took twenty minutes to say how impressed he was by what he had seen and concluded by saying that 'as he looked at our young, eager faces, and knowing how dangerous our missions would be, he just burned with fierce pride'. The silence that followed this remark was broken by someone calling out '48', followed elsewhere in the hall by others shouting out '49' and '50', and then there was a unified roar of 'some shit!'

One of the Jeds then pinned a cartoon to the bulletin board which depicted two polar bears on a vast ice field looking into a crater in the ice. One was asking 'What happened?' The other said: 'I don't know. He just said he was burning with fierce pride and then he disappeared.'

Obviously, something had to give and the colonel was quickly and quietly replaced by a more suitable, and sympathetic, Commandant. It should be added that the Commandant had previously commanded other SOE training schools with marked success but that, in the words of one Jed, 'he was miscast, poor fellow, to control rather wild young Americans'.

The first team into France from England was 'Hugh', which was dropped blind – that is, without a reception committee – near Châteauroux in central France in the early hours of 6 June. Its primary task was to help an SAS team which jumped with it to form a base from which raids could be mounted against German lines of communications, and to co-ordinate partisan support for this base. To further this end they were to contact Amédée Maingard, an F Section agent who ran the 'Shipwright' circuit in the Indre. The team also had to make an assessment of the resistance in that *département*, to act as a forerunner for the other Jed teams which were being dropped into the area, and to arrange reception committees for them.

The after-action report of 'Hugh' gives a clear description of the preparations for its mission which were probably similar to what all the teams experienced. Before it left, the team was given a detailed briefing on the topography of the area, what German army and air force units were located there, and information about the local police and Gestapo. It was also given details about the curfews and other restrictions in the Indre. It was then shown photographs of the F Section agent they were to contact, and of other important Allied agents in the region; was told how to inform London, by means of a hidden message, if the team were captured and was transmitting under duress; and was given instructions as what to do when its area of operation was overrun by Allied ground forces, as well as what actions to take if it were necessary to withdraw the team in an emergency.

On the night of 5 June the team was taken on the two-hour journey from Milton Hall to Station 61, a large country house used as a holding station for those awaiting air transport to take them into enemy-occupied territory. There it was given a good meal before being taken on to SOE's Tempsford airfield in Bedfordshire. At the airfield the men went to a dressing hut where they donned their jump suits after a security officer had made a thorough search of their belongings and pockets to ensure that they had nothing that might be of use to the Germans if they were captured. Besides their weapons – which were the same as 'Alan's – the men carried with them compasses, maps of the dropping zone and a road map of the area, escape and evasion kit, and extra crystals for the wireless sets. Other equipment, such as clothing and personal kit, wireless sets, and extra arms for the resistance were packed into canisters which were dropped with them. Each officer also carried with him in a money belt 100,000 French francs; the wireless operator had 50,000.

'Hugh' operated in the Indre for three and a half months, organising and supplying the local resistance, and until mid-August the *département* was of little interest to the Germans. 'Hugh' reported 500 rail cuts in its area between 6 June and 6 July. By August the numbers of resisters it was helping rose to 9,000, far more than it could comfortably cope with, and first 'Hamish', and then 'Julian' and 'Ivor', were dropped to help in the area. On 18 August the German 64th Corps was ordered to withdraw from south-west France and the routes that some of the Corps took went through or near the Indre. 'Hugh' made sure that their passage was impeded as much as possible and a report by a German staff officer from the Corps confirmed that it was largely successful in its efforts as troops had to be diverted from the Montluçon–Limoges–Châteauroux route 'a notable short-cut, and consequent saving of time' to one which used Poitiers as its pivot, with the troops passing through Bourges and Nevers.

'Hamish' parachuted into a DZ established by 'Hugh' near Bélâbre on the night of 12/13 June and subsequently worked in the Aigurande–La Châtre area in the south-east of the Indre and then at the southern end of the Cher *département*, near St-Amand, to which 'Ivor' was dispatched to help in early August. After 1 August the resistance groups in the area outgrew SFHQ's ability to sustain them, and one 300-man group even left to search for another Jedburgh team which could supply them. At first 'Hamish' could not find any Germans against which to deploy the Maquis it was arming. When the opportunity came in mid-July a group of 500, against the wishes of the Jeds, who wanted to wage hit-and-run guerrilla warfare, engaged a heavily armed German convoy in a pitched battle. Inevitably, there were casualties among the Maquis – some fifteen were killed – which was what the Jeds had wanted to avoid.

Fourteen teams of Jeds were eventually dropped into Brittany and these helped arm and organise more than 20,000 resisters. They carried out sabotage in the peninsula so efficiently that, as General Donovan later reported to the Joint Chiefs of Staff, they 'so paralyzed railroad lines that all German movements were by motor transport or on foot. Further, a major part of the German strength in Brittany was diverted and held to fighting the Resistance, both cleaning up ambushes and actually attacking Resistance centers in open battles... The intenseness of Resistance activity permitted General Patton's army, after its breakthrough at Avranches, to turn east with its main force and form the southern arm of the great encircling drive around the German forces in Normandy while mopping up in Brittany was left principally to the FFI.'

Once Brittany had been cleared Jed teams helped build up large groups of FFI personnel to contain the German garrisons which held on to the submarine ports of St-Nazaire, Lorient and Brest until the end of the war.

Typical of the Jed teams dropped into Brittany was 'Horace', which was parachuted into Finistère, the most western *département* in the Brittany peninsula, on the night of 17/18 July 1944. Its members were an American SO officer, a French officer, and an American SO wireless operator.

The team's mission was to contact two other Jed teams and elements of the Special Air Service which were already established in Brittany to help co-ordinate the potentially large resistance forces in the area, particularly those around the port of Brest. They were dropped 40 miles south-east of Brest and news of their arrival quickly reached the Germans who offered a million francs reward for information that would lead to their capture. Apart from some 5,000 unarmed partisans, there was no resistance organisation in Brest itself, all its leaders having been captured, killed or forced to flee because of the repressive measures the Germans had introduced.

With the supply drops they received, 'Horace' began to arm resistance groups and in mid-August these liberated a number of villages. Some ambushes were mounted but the fighting that took place was secondary to the value of the resistance protecting the flanks of US Army units, procuring intelligence, and harassing German patrols. On the one occasion the local resistance did try to attack a well-fortified area it was driven off with heavy casualties. However, it did surround and contain a powerful German coastal position at St-Pabu, west of Lannilis, until the arrival of the US Army. After threats and counter-threats by both parties, the Germans eventually capitulated and two members of 'Horace' were part of a group which received the garrison's surrender and then interrogated its commander. Later, 'Horace' members acted as guides for a combined force of 300 Rangers and 300 resistance fighters which attacked and silenced four coastal guns of the Graf Spee battery. The 'Horace' team returned to England on 15 September.

'Alexander', the 29th Jed team to be dropped into France, comprised one US Army officer, one French Army officer, and a US Army sergeant wireless operator. They were parachuted into the Creuse *département* in central France on the night of 12/13 August, with 30 members of the Special Air Service, to help harass German road and rail communications between Périgueux–Limoges–Châteauroux and Toulouse–Limoges–Châteauroux. The local FFI military delegate assigned the team to contact and then co-ordinate the efforts of two rival resistance factions in the Dordogne, the Maquis-controlled *Armée Secrète* and the communist-controlled FTP (*Francs-tireurs et Partisans*). Each controlled about 4,000 men, only half of whom were armed, and the 'Alexander' team managed to get both to agree to liaise for an attack on Angoulême defended by an estimated 2,500 Germans. Arms for the resistance in the town were smuggled in with the help of a parish priest.

'Looking extremely solemn and chanting Latin incantations,' the team's after-action report recorded, 'he would lead a mournful funeral procession into the cemetery in Angoulême, where the coffin would be interred with much loud weeping. The coffin, of course, contained arms and would be disinterred during the night by the resistance.' Three hundred Italians, who wanted to surrender, were also secretly exfiltrated from the town with their weapons which included anti-tank and heavy machine-guns. In due course the town was liberated when the Germans withdrew from it.

The first Jed teams into southern France from Algiers were 'Veganin' and 'Quinine', dropped on the night of 8/9 June, and 'Ammonia' the following night. 'Quinine' and 'Ammonia', dropped respectively into the Aveyron and the Lot, had missions which helped hinder the 2nd SS Panzer Division (*Das Reich*) moving from its base near Toulouse to the Normandy beach-head.

'Quinine' was commanded by Major Tommy Macpherson who had with him a British wireless operator, Sergeant Arthur Brown, and a young French officer who used the *nom-de-guerre* of Maurice Bourdon. His real name was Prince Michel de Bourbon, the nephew of the Pretender to the French throne. A member of the reception committee after greeting Bourbon ran back to his colleagues and shouted: 'We've got a French officer and he's brought his wife with him!' In fact, Bourdon's 'wife' was Macpherson who, being an officer in the Cameron Highlanders, had, quite properly to his mind, parachuted into France in his kilt.

Macpherson was a highly experienced fighting officer who felt 'I had a clear role of tip-and-run disruption, getting morale right locally. I viewed part of my job as being to move the psychology of the people. The vast bulk of the people were scared stiff to help us.' He therefore always moved around in uniform and when he acquired a car he decorated its bonnet with the Union Jack and the Tricolor, which did not endear him to local SOE agents who were used to working in extreme secrecy.

Macpherson soon found that he had an uphill struggle on his hands. 'With hindsight it was obvious that we had been very poorly briefed. The impression in London was that the *maquisards* were all keen volunteers, but it was immediately obvious that 90 per cent of them were there to stay away from the Germans, not to fight them. There was also a pretty false idea at home about what the *maquis* were for – there was too much Secret Army stuff, rather than concentration on hit and run attacks by small groups. The men we found when we landed were neither equipped nor trained for action.' Macpherson also had trouble preventing the supplies that were parachuted in to him from being pilfered by local resistance members, but later volunteers who genuinely wanted to fight did begin to come forward.

However poorly trained and equipped the local Maquis were, Macpherson immediately found sufficient numbers to mount an ambush on a small part of *Das Reich* which was making its way up the Figeac–Tulle road towards a bridge. He ordered two of the 27 Maquis with him to wrap wet cloths around the barrels of their Sten guns as he knew that this made them sound like machine-guns, and he personally positioned each man – some near the bridge, others behind trees – and laid a charge under the bridge. He also wired small charges to a line of trees which ran beside the road and told one man to detonate them when the Germans reached the bridge as this would cut off their retreat.

The ambushers waited for three hours in cold rain and when the column arrived at the bridge Macpherson blew it up and the leading half-track with it. The engagement lasted about half-an-hour before Macpherson ordered his party to withdraw when German infantry from the back of the column began to encircle it from the rear. The official after-action report of 'Quinine' states that 20 of the 27 Maquis were killed, though many years later Macpherson thought this was probably exaggerated.

'Veganin' was commanded by Major Neil Marten, who had with him a British wireless operator and a French officer, Commandant Vuchot, known by his *nom-de-guerre*, Noir. The operator was killed when the team was dropped into the Drôme near Beaurepaire on 9 June, his parachute having not been attached to the static line when he jumped. This preyed on Marten's mind to such an extent that SPOC withdrew him from the field at the first opportunity and the two Englishmen were replaced by 'Dodge' – comprising one American officer, Major Cyrus E. Manière and a French-Canadian wireless operator – on 25 June who, with Noir, carried out 'Veganin's mission to work with the Maquis to harass German traffic using Route 7, the main road which ran parallel with the east bank of the Rhône. After two months Manière was picked up by the French collaborationist police and deported to Germany. Noir remained at liberty and commanded a thousand-strong resistance force which aided the advance of American forces northwards after the Allied landings on the Riviera ('Dragoon') on 15 August 1944.

The next multi-national Jed team dropped from Algiers was 'Willys' (two Englishmen and a Frenchman) which was dropped in the Ardèche on 28 June to work with an Inter-Allied Mission and two OSS Operational Groups. The following night 'Chloroform', which comprised two Frenchmen and an American officer, Lieutenant Henry McIntosh, was dropped into the Drôme to assess why the command structure of the resistance in the southern Drôme was not functioning properly.

By the time the team arrived the main problem had been sorted out when one of the more controversial and outspoken resistance leaders, known as Colonel L'Hermine, was promoted and given a regional command over the Central Alps. The 'Chloroform' team were impressed by L'Hermine and he with them. He asked the team to accompany him to his new headquarters north of Gap, and they accepted, and the transfer was not opposed by SPOC.

Once the 'Dragoon' landings had taken place L'Hermine decided the time had come for a general uprising. Prior to attacking Gap, he gave 'Chloroform' and a small number of Maquis the task of destroying a strategically important bridge which carried the road from Gap towards Guillestre across the Durance at Savines. This was done on the morning of 16 August, but in fact the Germans never attempted to use the road because the garrison at Gap surrendered a few days later.

The delay about which Marten complained so bitterly now occurred as the next team, 'Packard', dropped in to Lozère, was not dispatched until 31 July. Then, on the night of 6/7 August, two more, 'Collodion', one of the few tri-national teams, and 'Novocaine', were dropped into the *départements* of Aveyron and Hautes Alpes respectively. 'Novocaine', consisting of two Americans and a Frenchman, was dropped near Seyne in the Hautes Alpes to work with an Inter-Allied mission and an SOE F Section circuit, 'Jockey', run by Francis Cammaerts. Cammaerts dispatched both the mission and the Jed team to a Maquis post at Vallouise from where they would harass German traffic on the roads to Briançon and the Montgenèvre Pass.

Seven more teams from Algiers were then dropped within the space of 72 hours (12–15 August), with the remainder following before the end of the month. At least two of these latecomers, 'Masque' and 'Scion', arrived much too late to be anything other than observers.

'Ephedrine' and 'Graham' were the first of the seven to be dropped, the former to Cammaerts' headquarters at Seyne, the latter into the Basses Alpes. 'Ephedrine' was led by a French captain, its other two members being an American officer, Lieutenant Lawrence E. Swank, and a French wireless operator. Shortly after it landed the team learned that Cammaerts had been arrested by the Gestapo that same day in Digne. It therefore moved with an Inter-Allied Mission which had landed with it, to join the groups already based at Vallouise, but on the way Swank was killed when a rifle accidentally discharged. At Vallouise both groups acquired mules to carry their equipment over the mountain passes and on 22 August they reached another Maquis camp south-east of St-Jean-de-Maurienne from where they attempted to harass the German garrison from Grenoble which was retreating into Italy.

On the night following the arrival of 'Ephedrine' and 'Graham', 'Cinnamon' was dropped into the Var and 'Citroen' and 'Monocle' to a Maquis supply drop zone at Lagarde which was situated north of Apt in the Vaucluse. 'Citroen', made up of two Englishmen and a Frenchman, was expected, but the arrival of 'Monocle', comprising two Americans and a Frenchman, was unscheduled after their aircraft had been warned away from their correct landing place. Even when the Lagarde DZ was found, the team's problems were not over as its after-action report recorded: 'We flew to our second ground, 'Armature'. There, we got a wrong signal. So, we circled for over an hour and getting no further signals, we jumped. The jump was ragged. Foster sprained his ankle and wrenched a knee. That field was not suitable for anything but supply drops and, naturally, the reception committee was not prepared for us. However, we made it.'

'Monocle' moved into the Drôme where the team's French officer remained at the FFI command post at Vachères while the two Americans accompanied resistance groups on sabotage and ambush attacks. At the same time 'Citroen', accompanied by two companies of Maquis, established a command post at La Bastide-des-Jourdans some ten miles north of the Durance. When an American battalion reached the area the Jeds' leader, Captain Smallwood, sent out a patrol with its commander in the direction of Cadenet where the Germans had placed an armoured rearguard. In Smallwood's words, these 'came rumbling down the street at us and we beat a hasty retreat', and he then went on to describe an act of outstanding bravery by a young member of the resistance. 'One of these tanks was knocked out of action by a man of the FTP when he came up behind it and slipped a grenade through the visor in front of the driver. The explosion probably killed the entire crew.' The rest were attacked with Gammon grenades when they reached Villelaure and this turned the column back. So impressed was the American battalion commander at the heroism of the *maquisard* that he removed his own decorations and pinned them to the young man's jacket.

Smallwood also noted in his after-action report that the French member of 'Citroen', Captain René Alcée, 'was kept busy with the need to maintain peace between the men of the FTP and the FFI who were at each other's throats most of the time over their political differences. His own troops bothered him much more than did those of the enemy', though, in fact, the Jeds in the Vaucluse helped achieve a unity of command which was all too rare elsewhere.

In north-eastern France eleven Jed teams were also dropped in August from London to help the advance of US 12th Army Group. Nearly all of them stated in their after-action reports that they had been dropped too late. The first in, 'Jacob', did not survive long. It comprised a British officer, Captain Victor Gough, a French officer, Captain Maurice Boissarie, and a British sergeant wireless operator, Ken Seymour. They were parachuted into the Vosges north of Epinal on the night of 12/13 August and two nights later reported that they had met up with the local Maquis south of Vexaincourt, but of the 800 available only 50 were armed. The Germans in the area were very active and attempts to drop arms to 'Jacob' were unsuccessful and on 15 September the team reported that Seymour had been captured and that Captain Boissarie and about 100 Maquis had been killed in a pitched battle with the Germans.

The following day Captain Gough reported that he had gathered about 200 Maquis and, with help from a local SAS team, had armed them. Then on 19 September he sent his last message: 'Have contacted 800 Maquis under Marlier. Sent message with SAS yesterday for arms drop. SAS will liaise with you. Great difficulty working alone. Can't come up on regular skeds [schedules]. Will come up on emergency when can. Please have your message ready for me on this channel. Have not had money yet. SAS having personnel drop to team here tomorrow. Please send money addressed to me with one of their officers.' But within days Gough had been captured and was executed that November.

Also on the night of 12/13 August a second Jed team, 'Aubrey', was dropped north-east of Paris to assist 'Spiritualist', an F Section (see Chapter 12) *réseau* whose leader, Major Dumont-Guillemet, arranged their reception. The team, which unlike most Jed teams were dropped in civilian clothes, consisted of a British captain, Godfrey Marchant, a French captain named Chaigneau, and a British sergeant wireless operator, Ivor Hooker. The leader of the 'Spiritualist' circuit had already armed about 1,500 potential resisters in the suburbs of northern Paris, and it was quickly decided that 'Aubrey' would be more useful, and safer, there than in the countryside. Marchant spent ten days or so instructing small groups of 'Spiritualist' resisters in sabotage techniques while Chaigneau acted as a liaison between resistance groups, but on 21 August, with the Germans retreating north-eastwards, the team moved back to the Meaux area to try and harass them. On 25 August, against SFHQ orders, the leader of 'Spiritualist' ordered his men into action, and two days later a large number of them arrived to set up an ambush position along a sunken road between Oissery and Forfry; and the 'Aubrey' team, now in uniform, assisted in this operation.

'The problems were twofold,' wrote the historian of the eleven Jed teams. 'The Maquis were basically unorganised and untrained, and the men really had no idea what would be coming down the road into their ambush. Only two Bren guns were operational, and only the Jeds knew how to operate the four Piats [Projector Infantry Anti-Tank].' The result was that the Germans' vigorous reaction to the ambush soon turned it into a rout in which Marchant estimated 86 men and women of the resistance lost their lives. 'Major Dumont-Guillemet directed a covering force to hold off the Germans while the remaining men dispersed. Captain Marchant said he would remain with the covering force and ordered Sergeant Hooker to leave the field. Hooker moved east along the streambed, where he met Major Dumont-Guillemet. They spotted Captain Chaigneau about thirty yards ahead of them. Captain Marchant and the covering force held their positions for a short while until another German tank approached and opened fire at close range, whereupon the covering force also fled. Marchant was forced to crawl north to a lake, where he hid for the next eight hours. The German armor continued to fire, killing Captain Chaigneau in the stream bed with a high-explosive shell. The mud in the stream bed was rather deep, so Hooker, Dumont-Guillemet, and the others crawled some two kilometers through the mud until they finally reached the shelter of the woods. From there, the group dispersed, with Hooker (who had discarded his codes) and Major Dumont-Guillemet making their way to a safe house.'

Two days later the US VII Corps arrived and before the end of the month Dumont-Guillemet and the two surviving members of 'Aubrey' were back in London.

On the night of 15/16 August the Jed team 'Augustus' – comprising a US Army major, John H. Bonsall, a French captain, Jean Delwiche, and a Technical Sergeant in the US Army, Roger E. Cote – was dropped, with three tons of supplies, some 25 kilometres south-east of St-Quentin. When the three men made contact with the local resistance leader he suggested that they move south. They agreed and went to the village of Crugny about 35 kilometres west of Reims, but the area was so crowded with Germans that they had no opportunity to raise any resistance forces. On 30 August SFHQ radioed them orders to carry out a counter-scorch operation in which they were to prevent the Germans demolishing five bridges across the Somme in the area of Amiens, but that night all three members of the team were caught in civilian clothes when the Germans stopped their horse-drawn cart in the village of Barenton-sur-Serre. They were carrying false identity cards and had with them their wireless and a quantity of arms and ammunition. The Germans shot them immediately.

That same night the only Belgian-British Jed team, 'Andrew', was dropped in the southern Ardennes to assist an Inter-Allied Mission, 'Citronelle', and served with it in the field for just over three weeks.

Both 'Benjamin' and 'Bernard' were Anglo-French teams. They were dropped together into a small field surrounded by the Argonne forest south of Clermont-en-Argonne on 20 August. 'Benjamin', led by a British Major, A. J. Forrest, was to operate east of the Meuse. Forrest had with him two French officers, Lieutenant Paul Moniez and Second Lieutenant H. Kaminski. 'Bernard' consisted of a British Captain, Jock Waller, a French captain, Etienne Nasica, and a British Sergeant, Cyril Bassett, and they were to work west of the Meuse. The drop zone had been chosen by the local resistance who had no experience of working with parachutists, and it proved to be much too small. Five of the two teams landed in the trees as did many of the supply containers that were dropped with them, and it took two days and three nights to collect everything.

The Gestapo and the French *milice* (collaborationist police) were soon on the trail of the two teams and they were constantly on the run until American ground forces arrived ten days later. On 31 August Captain Nasica was wounded in a skirmish with a German patrol as were Forrest, Kaminski, and Bassett when a German outpost fired on the Jeds' truck outside Clermont. They lost their truck but managed to infiltrate the German lines and reach safety. Nasica and Bassett had to be evacuated, but the others stayed on to help SOE's 'Pedlar' circuit, run by the second in command of F Section, Major Nicholas Bodington, before returning to England on 2 October.

The two Britons and one Frenchman of 'Alfred' who were dropped into the Oise valley north of Paris on 24 August were especially aggrieved at being sent into action so late in the day. 'This was the tale of the team Alfred,' they wrote at the end of their after-action report, 'not a very glorious one but not through any fault of the team. If we had been dispatched when we were first "alerted" some two weeks previous to our actual departure (team was "alerted" and "briefed" on 9 August but did not leave until 24 August) we could have done something useful.' It was certainly not their fault that they did not receive the arms they kept requesting nor that the retreating Germans were so thick on the ground that any movement was dangerous. But on 31 August, just as the Allied armies arrived, the team did mount two successful ambushes inflicting casualties on both occasions.

'Arnold', dropped into the Marne *département* on 24 August, was another team which complained that it had been dispatched too late. Sent to help the 'Pedlar' circuit, it was in the field only three days before the US Third Army overran the area. Its members also complained that because they had been dropped in civilian clothes they should have been provided with false identity papers.

'Archibald', one of the few Jed teams to be tri-national, was dropped near Nancy on 26 August, to two 60-man reception committees who were both anxious to receive arms. Although 'Archibald' was in the field for more than two months, it only worked for nine days behind the German lines and did not have time to accomplish much. But it did provide invaluable assistance in putting together a large force of Maquis which was subsequently used as conventional infantry with the US Third Army along the Moselle.

The last two Jed teams to be dropped into north-eastern France were parachuted in on the night of 31 August. 'Stanley', which dropped into the Haute-Marne, served just fifteen days in the field, while 'Rupert', parachuted into the Meurthe-et-Moselle *département*, served just two days longer.

With hindsight it can be said that the Jeds could have been – and should have been – sent into the field earlier than they were. The summation by one participant (Arthur Brown, the British wireless operator with 'Quinine') that 'The Jedburgh concept had been brilliant, the training superb but, between the limitations of the generals and posturing of the politicians, a wonderful opportunity came close to being frittered away', seems a fair one, as does his remark that it succeeded to the extent that it did because of 'the adaptability and determination of the men who had volunteered to carry it through'.

16
Guerrilla Warfare and the Characters of 'Character'

To help the advance to Rangoon of General Slim's Fourteenth Army through Burma in 1945, SOE's organisation in the Far East, now called Force 136, mounted three guerrilla operations behind Japanese lines. The most important of these was called 'Character', the nucleus of which had been in existence since 1942.

The original purpose of 'Character' had been to raise levies from the pro-British Karen Hill tribesmen who formed one of the most important minorities in Burma. They belonged to the same family as the Shans and the Siamese but were a distinct racial group, numbering over a million. They had spread from the Karen hills into Tenasserim and the Irrawaddy delta where most of them lived. In the Karen Hills – an area of some 4,000 square miles – they numbered 43,000, some 73 per cent of the local population.

The purpose of the levies had been to protect the flanks of the British forces as they retreated before the invading Japanese in the spring of 1942. When the Japanese began to overrun the Karen Hills, the tribesmen were told to return to their villages, hide their arms, and await the return of the British.

One of the officers who raised the levies, Major Hugh Seagrim, remained in the Papun area with a band of 200–300 guerrillas and W/T contact with him was eventually established in October 1943 at which time he estimated the potential fighting strength of the Karens to be about 5,000. Soon after contact had been made the Japanese discovered his whereabouts and began such severe reprisals against the Karens that Seagrim gave himself up in March 1944 to prevent any further suffering. He was subsequently executed in Rangoon, and the remaining two British officers with the Karens were killed in an ambush.

The planning and training for the reconstituted 'Character', whose British members were to arm, train, and lead the Karens in an open revolt against the Japanese, began in September 1944 and was launched the following February. In particular its mission was to harass the Japanese 15th Division withdrawing through the Karen Hills to Toungoo which was still held by a strong Japanese garrison. Once the division joined up with the garrison the two groups would be sufficiently powerful to delay the British advance to Rangoon until the monsoon

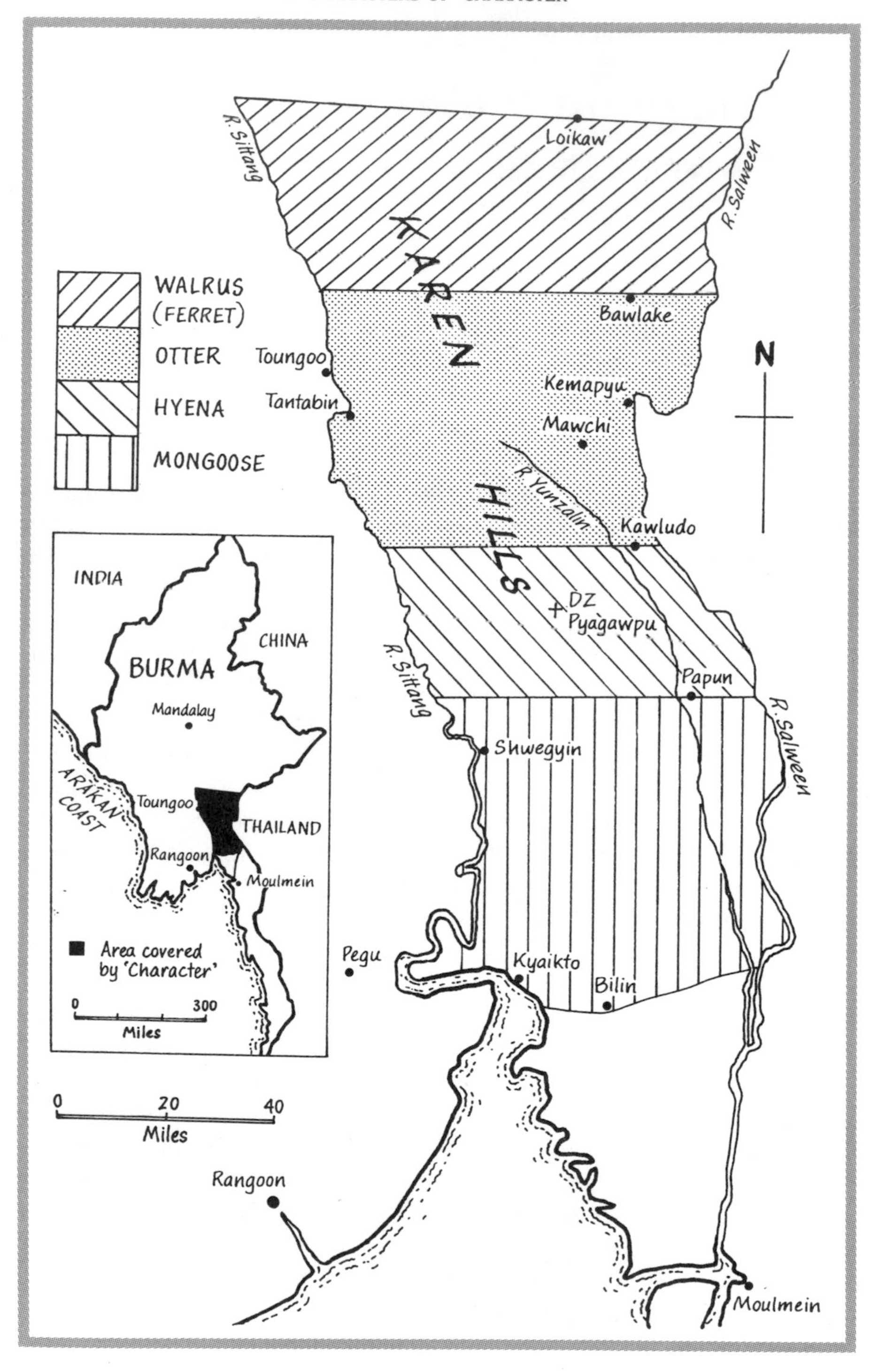

WALRUS (FERRET)
OTTER
HYENA
MONGOOSE
KAREN HILLS
N
R. Sittang
Loikaw
R. Salween
Bawlake
Toungoo
Tantabin
Kemapyu
Mawchi
R. Yunzalin
Kawludo
DZ Pyagawpu
Papun
Shwegyin
Pegu
Kyaikto
Bilin
Rangoon
Moulmein
0 20 40
Miles
INDIA
CHINA
BURMA
Mandalay
ARAKAN COAST
Toungoo
THAILAND
Rangoon
Moulmein
Area covered by 'Character'
0 300
Miles

rains arrived in May and bogged it down. If this happened it would have disastrous repercussions on the whole Allied strategy in south-east Asia.

To thwart the Japanese joining forces, the British blocked the direct route north of Toungoo with an armoured thrust. This forced the Japanese 15th Division to divert along a smaller road which curved eastwards through the Karen Hills before turning west to Toungoo.

'It looked as if they might beat us to it,' Slim wrote after the war. 'But I still had a shot in my locker for them... Over a long period in preparation for this day we had organised a secret force, the Karen guerrillas, based on ex-soldiers of the Burma Army, for whom British officers and arms had been parachuted into the hills. It was not difficult to get the Karens to rise against the hated Japanese; the problem was to restrain them from rising too soon. But the time had come, and I gave the word, "Up the Karens".'

To accomplish 'Character's mission effectively the area was divided into several zones where Special Groups, supported by Jedburgh teams (see Chapter 15), were to recruit, train, and lead into action local Karen levies, and an intelligence network was also to be formed in the area to keep track of Japanese movements and strengths.

Initially, it had been planned to divide the area into three zones. From north to south these were code-named 'Ferret', commanded by Major Eustace Poles, a big-game hunter from Rhodesia; 'Otter', commanded by Major (later Lieutenant-Colonel) Edgar Peacock, a Burma game warden and a member of the Burma Forest Service; and 'Hyena', commanded by Major R. D. Turrall who in peacetime had been a prospector.

Delays and the difficulties encountered in communications soon demanded changes in this arrangement. 'Ferret' was replaced by 'Walrus', commanded by Lieutenant-Colonel Tulloch, and Poles and his men then came under Peacock in the 'Otter' area. The southern half of 'Hyena' became part of a new area, 'Mongoose', commanded by Major (later Lieutenant-Colonel) Critchley, and the command of what remained passed to Lieutenant-Colonel G. W. Howell. Turrall was then given command of a sub-area within 'Hyena', all the operational zones being divided up as reinforcements were parachuted in and the numbers of levies increased.

It was the task of a Special Duties flight of Dakotas, based at Jessore in India and commanded by an Australian, Terence O'Brien, to drop the 'Character' teams. The idiosyncratic nature of the three commanders obviously impressed itself on O'Brien and it is worthwhile dwelling for a moment on his, and other people's, assessments of their characters. They seem to show that it was the oddballs who often made the best guerrilla leaders.

O'Brien described Turrall only briefly, as a wiry little man in his fifties who 'always wore a huge sombrero pushed down on his head and would peer up at you from under the brim'. But a report in an SOE file from a medical officer who tended to Turrall when he was wounded by grenade shrapnel reveals Turrall's testy, obstinate, almost cranky personality. The MO decided there were no fragments in Turrall. Turrall disagreed and refused to allow the MO to inform his HQ that there were none. The MO told Turrall to rest. Turrall would do no such thing, and then collapsed from exhaustion. When the MO expressed delight that Turrall's wounds were healing Turrall lost his temper. 'I am the patient', he snapped, 'and I know that I have a grenade fragment inside. Don't try to bluff me by saying it's healed.'

After Japan's official surrender on 15 August 1945, Turrall became so impatient with a local Japanese garrison, when it would not acknowledge their country's capitulation, that he arranged to contact a senior officer of the Japanese 17th Division to explain the situation. But when he arrived at the Japanese base the Japanese promptly roughed him up and only let him go some days later when they realised, from pamphlets dropped to them, that he was telling the truth.

Colonel 'Pop' Tulloch was the oldest of the three, being well on into his fifties, but just as fit and tough as the other two. He was a short – only five feet – dapper man with a neatly waxed moustache and was, wrote O'Brien, 'the most sharp witted of them all, and the best company'. He carried a monocle which was attached to the top button of his bush jacket by a black silk cord. His employment of it appeared to be arbitrary; sometimes he would raise it to his right eye to read or study a questioner – giving himself time, perhaps, to deal with an awkward inquiry – at other times he would glare or read without bothering to use it.

'Pop's passage to India had solved a delicate problem for his regiment back in England. The military future of Major Tulloch was extremely precarious when the head of 136 Burma Section, Ritchie Gardiner, arrived in England on a visit to SOE headquarters. He happened to hear of Pop's problem about a cheque, also about his bravery in action, and said he would be happy to take him for an operation he had in mind far away in Burma. So, with some relief, they allowed Pop to depart for foreign shores... There were gaps and anachronisms in his history, and his innumerable stories of financial jiggery-pokery carried a wealth of specialist detail surprising in a man who apparently had led such an active outdoor life.'

Tulloch's doubtful financial dealings were also touched upon by a sergeant wireless operator named Gibbs, who was with 'Walrus', and by O'Brien. Writing of his experiences many years afterwards, Gibbs relates that he had seen a report that Tulloch had been involved 'in nefarious activities against the Burmese government' and that subsequently he received a twelve-month prison sentence in Burma for embezzlement. O'Brien says that Tulloch didn't embezzle government funds but those of a Karen student.

But it was the third officer, Edgar Peacock, who could lay the greatest claim to being one of the war's outstanding guerrilla leaders. He was also in his fifties, 'a solid square chunk of a man' with a bristly moustache, whose eyes narrowed under his bushy eyebrows when he disapproved of something – which was often. He had spent his entire working life in Burma and could speak the language so fluently that, according to one old Burma hand, he was the only European he had met who, when speaking, was indistinguishable from a native. In 1914 the Burma government had refused to allow him to join up and because of this he nursed 'a bitter grievance' which was further heightened when in 1932 he was made redundant from the Burma Forest Service.

According to O'Brien, Peacock 'seemed to know every creature in Burma that walked, crawled, flew or swam; to have shot, trapped or hooked them at some time or another, and to have eaten them cooked in a variety of ways. His knowledge was practical; what fruits and plants could be eaten, what trees were useful – teak for ship decks, pyinkado for railway sleepers, padauk for gun carriages.' Though a keen hunter he later became more interested in game preservation, was a pioneer in shooting with a camera instead of a rifle, and was the author of a book on Burmese game. After Burma had been overrun by the Japanese in 1942 he trained troops for jungle fighting behind enemy lines for Force 136, then known as GSI (K), and subsequently 'commanded Guerrilla and Deep Penetration Troops in the Chindwin and Manipur campaigns in 1943-44'. Peacock noted with satisfaction in his final report that 80 per cent of the volunteers for the Special Groups were Burmans whom he had recruited in the Chindwin Valley in 1943.

Turrall and his 'Hyena' team successfully parachuted into their designated Drop Zone (DZ) at Pyagawpu on the night of 20 February, but the DZ which had been picked for the 'Ferret' and 'Otter' teams farther north at Kemapyu was found to be unsuitable, and fires burning in the area indicated possible Japanese encampments. The four aircraft carrying the two parties were therefore forced to fly back to Jessore, but returned on the nights of 23 and 24 February to Pyagawpu and dropped the two teams there.

The jump was later described by one of Peacock's officers, Captain Ansell, in vivid detail: 'The hills looked very beautiful to me standing in the open doorway, bathed as they were in the soft light of the moon. There was a shining silver river, too, over which we circled – the Yunzalin Chaung. How lightly and swiftly we skimmed over those mountain tops – and how slowly and with what toil we should climb them in the coming weeks! The lights below were clear and bright on the DZ set out in a letter T.

'Then the voice of the despatcher at my left shoulder, quietly wishing us luck; his staccato "Action stations Number One!" as the red light showed over the doorway. A momentary glimpse of green, the command "Go!" and then the swift rush of the slipstream, followed by that sudden, almost incredible stillness which comes on leaving the mighty noise of the engines and the rush of air past the door.

'A quick glance down the line showed the other 'chutes floating down, before the ground rushed up to meet me. Next moment I was on the dry, hard paddy field rolled up in the shroud lines of my parachute, like a rabbit in a net.'

There were several injuries, including Poles who broke a rib. Peacock found that Turrall and his 'Hyena' party had all arrived safely, but Turrall reported that the local Karens were 'in a dubious mood' and that he had only managed to recruit four of them. The arrival of the other two parties improved the Karens' morale, however, and there were soon more volunteers than there were weapons to arm them. Within a week 500 had been armed and by April more than 6,000 had been recruited.

After waiting for further supplies to be dropped to them Peacock and Poles began to move north with their Special Groups into their designated areas. Poles had soon recruited 200 levies, but his injury, and the fact that he was not going to be able to reach his area in time to harass the Japanese passing through it, brought about the change in plans already mentioned.

On the night of 24/25 March O'Brien flew 'Pop' Tulloch and his 'Walrus' team (two majors, a second lieutenant, three sergeants and fourteen Burmese other ranks) to a DZ where they could harass Japanese troops moving along the Loikaw–Kemapyu road. O'Brien later wrote: 'We were about midway to target when a waft of rum signalled the arrival of Pop in the cockpit, with his flask outstretched in offer. I was happy to chat but turned down the rum and advised that he save it for post-landing medical use; alcohol would be a pleasant anaesthetic, I suggested, while they were trying to reset the bones in his broken legs. He said he had broken his back once in a jump in Arizona and had to ride on a donkey twenty miles to hospital where they put a metal joint in his spine. When I asked if it had a hinge to allow him to bend he ignored the question and talked about prospecting in Alaska, then he gave his monocle a whirl and went back to the fuselage for a nap.'

When O'Brien saw that the intended DZ was very narrow, and that the position of a tree-covered hill at one end made it impossible to drop his stick with any accuracy, he abandoned the site immediately, flew eastwards, and found a more suitable one eight miles south of Loikaw. This was not the end of Tulloch's problems however; one man was killed and another injured, and then Tulloch had to leave the site immediately because collaborators from a nearby village alerted a Japanese garrison to his presence. Because he had not indicated that the rest of his team should be dropped, the other aircraft flew back to Jessore and returned 48 hours later to deliver the balance.

Although the Japanese had been alerted they were slow to react because they thought the party much larger than it was. Tulloch soon found a guide and shelter, and within two days a local chief had promised to raise 1,000 men. By 2 April, when the Group had its first clash with the Japanese, 400 Karens had been armed. They killed 30 of a party of 40, forcing the survivors to withdraw to Loikaw. By 13 April Tulloch had 2,000 armed levies under his command and five days later he received orders to concentrate his forces on the Loikaw–Bawlake road to delay the Japanese 15th Division as it moved down the road through the Karen Hills.

Meanwhile Peacock, who had been joined by Poles on 9 March, had heard that the Japanese were on his track. He therefore took both Special Groups into a mountain retreat, a 7,500-foot ridge, Sossisso, some three miles south-east of Nattaung, to avoid an immediate clash with Japanese patrols. This provided ideal defensive positions for the two groups and Peacock made it his main base for attacking the Japanese moving along the Mawchi road. It also had the advantage of overlooking Mawchi town, about eight miles to the east, and was a good area for the RAF to drop supplies to them.

By 23 March Peacock had recruited and partly trained 350 mobile levies and had issued rifles to 350 static levies (Home Guard). Until that date not a shot had been fired in anger, but three days later a Japanese force, about a company in strength, appeared from the south. They 'behaved in a very brave but foolish manner,' Peacock commented afterwards, 'deploying over the very steep open spurs and pressing up the escarpments to our advance positions. It was very good practice for our levies, most of whom had never fired a rifle before.'

One of the levies was killed, one of the British officers was badly wounded, and several other men were lightly wounded in this encounter which went on spasmodically, day and night, for 48 hours. Ammunition and food began to run short, but a Liberator, escorted by Mustang fighters, managed to make a drop at dusk. The Japanese, who had suffered numerous casualties, then withdrew and were subsequently harassed so badly by the Karens that they were practically wiped out.

On 7 April both 'Walrus' and 'Otter' were instructed to go over to the offensive and the following week one group from 'Walrus' destroyed a bridge on the road at milestone 84 and another destroyed a second at milestone 81. The Japanese entered Mawchi 48 hours later and the same day sent a convoy south, quite unaware that two bridges had been blown up in their path. The trucks were ambushed short of the first and hurriedly withdrew to Mawchi. Two nights later the Japanese tried again, having been preceded by a strong force of infantry which drove 'Walrus' and its levies from the road, and then put a heavy guard on the two damaged bridges while work began to repair them. Skirmishes continued for three days in the area of the bridges and once they were mended the Japanese tried to continue their withdrawal southwards.

Peacock had no intention of letting the Japanese off so lightly however. While the bridges were under repair he sent men further down the road to lay booby-traps which he had developed himself. These controlled explosive traps, as he called them, were made from No. 36 grenades (Mills bomb) from which the detonating mechanism had been removed and replaced by a three-foot length of detonating fuze (Cordtex). One end of the Cordtex was connected to the grenade, the other, at ten-yard intervals, to a much longer piece laid along the jungle path or track to be ambushed. A pull switch attached to one end of the long length was activated by someone hiding nearby, and the ambush was completed by weapons covering the length of the path.

Peacock's stock trap was 120 yards of Cordtex and ten grenades ten yards apart, but the same principle could be used against motor transport using charges of plastic explosive instead of grenades. These traps were, Peacock wrote, 'used with greatest effect on the Mawchi Road as witness the hundred-odd smashed Jap trucks in view between milestones 35 and 100 on that road. The same played havoc with enemy personnel following jungle tracks. The Japs could never fathom the use of these traps and for months walked into them with unfailing regularity. Ambushes in almost all cases were set in conjunction with Cordtex traps which is the simplest conceivable and the principles of which can be understood by any levy. The explosions and terrible effects of one hundred or more yards of Cordtex laid with grenades and heavy charges of explosive raises the morale of one side as much as it reduces that of the other. We used many hundreds of pounds of explosive and thousands of yards of Cordtex as an offensive weapon... These traps do not fall under the category of "booby" traps, because they are usually and most effectively operated by pull switches and lengths of cord pulled by hand at the right moment.'

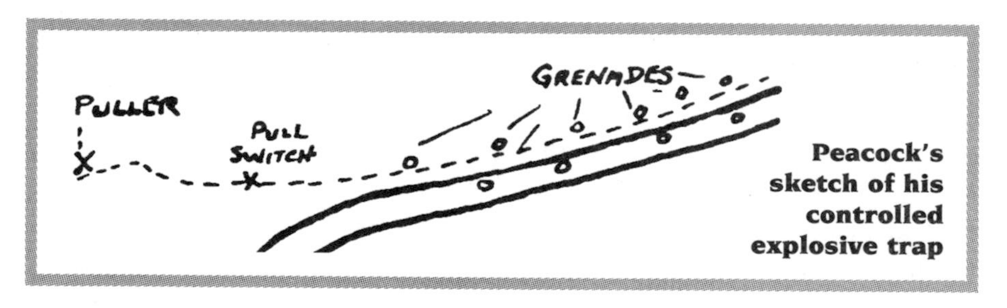

Peacock's sketch of his controlled explosive trap

It was ambushes and devices like these that delayed the Japanese 15th Division for a vital four or five days. It never did get to Toungoo, which fell to the British on 22 April, and the Japanese could do nothing to stop Slim's forces taking Rangoon which they did on 3 May. 'But for the contribution of the guerrillas,' wrote Charles Cruickshank, the official historian of SOE in the Far East, 'a considerable part of the Japanese forces would have confronted the advance guard of the Fourteenth Army, and possibly held it up long enough to put at risk the whole operation to recover Rangoon.'

This was just the beginning of 'Character's work with the Karens, for the Japanese, thwarted from reaching Toungoo, began to gather in the Karen Hills preparatory to making a break-out south-eastwards towards Moulmein. The guerrillas, as O'Brien so succinctly put it, were now caged with the tiger they had so successfully frustrated. It was a tiger that took time for the British to tame and meanwhile its sharp claws inflicted some grievous wounds on the lightly armed and isolated guerrilla forces. And once the monsoon broke, which it did early that year, the dropping of supplies became increasingly difficult. In May only half the supply operations launched from Jessore were successful and 25 aircrew were killed in crashes.

Recruits for 'Otter', which included Gurkhas from the nearby mines as well as Karens, continued to arrive and by the end of April Peacock had about 700 mobile levies who had been armed, trained, and organised into platoons. Under two British Jedburgh officers he then established a sub-area, 'Otter Green', so that the Japanese could be harassed below milestone 60 and possible escape routes via Yunzalin Valley to the 'Hyena' area could be blocked. One of these officers later wrote an abbreviated report which gives a flavour of what the fighting and the conditions must have been like.

'Towards the end of April, [Fourteenth] Army asked for a party to moved west from SOSSISSO to work on southern flank of Army. It was decided that Capts. Montague and Sell, with 50 levies go out to raise another group near Kolu. Supply drops were prearranged for the party which left 27 April. Near Tha Echi information was received that large enemy forces lay between us and our objective. So decision was made to open a DZ at Tha Echi and start recruiting and training immediately. Many recruits came but supplies of arms and food did not arrive until the 9 May, when small numbers arrived and were distributed. Reinforcements arrived from Sossisso. Capt. Montague immediately organised ambushes on the motor road and also the escape routes by the Myimgann Chaung. Many enemy were killed and M/T destroyed. Much intelligence was gathered about Jap positions along the Mawchi road and the plain between Tha Echi and Tantabin.'

As the monsoon worsened so did 'Otter Green's position. 'Transport problems were very serious and a heavy drain on available coolie labour. Many times food supplies were exhausted before drops succeeded. It was evident that weather was not wholly to blame, but inadequacy of air lift. All sorties to Tha Echi [by then the only DZ available because of monsoon conditions] were under enemy observation from about 5 miles. Several times strong parties of enemy entered Tha Echi valley and moved towards Tha Echi, but levies and homeguards drove them out.'

Refugees became an additional problem during June and July. About 1,000 had to be fed, before being sent off, with guides and escorts, to safety.

On 4 May, the day after Rangoon fell to Fourteenth Army, 'Otter' was reinforced by four officers and a platoon of 'V' Force (intelligence patrols drawn from the Assam Rifles), and on 11 May a British officer and eight Kachin guerrillas also joined it. Between 14 and 22 May the Japanese 15th Division guarding the Mawchi road was replaced by 113th Regiment of the 56th Division. In Peacock's terms this unit was a change for the better, as it was 'well worth fighting; a great improvement on the 15th Division. Their picketing along the road was good and cost us some casualties... [they were] a tough proposition.' Nevertheless, during the period 23 May to 23 June, Peacock estimated that 1,147 of them 'made, presumably, happy reunions with their ancestors', as he drolly put it.

By the end of May Major Poles' forces had, after many delays and deprivations, joined up with Peacock's, and sub-areas 'Otter White' and 'Otter Red' were established from his levies to press attacks on the Japanese. They were active in attacking the road from 25 May and 15 June respectively. By then the levies available to Peacock were distributed as follows: 'Otter Black': 1,263, 'Otter Green': 242, 'Otter Red': 330; 'Otter White': 215. If they had been properly supplied with food and the weapons they requested – particularly 3-inch mortars and medium machine-guns – there was little doubt that 'Otter' could have wreaked havoc among the Japanese who were, as Peacock described it, 'milling around us'. But because refugees were making constant inroads into the guerrillas' food and medical supplies, and because the necessary weapons were not available, Peacock estimated that his force's efficiency was reduced by half.

Now that the Japanese were concentrating their forces in the Karen Hills, and because Fourteenth Army, having captured Rangoon, 'appeared to rest on its laurels' as the official historian put it, 'Character's difficulties increased. For the Japanese had 50,000 troops in the area and without hindrance from Fourteenth Army they were able to re-organise and re-equip themselves and to start taking counter-measures against the guerrillas. They began to protect their convoys with armoured vehicles and were able to launch counter-attacks against the guerrillas whenever they sent large numbers of troops down the road. 'Walrus' had to give up control of the Bawlake–Mawchi road because of the strength of the Japanese attacks, and 'Otter' could only mount minor raids, for 'Otter Red' was driven from its HQ on 21 July and 'Otter White' had to abandon its ambushes of the road to defend its HQ. Neither 'Otter White' nor 'Otter Red' returned to the Mawchi road, but both were subsequently involved in heavy fighting with Japanese who, having crossed the Sittang River, were trying to escape through 'Walrus's area.

In the most southerly part of Burma covered by 'Character', Major John Lucas led a group code-named 'Mongoose Blue' which consisted of another British officer, three British NCOs, and eleven men from a Burmese regiment, the Burma Sappers and Miners. On 4 April Lucas was ordered by 'Mongoose's commanding officer, Lieutenant-Colonel Critchley, to take his group down to the coastal area to organise static levies, recruit mobile ones, disrupt Japanese lines of communication, and provide intelligence.

The area in which 'Mongoose Blue' operated was unlike the others, being populated by a mix of Karens, Shans and Burmans of whom only the first were reliable. But even the Karens proved reluctant recruits and Lucas found himself having to rely on 60 members of the Burma Defence Army who had defected from the Japanese and were badly trained and very edgy. The area included not only the road between Kyaito and Bilin, which Lucas ambushed frequently, but the Pegu–Moulmein railway line which, employing the only train available, the Japanese were using to retreat from the British forces pressing towards Rangoon.

On the night of 2/3 May Lucas laid a demolition charge on the line which derailed the train, and then hid while the Japanese survivors from it scoured the surrounding countryside for him. At one point they came so close that, determined not to be captured alive, he put the muzzle of his loaded pistol in his mouth and lay hidden in the grass with his finger on the trigger.

He escaped unseen, but the following month, when Fourteenth Army did not pursue its retreating enemy across the Sittang River, the Japanese forces ceased to withdraw and began to consolidate in Lucas' area just as they had farther north. Then on 6 June they launched a concerted attack on him from three sides. He had to abandon most of his equipment and stores, and to split up his party into small groups to avoid detection as he retreated northwards. Critchley, who had moved his headquarters near Papun, was driven into the nearby hills by similar attacks; and 'Hyena', which had been maintaining as many as 33 ambush parties on the main track between Kemapyu and Papun, was also forced to withdraw and hide.

The serious position in which the Special Groups now found themselves was exacerbated by the lack of aircraft to drop supplies to them and by the onset of the monsoon. So critical did it become that on 21 July General Stopford, who commanded Fourteenth Army's XXXIII Corps, informed South East Asia Command that he feared 'Character' would simply stop functioning because it could not make good the losses it had incurred in the field and from over-strain. Despite the fact that the previous month the guerrillas had managed to inflict more casualties on the Japanese than had the regular forces, a report written on 13 July 1945 by the two senior officers in 'Otter White ('Ferret 2') reveals that many had reached the end of their tether.

They had, they said, heard that Colonel Peacock intended to follow the Japanese withdrawing across the Salween River. 'The weather is too well known to need description, but it appears the difficulties it arouses are not. The tracks are often knee deep in mud, and almost impassable. Since there are so many of the enemy in the area, the practice of lighting fires is fraught with considerable danger.'

But the Karens needed to cook (because they could not live on K-Rations) and their officers could not be expected to remain soaking wet in the low temperatures which prevailed at night, nor was it possible for them to sleep without warmth. As a result, despite an excellent medical officer and available drugs, there was much sickness and a marked lack of enthusiasm. The Karens were suffering especially, and the writers of the report thought that 'there is a definite limit to the amount that can be asked of these men who are not trained soldiers. The few ex-soldiers, like ourselves, are well nigh worn out already.' Not half a dozen of their men, the report concluded, would follow their leaders across the Salween: it was not a matter of pursuing the Japanese but of surviving until they were relieved by Fourteenth Army.

According to Peacock's report no such follow-up was mounted. But the largest action in which the 'Character' guerrilla forces were to be involved, in terms of Japanese casualties, was still to take place when what remained of the Japanese 28th Army tried to cross the Sittang River to reach Moulmein at the end of July. South-east of Shwegyin 750 guerrillas belonging to 'Mongoose' were waiting for them, and when the Japanese reached the river's west bank, and began to cross on improvised rafts, the Karens pinned them down and made them ready targets for the RAF.

Altogether, the guerrilla forces belonging to 'Character' killed an estimated 10,964 Japanese troops and wounded 644. Peacock's tally for the 'Otter' area was 2,876 Japanese killed for the loss of 34 Karens and four of his force, an astonishing achievement which, together with his part in delaying the 15th Division advance to Toungoo, must put him in the same league as Orde Wingate as one of the war's most outstanding guerrilla leaders. Poles thought him 'one of the great guerrilla leaders of the last war, one of the greatest, I would say. He risked more and achieved more, and he conducted his campaigns at one moment like a Viking, raiding with a mere handful of trusty men... at others he held a peak overlooking a Jap Divisional position [Mawchi] for months, defying the Japs like a medieval baron in a border keep – forever taking toll of his enemy in sorties and forays, yet himself remaining impregnable against their assaults.'

But the success of 'Character' was also due to the sterling qualities of the Karens, and Peacock later paid tribute to their fighting abilities and toughness. 'The Karen can move about faster on these high hills than any Jap, and knows far more about jungle craft than he does. No sooner did our levies learn a measure of discipline and control than their natural attributes and cunning in the jungle gave them supremacy over the Jap to an almost unbelievable extent.' It was, he said, difficult to kill a Karen, and described how one of them was shot in the right lung, through the jaw, and through the left hand, and was left for dead. He was, however, far from dead, and walked up nearly 2,000 feet and three miles during the night to Peacock's forward section, where Peacock found him. He eventually recovered.

Appendix
Summary of OG Operations in Greece, April–November 1944

Group	Totals	I	II	III	IV	V	VI	VII
Number of operations	76	15	14	12	1	12	6	16
Trains attacked	14	0	5	0	0	3	4	2
Engines destroyed	11	0	3	0	0	2	5	1
Vehicles destroyed	32	0	31	0	0	–	–	1
Armoured cars destroyed	2	0	0	0	0	0	2	0
Convoys attacked	5	3	1	0	0	0	0	1
Trucks destroyed	61	19	6	31	0	0	0	5
Bridges destroyed	15	0	1	1	1	7	2	3
Roads mined	5	0	1	1	0	0	0	3
Rail track destroyed (in yards)	9,920	0	7,400	0	20	1,000	1,500	0
Garrisons and pillboxes attacked	3	0	1	0	0	2	3	0
Prisoners	106	0	0	0	0	105	1	0
Enemy killed and wounded	1,794	76	675	201	0	574	200	68
OGs killed and wounded	13	0	7	0	0	5	1	0

Miscellaneous destroyed

4 German Billets
2 Power Plants
2 Mineshafts
1 Blockhouse
1 Wall

Notes on Sources

Secrecy has been called a British disease and the records of SOE have certainly been one of its victims. Such documentation as survived the war and the immediate post-war years probably amounts to no more than 15 per cent of the total. For decades these surviving records have been kept from the public by the Foreign Office, though a friendly SOE adviser in the Foreign Office always answered what questions he could. But in 1993, after a government initiative for greater freedom of information, most of the surviving files – a few are still withheld – began being released to the Public Record Office at Kew. This process is continuing. At the time of writing those files concerned with SOE operations in the Far East, in Africa and the Middle East, and in Scandinavia have been released. Luckily, some of SOE's most interesting and important operations were carried out in these areas and it is upon them that this book focuses.

Against this dearth of SOE documentation there is a mass of autobiographical and biographical material by or about those involved in SOE during the war, some of it accurate some of it quite fanciful. There are also a number of official histories whose authors were allowed access to the files, though they were not necessarily allowed to publish what they found there. I have drawn from the more reliable of the former to leaven official narratives with eye-witness reports; and from the latter where, as in the case of France, the documentation is still not available.

In contrast to SOE, nearly all the records of the OSS in the National Archives have been available to the public for some years – the Central Intelligence Agency began releasing them in 1980 – and its official history, written in 1947, was published in two volumes in 1976. With few exceptions, no one was allowed to be named in this history, which was censored before publication, but it is not difficult, from the information available elsewhere, to piece together who was involved in what operation. And as with SOE there are many biographies and autobiographies which cover the activities of OSS individuals as well as several extremely detailed publications on the special weapons and devices that were designed and developed for them to use in the field. All these have proved invaluable to me to reconstruct how the OSS went about its sabotage and subversion operations and how they were executed.

Introduction and Chapter 1

Dalton, Hugh. *The Fateful Years* (London, 1957); Foot, M. R. D. *SOE in France* (London, 1966) from which I took the extract from SOE's War Diary; Funk, Arthur. *Hidden Allies: Special Operations, the Resistance, and Southern France, 1944* (London, 1993); MacDonald, Elizabeth P. *Women in Intelligence*, privately published; the official history of the OSS, *War Report of the OSS*, 2 vols. (Washington, 1976) edited by Kermit Roosevelt, from which, except for Barbara Lauwers, I extracted the examples of OSS operations; Stafford, David. *Britain and European Resistance, 1940-45* (London, 1980) from which I took Portal's remark; and Sweet-Escott, B. *Baker Street Irregular* (London, 1965). The draft history of SOE and the London staff officer's letter is in HS1/333 at the Public Record Office at Kew. I have also taken information from the 'Summary of Allied Aid to French Resistance' by Colonel Joseph F. Lincoln which is in OSS archives (RG226, Box 741, A-1, Entry 190, Folder 2)

Chapter 2

I took the Hugh Seton-Watson quote from *British Policy towards Wartime Resistance in Yugoslavia* (London, 1975) edited by P. Auty and R. Clogg, and the quotes about Brooker and the OSS's Schools and Trainings Branch from David Stafford's *Camp X* (Toronto, 1986) as I did much of the information about the camp and one of the quotes about Fairbairn. Details about Fairbairn's background and training techniques came from the March and September 1979 issues of the magazine *Soldiers of Fortune* and from Aaron Bank's *From OSS to Green Berets* (USA, 1986); the OSS Manual quote from John Brunner's *OSS Weapons* (USA, 1994); and details of SOE parachute training from Issues 8 and 9 of the Study Group on Intelligence. I have also drawn information from *Behind the Burma Road* (London, 1964) by William R. Peers and Dean Brelis; SOE: 1940-1946 (London, 1984) by M.R.D. Foot; *War Report of the OSS* (Washington, 1976) edited by Kermit Roosevelt; *The Secrets War* (Washington, 1991) edited by George Chalou; and *Knights of the Floating Silk* (London, 1959) by George Langelaan.

Chapter 3

I have relied a good deal for this chapter on Dr John Brunner's *OSS Weapons* (USA, 1994). I have also taken information from *Clandestine Warfare: Weapons and Equipment of the SOE and OSS* (London, 1988) by James Ladd, Keith Melton, and Peter Mason; *Secret Warfare* (London, 1984) by Pierre Lorain; *OSS Special Weapons & Equipment* (USA, 1991) by Keith Melton; *SOE in the Far East* (Oxford, 1983) by Charles Cruickshank; *SOE in France* (London, 1968), SOE: 1940-1946 (London, 1984) and *Resistance* (London, 1977), all by M. R. D. Foot; *Of Spies and Stratagems* (USA, 1963) by Stanley P. Lovell; *Beyond the Burma Road* (London, 1964) by William R. Peers and Dean Brelis; and *The Jedburghs: Masterstroke or Missed Opportunity* (privately published) by O. Arthur Brown.

Chapter 4

At the time of writing the SOE files on Greece have not been released. I have therefore drawn my information on the Gorgopotamos operation from a number of books written by the participants. They are: Myers, E. C. W. *Greek Entanglement* (London, 1955); Woodhouse, C. M. *Something Ventured* (London, 1982), and *Apple of Discord* (London, 1948); Marinos, T. *Harling Mission* – 1942 (Athens, 1993); Dimitris Dimitriou, *Guerrilla in the Roumeli Mountains* (Athens, 1978); and Hamson, D. *We Fell Among Greeks* (London, 1946).

Chapter 5

HS3/87, HS3/91–93, HS3/96 in the Public Record Office at Kew provided much of the information in this chapter. I took the quote from the BBC Radio 4 programme, *The Quest for Gus*, by Henrietta March-Phillipps, broadcast on 16 May 1972, from *The Commandos*: 1940-46 (London, 1985) by Charles Messenger, and I also used information from this book as I did from *Geoffrey: Major John Geoffrey Appleyard,* DSO MC *and Bar* (London, 1947) by JEA ; *Anders Lassen*, VC (London, 1988) by Mike Langley; and the Log of *Maid Honor* in Lance-Corporal F. C. 'Buzz' Perkins' file, Department of Documents, Imperial War Museum, London.

Chapter 6

HS2/253–256, HS2/262, HS2/269 in the Public Record Office at Kew provided much of the information for this chapter, but I am also indebted to Ralph Barker's *The Block Busters* (London, 1976) and Charles Cruickshank's official history, SOE *in Scandinavia* (Oxford, 1986).

Chapter 7

I have relied a good deal for this chapter on Sefton Delmer's *Black Boomerang* (London, 1962), but have also drawn on SOE files in the Public Record Office at Kew, Ellic Howe's *The Black Game* (London, 1982), Charles Cruickshank's *The Fourth Arm* (London, 1977), and *War Report of the* OSS (Washington, 1976) edited by Kermit Roosevelt.

Chapter 8

The main sources for this chapter are files in the Public Record Office at Kew: ADM1/16678, which contains the after-action reports of the participants, and SOE files HS1/232, HS1/257, and HS1/258. I have also drawn on Ronald McKie's *The Heroes* (Sydney, 1960), Brian Connell's *Return of the Tiger* (London, 1960), from which I took the extracts from Carse's log, Charles Cruickshank's official history, SOE *In The Far East* (Oxford, 1983), and Lynette Ramsay Silver's *The Heroes of Rimau* (Sydney, 1991) which concentrates on Operation 'Rimau' but includes chapters on 'Jaywick'.

Chapter 9

Much of the information in this chapter comes from a narrative of the Detachment's time in Burma which is in OSS archives (RG226, Entry 190, Box 33, Folder 4). I have also taken information from *The War Report of the* OSS (Washington, 1976) edited by Kermit Roosevelt, and James R. Ward's chapter in *The Secrets War* (Washington, 1991), edited by George Chalou. For background colour there are popular histories by the two commanders of the unit whose co-authors were novelists and former unit members: *The Deadliest Colonel* (New York, 1975) by Thomas N. Moon and Carl F. Eifler and *Behind the Burma Road* (London, 1964) by William R. Peers and Dean Brelis. Other sources include Richard Dunlop's *Behind Japanese Lines* (Chicago, 1979) and Roger Hilsman's *American Guerrilla* (London, 1991).

Chapter 10

SOE files (HS2/186-188) in the Public Record Office at Kew provided much of the information for this chapter. But I also took quotes and information from *Skis Against the Atom* (London, 1954) by Knut Haukelid, *Most Secret War* (London, 1978) by R. V. Jones, and *Heisenberg's War* (London, 1993) by Thomas Powers.

Chapter 11

Much of the material in this chapter comes from SOE files HS1/293, HS1/115, and HS1/198 in the Public Record Office at Kew, from *The Black Game* (London, 1982) by Ellic Howe, *Black Boomerang* (London, 1962) by Sefton Delmer, and *The Fourth Arm* (Oxford, 1981) by Charles Cruickshank.

Chapter 12

SOE files on F Section have not yet been released to the public. I have therefore relied on the official history, SOE *in France* (London, corrected edition, 1968), for much of the information in this chapter; its author, M. R. D. Foot, is the only person who has so far had access to these files and has been allowed to publish a book based on them. Except for those sources mentioned below unattributed quotes in the text are from his book. The quotes by Philippe de Vomécourt and Colonel Maurice Buckmaster are from F *Section*, SOE (London, 1985) by Marcel Ruby; Harry Rée's is from *Resistance in Europe*: 1939-45 (London, 1975) edited by Stephen Hawes and Ralph White. The reports of the SO officers working with SOE circuits are in the OSS archives (RG 226, Box 741, A-1, Entry 190, Folder 2). I also drew information from the second volume of *War Report of the* OSS (Washington, DC, 1976) edited by Kermit Roosevelt. There are, of course, a host of other books on or by most of the individuals mentioned in this chapter – some of them classics of their kind – as well as many equally good books on those I have not had room to include. There are, too, several excellent publications which cover just about every aspect of F Section's work in France, including several covering the betrayal of the 'Prosper' circuit. Except for the OSS official history, all the books mentioned above have bibliographies to which I refer any interested reader.

Chapter 13

SOE files in the Public Record Office at Kew (HS1/105, 135, 170,172, 288–293, and 297) and Charles Cruickshank's official history, SOE *in the Far East* (Oxford, 1983).

Chapter 14

Files in the Public Record Office at Kew – WO 204/2030B and WO 204/1970 – provided the after-action reports for the Greek OGs, 'Justine', and the Korcula raid. I took the quote in the first paragraph from Colonel Alfred T. Cox's report which is in OSS archives (RG226, Entry 190, Box 741, A-1, folder 7) as is the 'Percy Red' after-action report from which I also quoted (RG226, Entry 148, Box 83, Folder 1212). I have also used information and quotes from the *War Report of the* OSS (Washington, 1976) edited by Kermit Roosevelt; *One Man and His time* (London, 1960) by Serge Obolensky; and *Honorable Men: My Life in the* CIA (London, 1978) by William Colby. Details of the NORSO group in France and Norway also came from *The* OSS *Norwegian Special Operations Group in World War* II (London, 1994) by Bruce H. Heimark. Arthur Funk's *Hidden Allies: Special Operations, The Resistance, and Southern France,* 1944 (London, 1993) gave me a valuable overview of OG operations in southern France and the quote from 'Louise's after-action report was taken from this book.

Chapter 15

As SOE files on the Jedburgh teams have still to be released to the public, I have largely relied on OSS records, or on books based on these records, as well as autobiographies or monographs by some members of the Jedburgh teams. I drew details about Macpherson and 'Quinine' from *Das Reich* (London, 1981) by Max Hastings; the activities of the teams in central France from theses written by Major Wyman W. Irwin and Major Michael R. King; the activities of 'Alexander' and 'Horace' from *The War Report of the* OSS (Washington, 1976) edited by Kermit Roosevelt; and the activities of the eleven teams dropped into north-eastern France from *Jedburgh Team Operations in Support of the 12th Army Group, August* 1944 by Dr S. J. Lewis, a historian with the Combat Studies Institute at Fort Leavenworth, Kansas, which published his study in 1991. I also used information from Aaron Bank's *From* OSS *to Green Berets* (USA, 1986), Arthur Brown's *The Jedburghs: Masterstroke or Missed Opportunity* and *The Jedburghs: A Short History*, and Stanley Cannicott's *Journey of a Jed* (all privately printed), Peter Wilkinson and Joan Bright

Astley's *Gubbins and* SOE (London, 1993), M. R. D. Foot's SOE *in France* (London, 1968), and William B. Dreux's well-written and evocative memoir, *No Bridges Blown* (USA, 1971). Arthur L. Funk's *Hidden Allies: Special Operations, the Resistance, and Southern France,* 1944 (London, 1993) provided many of the details, and quotes, about the SPOC Jedburgh teams. I have also taken additional information about them from Major Marten's report which is in OSS archives (RG226, Entry 154, Box 56, Folder 945) as is General Donovan's report to the US Joint Chiefs of Staff.

Chapter 16

The official SOE reports on 'Character' are in HS1/10 and 11 in the Public Record Office at Kew, but I have taken most of Peacock's quotes and information about 'Character', and Captain Ansell's quote, from *The Life of a Jungle Wallah* (Ilfracombe, 1958) which is Geraldine Peacock's memoir of her husband and is based on his official report. I have also taken information, as well as a number of quotes about the leaders of 'Character', from Terence O'Brien's *The Moonlight War* (London, 1987) and have also extracted information and quotes from the manuscripts of J. P. Lucas and D. Gibbs in the Imperial War Museum, from Field Marshal Slim's *Defeat into Victory* (London, 1956) and from Charles Cruickshank's official history, SOE *In The Far East* (Oxford, 1983).

Index